Racial Politics at the Crossroads

Racial Politics at the Crossroads

Memphis Elects Dr. W. W. Herenton

Marcus D. Pohlmann and Michael P. Kirby

The University of Tennessee Press • Knoxville

Library of Congress Cataloging-in-Publication Data

Pohlmann, Marcus D., 1950–
    Racial politics at the crossroads : Memphis elects Dr. W. W. Herenton /
Marcus D. Pohlmann and Michael P. Kirby. — 1st ed.
        p. cm.
    Includes bibliographical references and index.
    ISBN 0-87049-926-2 (cloth: alk. paper)
    ISBN 0-87049-927-0 (pbk.: alk. paper)
1. Mayors—Tennessee—Memphis—Election. 2. Herenton, W. W.
(Willie W.), 1943- . 3. Mayors—Tennessee—Memphis—Biography.
4. Memphis (Tenn.)—Politics and government. 5. Afro-American
mayors—Tennessee—Memphis. I. Kirby, Michael P. II. Title.
JS1097.3.P65 1996
324.9768'19053—dc20   95-32505
                            CIP

To Richard Borys, consummate public servant, and to
Charles V. Hamilton, mentor, colleague, and friend

Contents

Preface   xi

Introduction   xv

Part I. The Political Context

  1. White Politics   3

  2. The Hackett Years   31

  3. Black Politics   52

  4. Dr. W. W. Herenton   74

  5. The Electoral Context   92

Part II. The Election of 1991

  6. The Hackett Campaign   119

  7. The Herenton Campaign   140

  8. The Election   165

Part III. Implications and Prospects for the Future

  9. Conclusion: Racial Reflexivity in Memphis   197

  Epilogue   205

  Notes   211

  Bibliography   251

  Index   263

Illustrations

Figures

 1. Memphis Population, 1830–1990   7
 2. Memphis Black Population, 1850–1990   12
 3. E. H. "Boss" Crump and His Wife, Bessie   16
 4. Mayor Henry Loeb   18
 5. Mayor Wyeth Chandler   21
 6. Mayor Richard C. Hackett   37
 7. George W. Lee   56
 8. George W. Lee and Fellow Republicans   61
 9. Jesse Turner Walks the Picket Line, 1963   67
10. O. Z. Evers with William Ingram, 1967   70
11. Otis Higgs Jr. Concedes on Election Night, 1975   72
12. Vote for Black and White Candidates, 1975–1991   93
13. Racial Polarization in Mayoral Elections, 1975–1991   95
14. Racial Bloc Voting in Mayoral Elections, 1975–1991   97
15. Voting-Age Population by Race, 1950–1990   99
16. Voter Registration by Race, 1951–1991   101
17. Registration as a Percentage of Voting-Age Population, 1951–1991   103
18. Voter Turnout by Race, 1979–1991   105
19. Turnout as a Percentage of Voting-Age Population, 1979–1991   106
20. Sources of Mayoral Campaign Contributions, 1991   128

21. Mayoral Campaign Expenditures by Category, 1991   130
22. Mayoral Campaign Expenditures, 1991   131
23. W. W. Herenton, Reverend Jesse Jackson, Maxine
Smith, and Others   161
24. Mayor-Elect W. W. Herenton and Campaign Assistant
Eddie Walsh   166
25. The Midtown Area   186
26. The Midtown Precincts in 1991   188
27. White Crossover for Elections in Midtown, 1991   189

Tables

1. Stages of Population Growth, 1830–1990   6
2. Area and Population Growth, 1826–1991   108
3. Racial Crossover Voting for At-Large Candidates, 1991   169
4. Viability of Black Candidates, 1971–1991   176
5. Absentee Ballots, 1983–1991   182

Preface

This work presents a case study of racial politics in Memphis. It seeks both to describe the developments that culminated in the 1991 election of Dr. W. W. Herenton and to explain the social and political history that prevented an earlier election of a black mayor. The study delves into Memphis history, sociology, economics, and politics. Given that breadth of scope, a wide variety of sources and methods had to be employed. Our approach is consistent with methodologists such as Eugene Webb, who argued that studies should not be method driven, but rather should select the methods which most appropriately answer the research questions.[1]

Existing academic literature on Memphis politics is cited throughout. That literature is strongest in detailing the history of Memphis from the Civil War to the demise of the Crump machine and in examining the events surrounding the assassination of Martin Luther King Jr. It includes books, dissertations, and master's theses on a variety of historical events, as well as specialized academic articles on topics from the yellow fever epidemic to the role of the churches in Memphis political and social life.

We also relied on various media sources for information. The most valuable of those were the *Press Scimitar* and the *Commercial Appeal*, which provided day-to-day accounts of politics in Memphis. In addition, the *Tri-State Defender* provided us with information on views in the black community during the 1991 campaign. Tapes from WMC television were transcribed to add more detail to our knowledge about events in the campaign. Further, the *Memphis Business Journal* provided information on both Memphis politics and economics.

The written information was then supplemented by interviews with a variety of insiders and observers who spoke with us both formally and informally. Most important, we were able to conduct far-ranging interviews with both of the 1991 mayoral candidates. Drafts of the chapters of this book were circulated among both political leaders and observers to check its facts. Although we did not collect polling data, it was made available as a result of an interview with a local political consultant and by utilizing the annual *Memphis Poll*.

The book is also informed by the professional observations of the two authors. Michael Kirby arrived in Memphis in 1970 and followed Memphis politics both at a distance, through his research activities, and by close involvement in a number of public policy issues. He was especially involved in politics during the Chandler and Hackett administrations. Marcus Pohlmann arrived in 1986 and immediately immersed himself in the study of the city's black political structure. His studies and contacts ultimately provided him with valuable access to the Herenton campaign organization. Thus, this is a work by political outsiders who have spent sizable portions of their professional lives collecting information about the politics of Memphis.

In addition, the qualitative information has been supplemented with considerable quantitative analysis, presented in the form of bar and trend charts. Demographic trends dating back to the mid-nineteenth century were examined by using census information. Registration information was examined from as early as the 1950s, when official collection of this data began in Memphis. In addition, voting turnout information by race has also come to be available and has been analyzed.

Voting patterns were examined through the use of a technique called "ecological regression analysis." This approach entails collecting racial and voting characteristics of precincts and estimating the voting patterns of black and white voters for each of the candidates. Although very complex to employ, the approach is used widely in voting studies and court suits challenging discriminatory practices in local elections. Essentially, the regression analysis involves determining how distinctly voting behavior changes when examining precincts with progressively larger proportions of African Americans. These resulting "regression" measures were then verified by examining voting behavior in precincts that had at least 90 percent black or 90 percent white registration.[2] Much of the quantitative data was collected by the authors as part of a lawsuit challenging discriminatory voting practices in Memphis.

We have arranged the chapters to emphasize how the history of Memphis affected contemporary racial politics, which in turn resulted in the election of Dr. Herenton in 1991. In particular, the organizational scheme points up how the black and white communities have developed quite separately in many ways, and how that separation has continued into the modern era of Memphis politics.

Chapters 1 and 2 trace the development of the city's dominant white political culture, concluding with a detailed look at incumbent Mayor Richard C. Hackett. Chapters 3 and 4 chronicle key events in the evolution of Memphis black politics, culminating in the emergence of Dr. W. W. Herenton.

Chapter 5 looks at specific demographic and rule changes that framed the 1991 election, while Chapters 6 through 8 analyze the two campaigns and the subsequent election returns.

Chapter 9 summarizes what we have found and discusses its significance in the light of previous scholarly conclusions about racial politics elsewhere.

• • •

We are grateful to Charles V. Hamilton, Lewis Randolph, Wilbur Rich, Kenneth Goings, Raphael Sonenshein, and Kenneth Jackson for their valuable suggestions at various stages in the process of turning this manuscript into a book. Eddie Walsh, Charles Crawford, Ron Walter, Mary Wilder, and Maxine Smith gave generously of their time in reviewing our historical accounts. Eva Mae Switzer provided extensive assistance as we gathered election data. Steve Gadbois was a great help with the regression methodology. Ric Crowder, Ashley Brian, Jay Mason, Chris Kirby, and Melissa Berry were terrific research assistants. Carol O'Connor was the best departmental secretary imaginable, and her contributions to all of our work are so pervasive as to make them impossible to isolate. We owe a considerable debt to both Richard Hackett and W. W. Herenton for their time and patience. And last, but certainly not least, we thank Barb Pohlmann, Jan Kirby, Justin Pohlmann, Tom Kirby, and Chris Kirby for their understanding and support throughout this entire endeavor.

Introduction

The election of Dr. W. W. Herenton as the first elected African-American mayor of Memphis, Tennessee, is of considerable social and historical significance. Besides being one of the very closest and most racially polarized mayoral elections in urban American history, it provides a unique opportunity to explore racial politics in one of the country's largest cities.

We employ an intensive case study method in order to analyze the 1991 mayoral election within the city's historical context. What we found was that Memphis has been unique in a number of important ways. The political evolution that culminated in the election of Dr. Herenton deviates significantly from scholarly conclusions about racial politics in other cities. In particular, Herenton's election itself deviates from others' conclusions about what is generally necessary to elect the first black mayor in a racially mixed city.

Racial Politics in Large Southern Cities

> Perhaps the most impressive feature of the black presence in the southern city . . . is not the harshness of white supremacy, but rather the resilience and perseverance of blacks.
>
> —Blaine Brownell and David Goldfield, *The City in Southern History*

Memphis is a southern city, and, as such, its politics has been influenced by regional patterns. As Roscoe Martin put it, "The politics of the South has a regional unity which necessitates its study over a broad area if there is to be maximum opportunity for understanding."[1]

One of the most consistent themes throughout the literature on southern politics is the prominence of race. From the Civil War to Reconstruction, from Jim Crow to the civil rights period and beyond, southern politics has long revolved in significant ways around the issue of race.[2] As V. O. Key writes, "Whatever phase of the southern political process one seeks to understand, sooner or later the trail leads to the Negro."[3] Following Reconstruction, for just one instance, state governments erected an elaborate array of voting impediments to minimize the political influence of African Americans.[4] Yet, as southern cities grew, urban blacks became more independent and politicized.[5] It was not long before there was considerable violent and nonviolent conflict between blacks and whites. Particularly when the job market was tight, this conflict often resulted in "race riots," whereby bands of whites would storm black neighborhoods, killing, burning, raping, and pillaging in order to vent their frustrations.[6]

Such violent intimidation, which also included lynchings, "night rides" by the Ku Klux Klan, and discriminatory law enforcement, appears to have led to a considerable amount of at least outward deference and adaptation on the part of southern blacks.[7] Despite social and political degradation, an aggressive race-conscious civil rights movement was slow to surface. According to Harry Holloway, "conditions tended to produce the accommodating individual expected by white supremacists."[8]

On the other hand, a body of scholarship is beginning to accumulate that suggests that black resistance to oppression—from protests to violent physical resistance—did not end with slave sabotage and revolts. In point of fact, this resistance may well have permeated the South during the dark days of Jim Crow. For example, individual blacks resisted trolley car segregation and mistreatment; black workers engaged in wildcat strikes; blacks fought the police at times; and mass rallies were held to raise money for legally defending arrested leaders.[9]

Turning specifically to urban voting participation, Bass and DeVries remind us, "[T]here are many places in the South where blacks voted long before the civil rights movement, [and] the black vote was often manipulated by white politicians."[10] Moreover, since the civil rights period of the 1960s, black and white voter registration rates have been reasonably similar in the urban South. Blacks, however, have tended to go to the polls less often than whites, and they also have been less likely to vote in the lower-salience races further down the ticket. When blacks and whites with similar incomes are compared, on the other hand, blacks actually vote at higher rates.[11]

One harsh reality, however, is that blacks remain more than twice as likely as whites to be poor.[12] And, in general, poorer people simply participate in the democratic process at far lower levels than those who are better off. This appears to be particularly true in the South and especially in the black South. Such regional variation has been due in part to the many voting constraints southern blacks have faced.[13] Further, the South has had very few political machines,[14] and it is wise to remember the general politicization that can occur by demonstrating to people, as the political machines often did, that their political participation would result rather directly in tangible political rewards.[15] But where machines did exist, reform devices, such as nonpartisan elections, have subsequently tended to reduce political involvement.[16]

Even when southern white politicians found it in their interest to allow black participation, Key and others have noted another problem for the African-American electorate. Not having to fight for the right to vote seems to have predisposed groups to turn out less and to vote less cohesively, as well as to make fewer political demands.[17]

Nonetheless, when focusing on those citizens who do turn out to vote, racial polarization in the voting of both blacks and whites is a well-established pattern nationwide. Racial polarization also has a tendency to increase with the relative size of the black population.[18] Thus, such polarization has often been quite marked in large southern cities with sizable black populations, especially where previous denial of the franchise has helped to unify the subordinate group.[19]

First Electing a Black Mayor

> We've waited patiently, voted for white candidates over and over. It's our turn now.
>
> —Harold Washington, 1983

Prior to 1967, no major United States city had elected a black mayor since a number of southern cities did so during Reconstruction. Then, a combination of circumstances came together. Many African Americans had been migrating to large cities since the turn of the century. A civil rights movement swept the country, knocking down barriers to black electoral participation, resulting in massive voter registration drives, and raising the level of black consciousness. At the same time, white middle- and upper-class residents were headed for the suburbs, leaving urban populations with a much higher percentage of African Americans.

Black mayors soon came to be elected in northern and southern cities alike. Carl Stokes in Cleveland and Richard Hatcher in Gary, Indiana, were elected first, and thereafter over the course of the 1970s, blacks were elected to the mayor's office for the first time in Newark (Kenneth Gibson), Detroit (Coleman Young), Atlanta (Maynard Jackson), Los Angeles (Tom Bradley), New Orleans (Ernest Morial), Birmingham (Richard Arrington), and Washington, D.C. (Marion Barry). Since 1980, Chicago (Harold Washington), Philadelphia (Wilson Goode), Baltimore (Kurt Schmoke), New York City (David Dinkins), Seattle (Norman Rice), Kansas City, Missouri (Emanuel Cleaver), Charlotte, North Carolina (Harvey Gantt), Oakland (Lionel Wilson), Dallas (Ron Kirk), and Denver (Wellington Webb) can be added to the list, not to mention smaller cities such as New Haven and Hartford in Connecticut, Flint, Pontiac, and Battle Creek in Michigan, East St. Louis, Illinois, Roanoke and Richmond in Virginia, Spokane, Washington, Little Rock, Arkansas, Pasadena and Berkeley in California, Camden and Atlantic City in New Jersey, and Tallahassee, Florida.

Moreover, the election of black mayors has not merely been a matter of waiting until a city had a black electoral majority. Where any of the largest fifty cities in the country had a strong mayor system and a population that was even 40 percent black, only Memphis and St. Louis had failed to elect a black mayor by 1991. Meanwhile, a good many of these black mayors were first elected in cities that had much smaller black populations.

Election Formula

The literature on urban mayors points to a number of similar conditions under which many black candidates were first elected to office.[20] Where African Americans achieved numerical majorities, the results were often all but preordained. However, the elections of black mayors in predominantly white cities have tended to have the following developments in common:

1) *At least two similar black candidate platform planks: pro-business growth and crime control.* These were two highly salient issues that appealed to both blacks and whites. They promised jobs and safety without implying a shift from social concerns or a crackdown on African Americans, underlying messages often heard when promised by white candidates.[21]

2) *An exceptionally large voter turnout in the African-American community.* Robert Starks and Michael Preston note that such historically high levels of African-American participation generally required not only massive registration and voter mobilization drives, but also a general belief among the black electorate that electoral victory would bring a significant restructuring, not merely representation, within the old structure.[22]

3) *Nearly all of the black vote going to one strong black candidate.* Early unity helped. In Newark and Chicago, for example, this unity was facilitated in each case by a community conference to settle on a single black contender. However, such conferences were by far the exception rather than the rule.

4) *At least 10 percent of the white vote.* Here, it was advantageous if the strongest white candidate waved the bloody shirt of race far too prominently, as was the case in Seattle in 1989.[23] This helped rally the "liberal"[24] white community. Chicago in 1989 is a classic case of the lesson well learned. Richard M. Daley went out of his way to appeal to black voters, even though he faced a strong black opponent and had little prospect of garnering many black votes. At least in part, Daley appears to have been appealing to white liberals who would not support a racist. Subsequently, more than three-quarters of the whites who had voted for Harold Washington voted this time for Richard M. Daley.[25]

In New York City the same year, all nine mayoral candidates took a formal pledge not to appeal to prejudice based on race, ethnicity, national identity, gender, or sexual orientation.[26] In part, this pledge no doubt reflects a genuine concern for the city's social harmony. However, it would be naive to think that such "restraint" is not at least partially motivated by a desire to appeal to urban liberals, a highly attentive and politically active urban electoral constituency who are likely to be offended by such pandering.

5) *Two or more strong white candidates splitting the rest of the white vote.* This is especially important if it is a multicandidate primary election without a run-off provision.

6) *A weak citywide party structure.* Historically, strong party organizations have tended to control both the black political leadership and the black vote, using them to secure the election of their own white candidates. In effect, such a tradition also reduced the likelihood of the kind of electoral insurgency that could produce a black mayor.

7) *No major media opposition.* Because it was essential to extract a large bloc of votes from liberal white "bookworms," as George Washington Plunkitt called them,[27] it was important that major local media sources took the candidacy seriously and then either were supportive or at least neutral once viability was established.

8) *Large group support.* finally, for financial contributions as well as help with turning out their voters on election day, it was very useful to have active and energetic assistance from groups like the AFL-CIO or the United Auto Workers (UAW).

This formula is predicated on an "accommodation" model of sorts. In this scenario, whether they intend to or not, African-American candidates run on a platform that is acceptable to a number of white liberals. Then, they subsequently win with a black and liberal white coalition.[28] In more current parlance, blacks benefit from at least a partial "deracialization" of local politics.[29] As Robert Smith describes this scenario in practice, "by and large, [successful black mayoral candidates] were pragmatic, experienced politicians who appealed to the white electorate in terms of citywide concerns, who emphasized that they would be 'mayor of all the people,' and who appealed to and successfully attracted some white liberal voter support."[30]

It is a myth, however, that the large majority of the African-American community automatically will vote for a black over a white candidate. In point of fact, there are many examples to the contrary. These include Philadelphia in 1967, Chicago in 1976, New York City in 1985, and

Memphis in 1987. Far more common is a low voter turnout in the African-American community if African Americans are uninspired by either the black or white candidates.

Racial Reflexivity

Our study of Memphis suggests an alternative scenario to deracialization. A history of serious racial conflict in an area, including at least a perception that the other racial group is likely to act in bad faith if given the chance, may well lead to a threshold of racial divisiveness that all but precludes interracial accommodation. We will refer to such a threshold throughout this work as the "point of racial reflexivity." At that juncture, because of that area's interracial history, any candidate's attempt to gain support across racial lines is immediately met with considerable suspicion within that candidate's own racial group. The candidate making such an appeal is seen as naive at best or as "selling out" at worst. As a consequence, it becomes more difficult to register and turn out large numbers of that group's members. It is also important to note, however, that a condition of racial reflexivity can exist even if it is a phenomenon that affects only one of the racial groups, and even if it affects only a portion of that group. If that portion of one group is significant enough to sway elections, and if it is unbending in its suspicion, then this subset of the group can deter the group's candidates from making overt cross-racial appeals.

Our study uses the concept of racial reflexivity to help explain the politics of Memphis. The city's 1991 mayoral election and the political history that preceded it deviated in significant ways from earlier scholarly conclusions about racial politics in southern cities in general, as well as from earlier conclusions about a city's initial election of an African-American mayor in particular. Most striking is the level of racial polarization that has persisted in Memphis, and the degree to which that polarization spawned a clear measure of racial reflexivity in the city's electoral politics.

The City of Memphis

The historical prominence of interracial conflict in Memphis politics, as in most southern cities, is undeniable. Yet, Memphis is unique in a number of ways as well.

At the turn of the century, Memphis was a southern city that had its Jim Crow system of segregation, lynchings, and race riots. Yet, as was the case in a number of other southern cities of the time, it also experienced a notable degree of early violent and nonviolent resistance to such oppression. This resistance appears to have been most common among poorer blacks who had more recently immigrated to the city.

As for voting patterns, the city's discriminatory past and service-based economy combined to spawn a large and exceptionally poor African-American lower class; this would lead one to expect relatively low levels of political participation. Yet, for a variety of reasons, this has not been the case. In particular, the overall history of political participation in the city's African-American community has been relatively remarkable.

Memphis was one of those southern cities that allowed early black suffrage when it served the interests of white politicians. For example, African Americans were selectively marshaled to the polls in the first half of the twentieth century by the political machine of E. H. "Boss" Crump. Despite their exceptionally low economic status as a community, blacks not only have registered at surprisingly high rates, but they also have voted at relatively high rates as well, even after the demise of the Crump machine.

Reformers launched an interracial grassroots movement in 1965, however, and it culminated a year later in a new electoral system that included a runoff provision for all citywide offices. Thus, no one could be elected mayor without receiving a majority of the votes cast, requiring a runoff election between the top two candidates if neither had received such a majority in the nonpartisan general election. That system, combined with frequent annexations of predominantly white suburbs and racially polarized elections with relatively high levels of voter registration and turnout, functioned for years to minimize the number of black elected officials.

Then, two important changes occurred. The United States Justice Department joined a group of prominent local African Americans in a legal challenge to important aspects of the electoral system. Although only partially resolved at the time of the 1991 mayoral election, that partial resolution, along with a significant change in the state's annexation law, helped elect Dr. Herenton in a city where the voting-age population had finally reached parity along racial lines.

The First Black Mayor in Memphis

It is clear that Herenton's victory deviates from the standard formula for electing an African-American mayor for the first time in a racially mixed city. Herenton's election began with two unity conventions, which delivered a single African-American candidate but also risked alienating many of the city's liberal whites, a group that was already quite small. Herenton ended up with very limited large-group support, white endorsements, or white votes. Meanwhile, there was no strong second white candidate to split the white vote. The only mass-circulation newspaper endorsed the white incumbent, and it had recently run a series of highly critical articles on Herenton's private life as well as on his tenure as school superintendent. Although race was a powerful undercurrent throughout, the two campaigns ran parallel to each other, with few attacks or discussion of issues. Instead, both camps concentrated on registering and turning out their own racial constituencies.

Then, in one of the closest and most racially divided electoral outcomes in big city history, Memphis chose its first African-American mayor. Dr. Herenton won without making accomodationist compromises with the white community. This was possible thanks to an extraordinary level of black support, including the mobilization of large numbers of lower-income blacks. Yet, if the city had been able to continue its annexations of predominantly white suburbs, our findings indicate that it is nearly certain that Herenton would have been defeated. It is less clear what a runoff election would have meant; but, in an electorate this closely divided, a runoff may well have led to a reversal as well.

Memphis appeared to have reached that threshold of racial divisiveness, or the "point of racial reflexivity," as we have chosen to call it, which all but precludes successful interracial accommodation. That political reality severely limits the chances for deracialized city politics, at least at the mayoral level. Whether a period of African-American governance will help reduce that racial divide remains to be seen.

Racial Politics

As the city had evolved, so had the dominant white political culture, and in many ways incumbent mayor Richard "Dick" Hackett embodied the contemporary version of that ideology. He was ultimately beaten by a combination of demographic and rule changes and a well-run, crusadelike Herenton campaign that successfully tapped generations of African-American frustration. As the *Memphis Commercial Appeal* put it, the election "signaled the end of the white conservative domination that has existed in most Memphis elections in this century."[31]

Yet, two realities are important to remember at the outset. First of all, as will be discussed at length in chapter 1, a historical quirk contributed to Memphis having an exceptionally small number of white liberals. Thus, over the years, blacks were left largely to their own devices, including their participation in Boss Crump's political machine.

Second, it is also important to remember that the Memphis black community has long contained its own significant social and economic fissures. In particular, there regularly has been a small group of relatively prosperous leaders, most of whom have been inclined to political pragmatism. At the other extreme, there has been a sizable core of very poor people. This latter group has often been militant, rebellious, and difficult to incorporate into mainstream electoral politics.

Part I

The Political Context

1 White Politics

The worlds of the cotton field and of the skyscraper are essentially the same. They both sprang from the rural traditions. . . . The southerner carried the burden of his past into the present and left its legacy for the future. In no other region is the past so much a part of its present, and its cities so much a part of both.

—David Goldfield, *Cotton Fields and Skyscrapers*

A community's political culture reflects the values and beliefs of that population and shapes the nature of its political behavior. We will analyze the evolution of the dominant political culture in Memphis and then examine its impact on the city's racial politics.

As David Goldfield has noted, southern urbanism developed relatively late, and its lifestyle and cultural values were transplanted from the rural South. Most important, like its rural counterpart, the southern city ended up as a biracial caste system. Whites would be dominant, blacks subordinate, and change would be impeded by the peculiar nature of the southern economy.[1]

Historical accounts of Memphis provide much support for Goldfield's arguments. The city's political culture has long reflected the values held in surrounding rural areas. For years, whites controlled the city's primary political and economic institutions, keeping blacks subservient through a variety of devices. Such a biracial caste system survived wave after wave of black migration to the city. Yet, beginning in the 1970s, a few cracks began to appear in this wall of racial constraint.

Historical Context (1794–1870)

Before beginning our analysis, we will briefly review the early history of the city to put it into context for the reader. As we will argue below, the history of Memphis provides an important precursor to understanding the city's racial politics as they have evolved in the twentieth century, ultimately leading to the election of 1991.

The land that is now Memphis once was inhabited by the Chickasaw Indian tribe. It was taken from them by the Spaniards, who were later routed by the United States Army. Fort Adams (renamed Fort Pickering) was then established on a key Mississippi River bluff at this location. The state of North Carolina subsequently purchased the land and sold a tract to John Rice. In 1794, he sold five thousand acres to Judge John Overton and Generals Andrew Jackson and James Winchester, who, in turn, established the city. The Memphis town plat was laid out in 1819, a town charter was granted in 1826, and a city charter was ceded in 1849.[2]

Memphis soon became a major river port and railroad center, with the local economy thriving on cotton and slave trading in particular. Two center city streets still bear names that defined this commerce: Exchange and Auction Streets. In addition, given the transient nature of such a commercial center, the city developed a reputation as a tough river town, with many honky-tonks and a high level of violent crime. Yet, apart from transitory traders, the city's own permanent population soared in the 1850s and 1860s, including a relatively rich ethnic mix of African Americans, Germans, Italians, and Irish.[3] Whereas in 1820 there were fewer than one hundred people and there was virtually no commerce, by 1860 there were approximately twenty-three thousand residents and fifty million dollars in annual trade.[4]

During this period of extraordinary growth, John Deaderick purchased five thousand acres in an adjacent area later known as "Orange Mound." Deaderick held a large number of the area's slaves, and, like many of his fellow slave masters, he would hire them out at times. However, given the availability of indigent Irish workers to do much of the manual labor, the urban demand for slave labor was limited.[5]

As civil war lurked on the horizon, Memphis whites supported slavery and even placed restrictions on free blacks (e.g., education was forbidden and a curfew was imposed).[6] Nevertheless, the city initially did not endorse secession, though local support for the Confederacy did build once the war began. By 1862, the city had fallen to advancing Union troops. Fortunately for Memphis, the early Union takeover helped the city avoid the kind of wartime destruction that befell cities such as Atlanta; and, along with the entire state of Tennessee, the city was not subjected to congressional Reconstruction following the war.[7]

Sizable Freedmen's camps quickly sprung up around the outskirts of the city, with large numbers of these former slaves opting to reside in and around the city following emancipation. In 1865, for example, the city's African-American population grew by 500 percent.[8] Brownell and Goldfield refer to such movement as the first phase of the Great Migration.[9] With the possible exception of New Orleans, Memphis soon had more black residents than any other city in the nation, with Beale Street becoming, as George Lee put it, "the main street of Negro America"— the center of black Memphis business, religion, entertainment, and vice.[10]

Population Trends and Political Culture

Numerous historical analyses suggest that a rurally based political culture became embedded in the politics of Memphis.[11] To help frame that evolution, figure 1 shows the growth of the Memphis population over time. Table 1 demarcates five specific stages during that growth and indicates both the population level and percentage of population change during each stage.

Stage One: Initial Growth

Stage one lasted from just before the Civil War until the 1870s. During this period Memphis became a large city by southern standards.[12] As of 1860, on the eve of the Civil War, Memphis had grown to a population of 22,623; further, that figure would double by the following census.

The composition of the population during this stage was much different from any subsequent time in Memphis history. A large number of

Table I

Stages of Population Growth, 1830–1990

Historical Stage	Year	Total Population	Population Growth	Percent Growth
1. Initial Growth	1830	663		
	1840	1,799	1,136	171
	1850	8,841	7,042	391
	1860	22,623	13,782	156
	1870	40,226	17,603	78
2. Yellow Fever	1880	33,592	-6,634	-16
3. Moderate Growth	1890	64,495	30,903	92
	1900	102,320	37,825	59
	1910	131,105	28,785	28
	1920	162,351	31,246	24
4. Urban Growth	1930	253,143	90,802	56
	1940	292,942	39,789	16
	1950	396,000	103,058	35
	1960	497,524	101,524	26
	1970	623,988	126,464	25
5. Population Loss	1980	646,356	22,368	4
	1990	618,682	-27,674	-4

foreign-born immigrants provided a heterogeneity that was unusual for the South.[13] In 1860, foreign-born residents constituted more than 36 percent of the city's white population. The largest groups were Irish, with 5,242 people, and Germans, with 2,596.[14] There were also 3,822 African Americans, more than 3,600 of whom were slaves.

An analysis of these two key white ethnic groups reveals that the Irish immigrants were initially lower-class workers who often lived in racially integrated neighborhoods and competed directly with blacks for lesser-skilled jobs. They generally sought manual work and had a reputation for exhibiting unruly behavior. For example, the mayor of Memphis called out the militia when 200 Irish laborers arrived to work on the Mississippi river levee.[15] The smaller German population, by contrast, was seen as having a modernizing influence on the city. They brought with them their musical heritage, for instance; and Clayton Robinson describes the sounds of Haydn and Schubert emanating from German

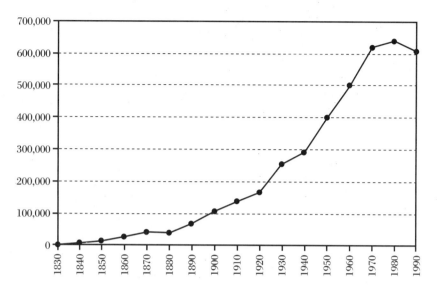

Fig. 1. Memphis Population, 1830–1990.

households. They also brought with them ideas, such as trade unionism, that were alien to the native Memphis culture.[16]

Stage Two: Yellow Fever

Meanwhile, most of Memphis lacked even the most elementary sanitation facilities. In particular, an area known as Bayou Gayoso drained five thousand acres of an open sewer, receiving deposits from thousands of private privies. This created a fertile breeding ground for mosquitoes carrying yellow fever.[17]

Disaster hit from the late 1870s into the 1880s, as a series of yellow fever epidemics devastated the city. The 1878 epidemic alone produced the highest death rate from an epidemic that any city in the United States had ever seen. Between deaths and departures, Memphis recorded a huge loss of population in the 1880 census. From an estimated eighty thousand people before the fever struck, Memphis shrank to thirty-four thousand residents.[18]

As a result, among other things, the heterogeneity of the city would change dramatically. With the exception of those Irish immigrants who were too impoverished to flee, virtually all the members of the white ethnic groups departed. Overall, more than twenty-four thousand people fled, and few ever returned. This exodus left only six thousand whites. Most blacks also were too poor to leave, but a much higher proportion of them survived, as they proved to be more resistant to the disease. Where whites contracted yellow fever, the death rate was 70 percent; while, for unknown reasons, the death rate was only 7 percent for afflicted African Americans.[19]

Stage Three: Moderate Growth

The years between 1880 and 1920 marked the third stage, as the population increased by approximately thirty to forty thousand per decade. The nature of that moderate growth, however, had a lasting impact on the city's political culture. The better-off and more cosmopolitan whites who had fled were replaced by poorer and more parochial whites from the surrounding rural areas of Tennessee, Mississippi, and Arkansas.[20] By 1900, the city's foreign-born population had declined to 15 percent, while 80 percent of its residents now hailed originally from the Tennessee and Mississippi countryside.[21]

Roger Biles indicates that "Memphis developed a personality determined in large measure by its southern location."[22] John Harkins observes that, among other things, "the newcomers' conservative rural values were at odds with the urban conception of the good life with its conspicuous consumption and conspicuous leisure. The resulting sense of disorientation and alienation may have contributed to high rates of crime and violence which troubled Memphis well into the 20th century."[23] In the latter part of the nineteenth century, for instance, the Ku Klux Klan was active locally and was even openly involved in electoral politics.[24]

Stage Four: Urban Growth

Stage four, from 1920 to 1970, was marked by the largest population increases in the city's history. Its population increased by approximately one hundred thousand per decade, except during the Depression years. Much of that growth continued to originate from the rural South, and a sizable share of it resulted from the annexation of surrounding areas.[25]

Among other things, this pattern continued to produce a very conservative electorate. In 1968, as a case in point, Democrat Hubert Humphrey received 12 percent of the white vote, Republican Richard Nixon received 46 percent, and American Independent George Wallace received 42 percent. The votes for Wallace, and to a somewhat lesser degree a number of the votes for Nixon, reveal the conservative nature of the white electorate overall. In addition, Wallace's support cut across all income lines, although it came disproportionately from working-class whites.[26]

Stage Five: An Era of Change

In stage five of the city's urbanization, we find a degree of gradual demographic, political, and social change. In terms of demographics, figure 1 shows that, beginning in the early 1970s, population growth slowed to a trickle, while the city actually lost population over the course of the following decade. Part of this change may have been related to adverse publicity following the King assassination. National publications, for example, often referred to Memphis as a "backwater town." Even more directly, however, there was the continual movement of wealthier black and white citizens to the suburbs surrounding Memphis, while the city's reliance on annexation slowed considerably.

The Memphis Economy and the Political Culture

Besides the transplantation of rural culture into southern cities, Goldfield also notes how the nature of the southern economy limited both economic and social development.[27] In Memphis, historians have indeed found the political culture intertwined with the city's economic system, thus creating Goldfield's social and economic constraints.

In 1873, local merchants established a cotton exchange that was to become the largest "spot market" in the world.[28] An economic system developed, which financed and marketed cotton from planting to production. It was a highly lucrative process since commissions and profits resulted from the variety of businesses built around cotton even in years when the price of the commodity itself was low. Because of the stability of such profit, there was little reason for Memphis financiers to industrialize the city.[29]

The family names of these planters and financiers are still recognizable among the prominent families, historical institutions, and named streets of Memphis. They include Fontaine, Norfleet, Brinkley,

Donnelson, Dunnavant, Fargason, Farnsworth, Galbreath, Neely, Orgill, Overton, Snowden, and Trezevant. These families controlled the cotton trade, banks, real estate, transportation, and insurance businesses.[30] And many of these names continue to be found among the city's economic elite, as well as among the list of large campaign contributors in Memphis politics.

The physical modernization of Memphis took place during the post–World War I era. It was a time when Memphis constructed some landmark downtown buildings, such as Lowenstein's department store, the Cotton Exchange Building, and the Claridge and Peabody hotels. The industrial base of the city expanded with the Buckeye, Swift, and Humko companies, as well as a large Sears distribution center. Further industrial growth after World War II brought industries such as Du Pont, Firestone, and International Harvester.

Memphis economic elites wanted to partake of the profits of a growing economy; yet, they were also cultural traditionalists who wanted to keep their rural values.[31] This conservatism was related to the type of boosterism they employed. For example, one of the members of the conservative economic elite composed the following poem that provides some insight into the elites' view of the city: "Before the dawn of Christianity; the boast of man was I am a Roman; Today; the same man would have said; I am a Memphian."[32]

Although benign on its face, this type of boosterism reflected a blind spot. These elites were either out of touch with the serious problems faced by many in the city or they were simply choosing to ignore those problems. As late as 1941, for instance, the Chamber of Commerce maintained that "Memphis is well housed; Memphis has no housing problem."[33] As late as the 1970s, city officials called Memphis "[t]he city of Good Abode." Such rhetoric, however, simply ignored the residential squalor faced by thousands of severely indigent Memphians.

The types of employers coming to Memphis also reflected this adherence to traditionalism. They were companies who manufactured machinery and chemicals for the agricultural base of Memphis or processed the farm commodities that were eventually to include more than cotton.[34] Rather than being harbingers for social change, however, most of these companies were drawn to Memphis, at least in part, because of low wages and the lack of labor unions.[35]

After studying a variety of United States cities in 1970, Daniel Elazar concluded that Memphis was one of the only large southern urban centers to retain what he termed a dominant "traditionalistic" political culture. He defined this type of political culture as including domination by a small group of business elites, a weak white working class, exclusion of blacks whenever possible, and a penchant toward providing only a minimum of public services.[36]

Race and Political Culture

In addition to showing how rural culture was preserved in southern cities and how the southern economy limited social and economic development, Goldfield develops a third theme that deals specifically with the impact of race. He argues that a biracial society and its established hierarchical relationships moved from the rural South into the region's urban settings.

Memphis has had a large African-American population since the decade of the Civil War, when that population reached almost 40 percent, a proportion that held for most of the city's subsequent history. The 1900 and 1980 census figures for blacks showed that they made up approximately 50 percent of the population, while the 1990 figure of 55 percent was an all-time high (figure 2).

The historical literature on Memphis does not paint a pretty picture of the white response to this formidable black community. It suggests that tenets of white supremacy affected the Memphis historical landscape, particularly after 1880. Yet, there were racial problems even before then.

Despite efforts by the Freedmen's Bureau, for example, interracial strife developed, particularly between the blacks and the Irish, who resided in many of the same neighborhoods and competed for many of the same job opportunities. In 1866, for instance, struggling Irish residents turned their frustrations on many of their more recently arriving black neighbors in a three-day riot that left forty-six blacks dead, nearly twice that many injured, five women raped, approximately one hundred blacks robbed, and ninety-one homes, four churches, and all twelve black schools destroyed.[37]

Then, beginning in the latter 1800s and lasting for more than half a century, an elaborate "Jim Crow" system of legally mandated racial segregation developed. Public facilities—from streetcars to parks, from li-

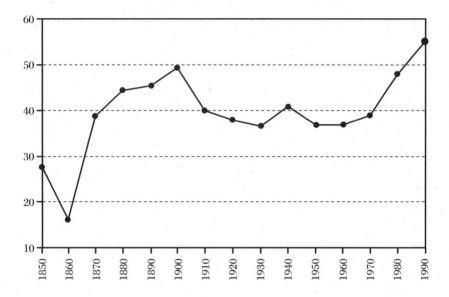

Fig. 2. Memphis Black Population, 1850–1990.

braries to theaters, from shops to restaurants—were all formally segregated. Until 1923, LeMoyne High School was the only accredited four-year high school blacks were allowed to attend, and there were no college opportunities until LeMoyne added a college level in 1932. Not until legal pressure began to build in the 1950s and 1960s were Memphis facilities finally desegregated.[38]

Violent intimidation occurred as well. For example, there were well-publicized lynchings of blacks in 1892 and 1917. There also would continue to be a number of controversial killings of black suspects by white police officers, even in recent years. Some of the most prominent examples include the killings of Levon Carlook (1933) and Elton Hayes (1971), as well as the Shannon Street Seven (1983), an incident remarkably similar to another such event in August of 1916.[39]

Twentieth-century laws and public policies, regardless of intent, reinforced white dominance. For example, repeated annexations of predominantly white suburban areas helped maintain a white majority, while at-large city elections and a runoff provision helped insure that the white majority would be able to have its way electorally.[40]

Beneath such policies, laws, and behavior stood a bedrock belief system that had been nurtured by continued rural white in-migration. As late as the 1940s, Gerald Capers described the dominant Memphis ideology as a combination of "Protestant Fundamentalism, loyalty to a fantastic ideal called the Old South, and uncompromising insistence upon the preservation of white supremacy."[41] William Miller's study of Memphis during the Progressive Era argues that "[t]he white supremacy ideal as it became defended in the Old South was an inevitable folk response to a difficult social problem produced by two racial groups living together in a master-servant relationship...."[42]

In some quarters, an important component of this racial superiority was the ideal of noblesse oblige. Those southern whites believed they had an obligation to protect, uplift, and care for what they perceived to be the less fortunate race. John Terreo reported a quotation from the *Daily Appeal* in 1889 suggesting that African Americans "must be educated and Christianized, and so fitted for the duties of life."[43]

But noblesse oblige extended only so far and, in some ways, reinforced other white supremacist views. Considerable documentation of a white supremacy viewpoint can be found in the pages of the local press. As late as 1918, a prominent white businessman called for repeal of the fifteenth Amendment "in order that normal political life might be restored to the South."[44] More than a decade later, the *Commercial Appeal* declared that "the Anglo-Saxon will not be ruled no matter what the odds are against him. He possesses the imperious and unyielding despotism of conscious superiority."[45] Local white newspapers also regularly used terms like "darkey" and "nigger," called Booker T. Washington an "Alabama coon," and the *Commercial Appeal* ran a degrading "Hambone" cartoon strip from October 1915 until a week after the King assassination in 1968.[46]

Nonetheless, at least since the mid-1920s, neither the White Citizens Council nor the Ku Klux Klan were political forces in Memphis, and the city's white politicians did not participate in the worst of the overt race baiting that was prevalent among vocal southern segregationists such as Lester Maddox and George Wallace. As a matter of fact, Harry Holloway concludes that Memphis "lacked the ardently conservative factions, whether racially or economically oriented, that were present in [cities like] Atlanta and Houston."[47] He even goes so far as to label contemporary Memphis a "prototype of a modern southern community," where "the white population tends to be chiefly concerned with progress and making money."[48]

But where were the white "liberals"? In his study of Memphis between 1900 and 1930, Lester Lamon concludes that "Memphis was almost totally lacking in white liberalism."[49] By 1960, for instance, the Dedicated Citizens' Committee, as liberal a white group as had ever existed in the city, would not allow an African American on its executive committee and supported the maintenance of an all-white school board.[50] In addition, Memphis business groups did not endorse a single black candidate for any office from 1950 through 1980.[51] And, as late as 1993, the Memphis City Council split precisely along racial lines when considering whether to bar members of discriminatory private clubs from being named to city boards and commissions.[52]

Race and Political Leaders

Some of these racial themes found in the political culture have been reflected in the city's political leadership. Two of these leaders, Boss Crump and Henry Loeb, reflected the traditional southern nature of the Memphis political culture.

E. H. "Boss" Crump

A Mississippi-born Irishman, Edward H. "Boss" Crump arrived in Memphis at the age of eighteen and rose from bookkeeper to business president in a mere seven years. He first won city political office in 1905 and soon led the ouster of Mayor Joseph Williams's city hall machine. Oddly enough, Crump was elected mayor in 1909 on a "reform" ticket, and he was the first mayor to serve under the new commission system. He served as mayor of Memphis from 1909 to 1915, when the state legislature removed him from office for failing to enforce the Tennessee prohibition law.[53]

By the late 1920s, he had consolidated his political power; without holding public office himself, he proceeded to dominate Memphis politics from then until his death in 1954. For example, his mayoral candidates lost only two precincts between 1928 and 1948, and those precincts were subsequently abolished upon redistricting. In four of the mayoral races, his candidates actually got approximately 99 percent of the votes cast.[54]

In constructing his own political organization, Crump successfully registered the number of black voters he needed, and he turned them out to vote with the help of a number of prominent blacks.[55] His base of support was an odd mix of blacks, Irish immigrants, and rural southern whites, and, like most bosses of the day, he held his coalition together with selective patronage.[56]

In many ways, Crump was a paradox. On the one hand, he ruled with absolute and ruthless power. He was known to use regulatory agencies, personal attacks, and even henchmen to harass his enemies.[57] For example, he used physical force by the police to stop the CIO from organizing workers, and when black clergyman G. A. Long defied Crump's wishes and dared to allow union activist A. Phillip Randolph to speak from the pulpit of his church, Crump responded by having Long physically assaulted, the police harass his congregation, and fire inspectors require thousands of dollars in church repairs.[58]

Yet, on the other hand, Crump was also progressive in a number of ways. He improved the streets, enhanced fire and police services, attacked the violent crime that had long plagued the city, made Memphis one of the "cleanest" and "quietest" cities in America,[59] and formed a model public utility that exists to the present. According to Capers, he was "spectacularly efficient, economical and honest."[60]

In addition, he had overt populist leanings, leanings that occasionally put him at odds with a number of the city's monied elite.[61] Crump denied being a "boss," claiming instead to be "just an unassuming good citizen working with and for the people."[62] He also claimed he was in "favor [of] submitting anything to the people."[63] Overall, a significant part of his appeal stemmed from the fact that he had a good sense of what would be politically popular and was trusted by his loyal base of supporters.

Even more important, Crump fit the political culture of Memphis. His Holly Springs, Mississippi, roots appeared in his southern gentry attire and in his unabashed gallantry toward women. Further, he was quite accessible to citizens. He staged parties and barbecues, had a high public profile, and was plainly outspoken.[64] In addition, he understood the parameters of the political culture and eventually ended machine reliance on vice and liquor so as not to alienate fundamentalist preachers and their congregations.[65]

In terms of race, Crump was an avowed segregationist. For example, despite his fervent patriotism, in 1948 he made Memphis the first United States city to cancel a visit by the red, white, and blue Freedom Train, which carried the original United States Constitution, Declaration of In-

Fig. 3. E. H. "Boss" Crump and His Wife,
Bessie. Courtesy of The University of Mem-
phis Libraries, Mississippi Valley Collection.

dependence, and other historical documents. He simply refused to comply with the American Heritage Foundation's requirement of desegregated viewing, even though such cities as Atlanta and Jackson, Mississippi, had made that concession.[66] He never allowed an African American to hold any position of power within his political machine. And he also worked hard to purge the city of black leaders perceived to be militant in any way (e.g., G. A. Long, Robert Church Jr., Dr. J. B. Martin, Harry Gibson, and Howard Perry).[67]

Nonetheless, he stifled white attacks, and events similar to the riot of 1866 and the lynching of 1892 did not occur under Crump's leadership; he kept the Ku Klux Klan at bay in order to protect both blacks and Irish Catholics; he delivered selective patronage to the black community; he tacitly allowed much illicit trade on Beale Street; and he hired the city's first black police officer in 1948.

Henry Loeb

The themes we find in the Crump era—adherence to the old southern values, populism, and the subordination of African Americans—recur with Henry Loeb. Loeb, however, did not rule as long as Crump nor did he have Crump's political style or organization.

Loeb was elected public works commissioner in 1955, one of five commissioners that governed the city of Memphis under the form of government it had employed since 1909. He was considered a racial moderate during those years, although he became increasingly segregationist in his public views during his 1959 mayoral campaign.[68] He won that mayoral race, making him the strongest of the commissioners and the spokesperson for the city. Yet, even though he was popular during his first term and could easily have been reelected, Loeb chose not to run in 1963, apparently because his wife wanted him to leave public life.

Four years later, Loeb was back in the political fray. Increasingly conservative and segregationist, he became mayor after winning a runoff against a moderate white candidate, William Ingram. In that runoff, Loeb won 80 percent of the white vote, while Ingram won 99 percent of the black vote.

These were difficult times, as Memphis was becoming a racial powder keg. During the preceding summer, for example, there had been several acts of random racial violence. Harkins indicates that many white Memphians began purchasing guns and ammunition in anticipation of a race war.[69] The 1967 election itself took place after the city changed to a mayor–council form of government. The change, discussed at length in chapter 3, was at least partially orchestrated by moderates who hoped that it would professionalize city government and move Memphis forward in race relations.[70]

Then, an event in 1968 propelled Memphis and Loeb to a place of infamy in American political history. Low-paid black workers attempted to organize a sanitation workers' union. Loeb opposed unions on philosophical grounds and because state law outlawed municipal unions. He also was concerned about the need to balance the city budget and thus was offering only limited raises for city workers. When Martin Luther

Fig. 4. Mayor Henry Loeb Speaking with College Students. Courtesy of The University of Memphis Libraries, Mississippi Valley Collection.

King Jr. came to Memphis to march with the workers, he was assassinated at the Lorraine Motel. Memphis became the shame of the country, and Loeb was at the center of this maelstrom.[71]

Loeb was a traditional southerner, a fact mirrored in a plaque given to him by Southern Airways that characterized him as a "southern aristocrat."[72] Harkins describes him as a man who "emphasized old-fashioned virtues—pride, thrift, hard work, decency and patriotism."[73] A staff member close to Loeb suggested that he was so honest that he would not even drive a city car to pick up an item at a convenience store. He was conservative with city funds and brought a businesslike approach to city government, with line-item and capital budgeting.[74]

His unbending convictions created problems for him politically, however. *The Commercial Appeal* called him "conservative, benevolent and sometimes crude," inclined to do whatever he felt was "right" rather than popular, regardless of the personal or public cost.[75] In 1980, Mori Greiner, editor of the *Commercial Appeal*, called Loeb "intolerant and oppressive," a man who "almost destroyed this city and poured it down the drain."[76] Thomas Cowan characterized the Loeb period as a time of "super intolerance."[77] And a local political analyst said that Loeb had "hurt this community more than any other person in the history of Memphis. He made the people proud they were racist. He contributed massively to the racial polarization of this town."[78]

Nevertheless, Loeb was also a populist who had a solid base of support in the Memphis white community. Harkins suggested that his appeal was so immense that he "acted as a one-man political machine."[79] Loeb himself said that he "was a typical Memphian. No doubt that was one reason I had a lot of support. I thought like an average Memphian."[80] Even after leaving office, he commanded adulation among many older white residents. *Memphis Magazine* described a speech he was to give at Wesley-Highland Towers, where he was introduced as "your friend and mine and everybody's friend."[81] Nowhere was this adulation more apparent than at the many Loeb Dutch Treat Luncheons, which featured various public speakers. Started in the mid-1950s, they continue today, although, at Loeb's death, his family asked the group to remove his name from the title. The former mayor referred to fellow conservatives who attended these luncheons as "200 crazy nuts over there who want to eat with me."[82]

Among other things, Loeb was a practitioner of a form of noblesse oblige. Although he was a self-proclaimed segregationist, Harkins argues that he was not a racist in his personal life.[83] Joan Beifuss indicates that he was not a well-read person and thus could not see that "genteel structural racism" had the same impact as "blatant racism."[84]

His defenders, on the other hand, overlooked the negative side of his views. City council member Jerred Blanchard said that he was a "very decent guy. Decency is essence to him. They call it the plantation kind of thing, but this is just decency as Henry Loeb understands decency." Referring to the workers during the sanitation strike, Blanchard said Loeb "never cut off utilities [of the workers]; he increased contributions for food stamps and got waivers on insurance policies."[85] Other anecdotes concerning Loeb's "decency" abound. A staff member close to Loeb suggested that he had a paternalistic view of blacks. He once fired a sanitation supervisor who was lending money to workers at usurious rates. During the sanitation strike that took place in the cold winter weather, he invited a picket walker to his office for hot coffee.[86]

Overall, however, he did not look to acclimate white Memphians to a sharing of power with the African-American community. Not only was he an avowed segregationist, but a number of white Memphians understood his motto, "Be Proud Again," as a "white-power" protest against civil rights. And as late as 1980, the Loeb Dutch Treat Luncheons were punctuated by racial epithets from the audience.[87]

In point of fact, he actively worked to keep blacks out of public life. In 1959, for instance, black candidate Russell Sugarmon ran for Loeb's former position as public works commissioner against a number of white opponents. There was no runoff provision at the time, and mayoral candidate Loeb was concerned that a black might succeed him in office. Since he wanted the white popular majority to prevail, he asked the governor to call a special session of the state legislature to pass a runoff requirement. He also called a meeting of the white candidates seeking his former post; and, in the face of considerable pressure, one of the two leading white candidates dropped out of the race.[88]

In 1960, Sugarmon and other blacks met with Loeb and his fellow city commissioners to propose gradual desegregation, starting with parks and museums. The mayor listened to the presentation, emphatically said "No," and then proceeded to turn his chair so his back was facing the black visitors.[89] In 1961, when the other commissioners endorsed black A. W. Willis for a vacancy on the Memphis Transportation Authority board, Loeb vetoed the appointment because of Willis's desegregation activities.[90] Loeb's insensitivity to blacks' social situation was matched by his insensitivity to their political position. In 1970, a black youth fleeing police was beaten to death by law enforcement officials. Fires and other disturbances resulted in the black community. Loeb was fast to call a curfew, but appeared to ignore the underlying problems in the police department that were perceived to have contributed to the death.[91]

Wyeth Chandler and the Politics of Transition

Change was beginning to take place in the political and social arenas, however, although it tended to be incremental and subtle. At the leadership level, the transition began with the 1971 retirement of Henry Loeb

*Fig. 5. Wyeth Chandler, Mayor of Memphis,
1971–1982. Courtesy of the Memphis/Shelby
County Archives, Memphis/Shelby County Public
Library and Information Center.*

as mayor and his replacement by Wyeth Chandler. Loeb hand-picked
Chandler after a meeting that included Loeb, Chandler, conservative city
council member Bob James, city council member Downing Pryor, and
grain industrialist Ned Cook.[92]

In his initial municipal election, Chandler won two-thirds of the vote
in the more affluent white areas and about half the vote in white working-class areas such as Frayser. One of his main opponents was future
county mayor William "Bill" Morris, who received labor endorsements
but not the majority of labor votes. Morris also had expected to win much
of the black vote, but it ultimately went to Judge Kenneth Turner.

Judge Turner had contact with the black community from his years as
a very prominent juvenile court judge in Memphis. As a result, he received endorsements from such prominent black political organizations
as the Unity League, Democrat Council, Kennedy Democratic Organiza-

tion, and the Eighth District Political Association.[93] Ultimately, he captured the bulk of the African-American vote in both the 1971 general election and in the runoff.

Chandler, on the other hand, was a product of the city's traditional political culture. *Memphis Magazine* referred to his "good ole boy pose" and lack of creativity in politics.[94] A staff member in his administration described his lack of a philosophy and vision.[95] Chandler's response was that "I don't want to be thought of as some intellectual," and "what makes a city strong and viable isn't the anything goes–cosmopolitan attitude." He described Memphis as "not a cosmopolitan city. It's a city of people with rural backgrounds, of people from southwest Kentucky, from southeast Arkansas, from northwest Mississippi."[96]

His views on race were of the same school as Loeb's, although he did not possess Loeb's level of rigidity. One staff member claimed that Chandler could see the African-American side of issues. The same staff member believed that Chandler was resigned to the fact that blacks would not support him, however, because of the Loeb endorsement. Mayor Chandler said, "I try to represent everybody," yet he did not have black staff members, and his only black department head administered a small human services program. Further, Chandler often characterized whites as "we" or "our people" and blacks as "they" or "your people."[97]

As mayor, Chandler did not appear particularly interested in the details of the job and had a social life that led one staff member to call him a "fun loving tom cat."[98] He left the running of the city to two very capable chief administrative assistants, Clay Huddleston and Henry Evans, and some talented department heads, such as Sanitation Director Maynard Stiles and Police Director Buddy Chapman.

The modern development of downtown Memphis, including the Mud Island recreation area and museum, the downtown walking mall, and the renovation of the Peabody Hotel, were directly attributable to the Chandler administration. Thus, changes in public policy came much faster than changes in racial politics.

W. Otis Higgs and Coalition Politics

In 1975, black Criminal Court Judge W. Otis Higgs ran against Chandler in a race that was to provide many elements of subsequent black versus white elections.[99] The reaction of the white community was at least as interesting as the dynamics in the black community.

Higgs was impressive and articulate and had excellent credentials. For example, he had founded the acclaimed Pretrial Release Program and Project First Offender, two programs that combined to streamline the bail and probation systems in Shelby County. He was also a criminal court judge, the youngest and the only black judge in the state at the time of his appointment.

Higgs decided to run only hours before the filing deadline, and in the process he undercut Judge Kenneth Turner, who had expected the level of black support he had received four years earlier. Higgs's late entry meant that he would have only limited funds and would have to put together his media material in the midst of the campaign.

In addition, he had to gain white support because the demographics of the community showed that only 38 percent of the voting-age population was African American. Thus, there was a debate in his camp, for example, concerning whether even to put his picture on his leaflets, as he did not want to be seen as solely the candidate of the black community.[100] Meanwhile, he ran a race-neutral campaign, focusing on the lack of progress and poor quality of life in Memphis, as well as on the lack of quality in the city's public policy. He also referred to Chandler's tunnel vision and called him the guardian of the status quo.[101]

Although he entered the race very late, Higgs enjoyed support from a number of whites, including lawyer Bill Bruce, pollster Berje Yacoubian, councilperson Jerred Blanchard, state legislator Pam Gaia, and lawyer John Dice.[102] Much of the support for his door-to-door campaign came from committed young staff members and volunteers involved with Pretrial Release and Project First Offender. He addressed whites directly through a low-profile campaign in which he met with small groups of neighbors in their homes.[103] At a typical meeting, Higgs would focus on public policy and the need for leadership. He portrayed himself as a serious person with sense of humor, and definitely not a radical.[104] Although effective at cementing the votes of those attendees who were leaning in his direction, this strategy was time consuming, and time was a commodity that he did not have because of his late entry into the race.

Meanwhile, Chandler raised large sums of money for a media blitz, worked the phones in the white community, and held backyard receptions in the more affluent white areas. He ignored the black vote and made few overt attempts at race baiting. "Instead," according to John Daniel, "he attacked Higgs's qualifications calling the move from judge to mayor a vast leap."[105] In addition, Chandler questioned Higgs's knowledge of city government; a prominent member of his organization said, "[I]f he were white, [Higgs] wouldn't have [gotten his votes] because he lacked the true qualifications that a mayor needs."[106]

The behavior of white candidate Kenneth Turner was paradoxical. He had positioned himself as a moderate in 1971 in order to get the black vote. Beginning in 1975, however, a white moderate would have a much harder time attracting many black votes as there were now viable black candidates. At the same time, the large majority of the white vote continued to go in the direction of conservative white candidates. In apparent frustration, Turner ran an exceptionally negative campaign against Higgs.[107]

Chandler and Higgs were the two top vote getters in the general election and therefore met in a runoff. In the final voting, Chandler triumphed on the strength of his solid base in the white community.

Dick Hackett and the Conservative Legacy

Chandler finally tired of being mayor altogether and accepted a judicial appointment in 1982. At that point, it appeared that the city council planned to name one of its members, Oscar Edmonds, as mayor. A lawsuit filed by public-interest attorney Dan Norwood, however, succeeded in requiring an election to fill the post.[108]

In the subsequent special election, the conservative torch passed to Richard C. "Dick" Hackett, a county clerk in charge of license plate distribution and car registration. Hackett had reformed a previously inefficient office, eliminating the long lines that had come to characterize the license-renewal process. He also had an enormous grassroots following in Memphis since he had once worked for Chandler's Mayor's Action Center, an agency that responded to citizen complaints about city services. In addition, conflicts with his staff suggested he was not sympathetic toward unions or black workers, a political plus among conservative Memphis whites.

Hackett's black opponent was a member of the city council, J. O. Patterson, who was chairperson of the council when Chandler resigned and thus served briefly as interim mayor. He served as a state legislator during the same time and thus seemed somewhat uninvolved in city government because of his many absences.

More serious opposition to Hackett came from a moderate white candidate, Michael Cody, who was a city councilperson, a member of a highly visible law firm, and very photogenic. Cody's legal contacts and attractive personality made him an effective fund-raiser in the white business community. Whereas Hackett had to depend upon his grass-roots effort, Cody used his money for an extensive media campaign.

In the end, Hackett captured the white conservative vote, Patterson captured the smaller black vote, and Cody finished a close third. Hackett then went on to win the runoff against Patterson, with Patterson receiving few white crossover votes and failing to generate even the black turnout that Higgs had inspired just three years earlier.

As an incumbent mayor, Hackett ran in 1983 for a full four-year term and triumphed over a split black community without needing a runoff. Black candidate John Ford received the most black votes, and W. Otis Higgs ran second in a bitter campaign. J. O. Patterson did not run, but he apparently was angry with John Ford, who had not acceded to a Patterson candidacy in the 1978 county mayor's race.

The pattern was similar in 1987 when Hackett ran against black city council member Minerva Johnican and black activist Teddy Withers; again Hackett won without a runoff. Moreover, he ultimately won with a relatively high black crossover vote, at least by local standards. He had received endorsements from the Shelby County Democratic Club, a black political organization, and from D'Army Bailey, a local black political activist and 1983 mayoral candidate, who said that it was "time to break the stalemate of race as a definition of our politics."[109]

Hackett's black support developed as he appointed African Americans to his administration and directed some highly visible public policy projects toward the black community. Although he depended upon white conservative voters, Hackett generally avoided overt racial appeals or even indirect racial cues in his electoral politics. In particular, he enjoyed a reputation for getting things done. His administration was widely credited with improving the city's economy; and, although blacks did not share equally in that improvement, various downtown and tourist projects did provide a number of low-skill jobs for the inner-city black population.

Political Change in Memphis

> The South, with all its distinctiveness and contrasts, has always been a
> region in slow motion. . . . [S]outhern leaders patiently constructed layers
> of cities.

—Lawrence Larsen, *The Rise of the Urban South*

Despite the dominant political culture, some groupings of moderate
white leaders have emerged from time to time, especially during stage
five.[110] The Memphis Committee on Community Relations, for instance,
hatched a plan for gradual desegregation in the 1960s. Yet, there is little
doubt that many of the city's small group of white liberals became alienated by the black nationalism of that period.[111] For example, the running
of black mayoral candidate A. W. Willis in 1967 was opposed as being
premature; and when black political leader Jesse Turner argued that
"[w]e're 40 percent of the population. We want 40 percent of the money,
40 percent of the land, and 40 percent of the jobs," long-time moderate
Lucius Burch responded that "you'll have to put a bullet in me to get
that [handed to you]."[112]

Nevertheless, the 1970s and 1980s brought a degree of political
change. This change did not replace the dominant political culture, but
it may have sensitized it somewhat as Memphis moved toward becoming a more modernized city.

To begin with, a group of black political leaders emerged who appeared to inspire more trust in the white community. They included
Higgs; Shep Wilbun, an innovative city council member active in housing
policy; the head of the city's Division of Housing, Robert Lipscomb, who
had been active in a delinquency prevention effort known as "Memphis
Partners"; Jerome Ryans, a head of the Memphis Housing Authority; former
county assessor Michael Hooks; city council member Myron Lowrey;
Judge D'Army Bailey, who was a driving force behind the creation of
the city's National Civil Rights Museum; former Juvenile Court referee
Veronica Coleman, nominated for a federal attorney's post; Judges Odell
Horton and Bernice Donald; public defender A. C. Wharton; and Greg
Duckett, the chief administrative officer in the Hackett Administration.

As for white political leaders, the Crump years had been disastrous because Boss Crump had not tolerated competitors to his political rule. Although he may have produced technicians who could administer services, there was a dearth of political leaders who could lead the city out of its traditional political culture. The result was a vacuum that provided an opportunity for a man as rigid as Henry Loeb to exercise political power once Crump departed.

While Wyeth Chandler was only a transitional figure between the traditional political culture and an unsettled future, finally a more moderate white leadership cadre began to emerge. This group included Hackett, economic leaders such as Henry Turley and Fred Smith, and city council members such as Barbara Sonnenberg and Jack Sammons. Moreover, Shelby County Mayor Bill Morris brought county resources to bear on problems in the black community, including full county funding of the area's lone public hospital and an innovative study of local poverty that resulted in a proposal, "Free the Children," that outlined a comprehensive set of steps for gradual reduction of poverty in a north Memphis area.[113]

In addition, the city hired a number of highly competent professional administrators. Chandler, for example, had recruited competent administrative officers who ran the city while he played his political and personal roles. Hackett cultivated a solid working partnership with the Memphis business community that spawned innovative policies in areas such as downtown development. Meanwhile, the 1993 *Memphis Poll* showed that there was widespread satisfaction with the resulting public services, satisfaction that cut across racial lines. Over 90 percent of the respondents thought that the fire department was doing a competent job, and the same percentage was satisfied with the zoo and Pink Palace Museum. Other major services also received impressive rankings by Memphians, as did downtown development, projects to assist businesses to relocate to Memphis, and efforts to promote tourism.[114]

Moreover, Memphis gradually became somewhat more diverse. Although it remains nearly the most ethnically homogenous large city in the nation,[115] its political landscape did come to include Southeast Asians, Native Americans, Hispanics, gays, an artist colony, and professionals from across the United States. Memphis colleges and universities prospered and brought cultural diversity to their students and the community as a whole. Beyond these demographic factors, Memphians developed new political and social institutions, such as a rich fabric of neighborhood organizations.[116]

The churches were important agents of political change as well. While Selma Lewis's study of the 1968 sanitation strike indicated that white churches played a very minimal intervention role in that tragic series of events,[117] the 1970s and 1980s brought a much greater commitment by those white churches. The Memphis Inter-Faith Association (MIFA) formed and has been particularly effective at providing food for the indigent. Calvary Episcopal Church developed programs for the homeless, while the Catholic diocese worked with Vietnamese and Hispanic immigrants. Churches founded VECA, the city's largest integrated neighborhood organization. Further, the Alinsky-type group, Shelby County Interfaith, brought together white and black churches to address community problems.[118]

Another major source of change was a new generation of businesses that chose to locate in Memphis. The 1920s and 1940s had brought to Memphis firms looking for a city with low taxes, low wages, and a lack of unions. Many of those manufacturing companies had since left Memphis, and they did not leave a legacy of enlightenment or community improvement. The 1970s and 1980s found companies more interested in using and improving the city's amenities. These companies and their employees played a role in supporting the arts, improving community institutions such as the zoo and Pink Palace Museum, and participating in a variety of neighborhood and social groups.[119]

There were also indigenous companies that believed that their growth was dependent upon both a better educated labor force and an environment of greater tranquillity between blacks and whites. These companies included Federal Express, First Tennessee Bank, Malone and Hyde, Holiday Inn, Turley Real Estate, Auto Zone, and Schering-Plough. They funded innovative community programs like Memphis in May, which brought Memphians downtown; supported social activities through research and operating funds; and encouraged their executives to work with troubled institutions.

The Chamber of Commerce contributed to this evolution as well. Because of the bad press the city received after the garbage strike and the King assassination, these leaders marketed the city with a million-dollar advertising campaign. They hired an enlightened executive director, David Cooley, who spoke in a language not often heard in white Memphis: "The greatest barrier to a better Memphis is ignorance. What are some problems of urban growth? a deteriorating central city . . . bad housing for a large percentage of our population . . . lack of skills training . . . poor worker mobility . . . undereducated and underemployed people in large numbers . . . token acceptance of blacks in decision making positions."[120]

Prominent local families and individuals made contributions, too. For example, funds from the families of former mayor Edmund Orgill and crusading newspaper editor Edward Meeman allowed Southwestern College (now Rhodes College) to form the Urban Policy Institute. John Osman of the Brookings Institution conducted regular seminars using nationally recognized experts to discuss the social, political, and economic problems of Memphis. Participants included political leaders, economic leaders, small-town leaders, and a number of local black and white citizens.

Even though the Urban Policy Institute ceased to exist after Osman's death, the business community, along with many volunteers, came together in a communitywide group called Goals for Memphis. Initially called the Jobs Conference, it organized to spend state funds for capital projects in Memphis that had a potential for economic development. Then, the organization formed into a goal-setting group that examined a variety of community problems, including crime and delinquency, education, black economic development, and many others. In 1992, it launched a Memphis Race Relations and Diversity Institute to "address racism in the workplace and explore the competitive advantages of a diverse work force."[121]

Lastly, organizations like the Mid-South Peace and Justice Center and the local branch of the National Council of Christians and Jews provided the black community with a reliable group of white liberal allies. They were not large enough, however, to provide the base for a significant electoral coalition.[122]

• • •

Over the course of the twentieth century, Memphis began to change. In particular, it was once again becoming more demographically heterogeneous. At the leadership level, the 1970s and 1980s were periods of slow political change as both economic and political leaders worked to improve the reputation Memphis had acquired during the Loeb administration.

Nevertheless, on the eve of the 1991 mayoral election, white political attitudes in the community at large remained a product of a historically traditional political culture that had produced highly polarized voting behavior. Whites simply had been unwilling to relinquish political control to black elected officials. This fact could be seen in the very minimal white crossover voting for black mayoral candidates and the fact that only one black at-large city councilperson had been elected since 1967. Thus, most whites were not ready to vote for W. W. Herenton as mayor in 1991, although a significant number did finally cast their ballots for black city council members.

2 The Hackett Years

The conservative political culture of the city's white majority had long been a force in Memphis. Mayor Richard C. Hackett and a number of his policies were important transitional components in the emerging modernization of both the city's political culture and its economy. The following examination of the incumbent mayor's personal, political, and policy-making history helps confirm that point. It also provides an important context for our analysis of the 1991 mayor's race.

Hackett's Personal Background

Richard Cecil "Dick" Hackett was born in 1949 to William and Rosemary Hackett. He was one of five brothers who grew up on Rosemark Street in the middle of the then sparsely populated Whitehaven area. This was a white working-class neighborhood that was just beginning to develop. His father was a contractor who ran a one-person remodeling firm. His mother was a homemaker. Although far from wealthy, they lived in a comfortable home, and both parents spent considerable time with their children. Dick Hackett's older brother Bill went on to become a general sessions court judge, while his younger brother Mark was to follow in his political footsteps, albeit with far less success.

Dick Hackett attended a Catholic grade school and graduated from Hillcrest, a public high school. He was an average student, but a very industrious person. From an early age, he worked at odd jobs, such as mowing lawns and splitting wood. His brother Bill characterized him as a person who "always worked hard and was organized and efficient."[1] For example, he worked at a Bonanza restaurant clearing tables and later became its manager. His high school career, on the other hand, was less than noteworthy. His grades were mediocre, and he was not involved in school activities. He attended Memphis State University (later renamed the University of Memphis), where he once again made average grades, leaving school one semester short of receiving his degree.[2]

His academic interests were in education (he wanted to be a teacher) and social welfare. The latter interest led to a counselor position at St. Peter's Home for Children, where he spent several years as a live-in guardian to a group of approximately ten children.

He met his future wife, Kathy, at St. Peters. They had three children, Jason, Mary Shea, and William, who were eight, six, and three years of age respectively at the time of the 1991 election. The Hackett family first lived in Whitehaven and later moved to East Memphis.

An active member of St. Louis Catholic Church, Hackett was deeply religious. He was also a devoted family man. He set his priorities as "God, family and city."[3] In a similar vein on another occasion, he said, "I consider myself very much a family man. My number one love."[4] He was fastidious about carving out quality time for his family, and he was careful to keep his political and family lives separate. For example, his home phone was unlisted to protect his family from political phone calls; further, he canceled his home subscription to the *Commercial Appeal,* sparing both himself and his family the harshness of publicized personal criticism. In addition, his family normally did not appear at political events with the mayor.

Political Life

Hackett worked in the 1971 mayoral campaign of Wyeth Chandler. Chandler was searching for a staff member from the Whitehaven area, and Hackett was drawn to the campaign because his parents had admired Chandler's opposition to the annexation of Whitehaven into the city of Memphis. Once in the Chandler administration, Hackett created and became the first director of the Mayor's Action Center, a city complaint bureau. In 1976 he refused Chandler's offer to serve as interim city court clerk; but in 1978 he was elected as the Shelby County clerk and reelected again in 1982. When Chandler resigned in 1982, Hackett won a runoff election and became, at age thirty-three, the youngest mayor of any major U.S. city at that time. Memphians reelected him in 1983 and 1987. In 1992, following his mayoral defeat at the hands of Herenton, he went to work for St. Jude Children's Research Hospital as director of development.

Although he never declared a political affiliation, Hackett endorsed George Bush in 1988 and was generally presumed to be a Republican. His 1992 campaign financial disclosure form, for instance, listed four hundred dollars spent on tickets for local Republican Party events. On the other hand, he also had strong ties to a number of local Democrats, some of whom worked on his campaign. The wife of Democratic political leader William Farris arranged his campaign receptions, and Democrat Oscar Edmonds was his primary ally on the city council. One of his closest advisors and a member of his administration, Paul Gurley, ran for the state legislature as a Democrat.

As for ideology, Dick Hackett's defeat in 1991 marked the end of white conservative governance in Memphis. Yet, Hackett said as early as 1982 that he was not a "Chandler-type conservative." He labeled himself a "progressive moderate," although he actually appeared to be more of a moderate conservative.[5] For example, he prided himself on being very conservative with regard to fiscal matters, and he believed he had to constantly balance his concern for budgets against his concern for human services.[6] He was very outspoken about the need to eliminate parole and enact capital punishment, although his drug czar, Jerry Oliver, emphasized prevention and social programs. He participated openly in anti-abortion rallies.[7] With regard to race, he avoided racially derisive public statements; when he was asked racially insensitive questions, such as "why did you appoint black directors," he responded that such questions were "insulting." On the other hand, he depended upon conservative whites for the bulk of his votes.

Lastly, it is important to note that Dick Hackett was largely a loner, with only a few intimate friends. Among other things, this position facilitated his break from the old political regime and allowed him to steer a more independent and moderate course, as he was not tied into the social network that had long carried the torch for the traditional political culture of the city.

Hackett first won elective office in 1978. That year he won the Shelby

County clerk's position, obtaining 51 percent of the vote against eight other candidates. The office had a reputation for inefficiency, particularly because of the way it handled the yearly renewal of license plates. There were long waiting lines, as residents had to renew their licenses at the clerk's office at the same time each calendar year. Utilizing an innovative political sign of a license plate with his name on it, Hackett campaigned for the clerk's office on his performance in the Mayor's Action Center and suggested that he would bring the same energy and innovation to the clerk's position.

Once in office, he instituted a branch office, introduced a method whereby residents could mail-order their licenses, and staggered the dates that plates were to be renewed. In the process he reduced the clerk's expenditures by 20 percent, decreased the staff from ninety to fifty, and increased revenue by 60 percent.[8] He also instituted a dress code in the office, banned chewing gum and smoking, and worked on improving the office's common courtesy toward the public.

As a reaction, employees attempted to unionize. Among other things, they charged Hackett with discrimination and harassment. Hackett responded that these charges were only tactics designed to advance the unionization effort.[9] He was ultimately successful in this battle with his employees, and he went on to easily win reelection in both 1978 and 1982.

Mayor Chandler resigned from office on September 28, 1982. Hackett and a variety of other candidates then ran for the post. This election provided a number of important lessons about Memphis politics.

First, the white electorate quickly identified Hackett as its candidate. Hackett had the pulse of the Memphis political culture, which was essentially working class and "earthy." White Memphians liked his common-man approach, an image that he had cultivated at the Mayor's Action Center. With his sleeves rolled up and his tie undone, he had demonstrated an ability to slash government while still delivering services.

Moreover, Hackett seemed to benefit from his well-publicized battle with black union members over the behavior and dress standards he had imposed in the clerk's office. Although he made no racially polarizing public statements, it certainly appeared that some voters perceived an anti-black strain in Hackett and supported him for that reason.[10] The Hackett mayoral races, like other recent mayoral contests, showed high levels of racial polarization in voting results.

In addition, the 1982 election demonstrated the racial component of Memphis electoral politics in yet another way. Black candidate J. O. Patterson ran a rhetorically muted campaign until the end of the runoff. During the runoff, for instance, Hackett and Patterson treated each other so gently that the newspapers called the campaign a "love fest." Once he realized that victory was slipping away, however, Patterson made some racially polarizing statements. For example, he accused Hackett of having called a black employee a "Mau Mau." The outburst appeared to reflect a recognition that Patterson needed a polarized black community in order to maximize turnout—a technique used by a number of black candidates in subsequent Memphis elections.

Lastly, the 1982 race demonstrated that a qualified white moderate could not win a mayoral election in Memphis. Michael Cody, a Kennedy-esque candidate well liked by many of the city's corporate elites, ran with the intent of attracting enough black and moderate white votes to reach the runoff. He wanted to "bridge the gap between all segments of the community" and "step across the [racial] line."[11] Cody attempted to "show the nation that Memphis is a city that is trying hard to heal its racial wounds."[12] The conventional wisdom was that Cody lost because he was not a conservative. Exit polls also showed that 40 percent of the self-identified liberals in the community voted for Hackett.[13] This data indicates that the city's self-identifying liberals were either not particularly liberal on the race issue, or that they demanded a more populist approach from their candidate.

The 1983 election for a full term was uneventful, although the black community was deeply split. The 1987 election, on the other hand, was the apex of Hackett's electoral success. The city had just retained St. Jude Children's Research Hospital, which had appeared to be planning to move to St. Louis. International Paper had relocated its headquarters from New York to the Memphis area. A fifty-six-million-dollar propeller testing facility opened in an industrial area of Memphis known as Presidents Island. And, to top it all off, *Fortune* magazine had recently called Memphis a "boomtown."[14]

In addition, Hackett had dodged two racially charged political bullets: the police shootings of Joseph Robinson and of the Shannon Street Seven. A mentally disturbed person, Joseph Robinson was shot after brandishing a knife. Recognizing that this could become a politically incendiary event, Hackett visited Robinson's mother in the LeMoyne Gardens public housing project to express condolences. He also spoke with the state and federal prosecutors about investigating the incident. Similarly, with much help from Police Director John Holt, Hackett was able to defuse the highly volatile Shannon Street affair, in which police appear to have summarily executed seven black men who had themselves brutally tortured and murdered a police hostage. In the end, Hackett received an incredible 18 percent of the black vote to win handily in 1987.

Dick Hackett's political style encompassed an unusual mix of components. He was a down-to-earth working man on one hand, and yet a somewhat cold and distant technocrat on the other. He also had a relatively rocky relationship with the Memphis City Council, although this did not seem to detract from his broad-based popularity in the white community.

Thus, Hackett was a populist of sorts, albeit not a very charismatic one. The *Commercial Appeal* indicated that he had a distaste for "bluebloods," could be quite plain-spoken and blunt at business meetings, and surrounded himself with friends in city hall who were technicians and not very visionary or intellectual.[15] In addition, he leased a mid-sized car and put two of the three mayor's bodyguards back on the street when he took office in 1982.[16]

In sharp contrast to previous mayors like Loeb, Hackett developed a relatively solid working relationship with the city unions. Among other things, he utilized a personal touch in dealing with employee problems. Early in his administration, for instance, he went to the hospital to spend time with an injured fire fighter and his family.[17] He repeated this pattern throughout his years in office, visiting all sorts of ill or injured public servants, including fire fighters, police officers, and sanitation workers.

Despite his efforts to relate to people in a personal, immediate way, Hackett, insular by nature, did not especially like the ceremonial role of mayor. He said, "I don't enjoy the public aspect of political life at all."[18] He also claimed, "I don't consider myself a politician."[19] However, he became an increasingly effective public speaker and gradually warmed to his ceremonial tasks. On one occasion, for example, we had contacted the mayor's office to obtain some publicity photographs for a college brochure. Not only did the mayor patiently pose with our students, but he took them into his conference room and answered political and policy questions for a considerable length of time.

On the other hand, he never did learn to enjoy the travel required in

Fig. 6. Richard C. Hackett, Mayor of Memphis, 1982–1991. Courtesy of the Memphis/ Shelby County Archives, Memphis/Shelby County Public Library and Information Center.

his ambassadorial role. "When the Mayor boards an airplane, he goes coach . . . he takes the last flight that will get him there and the first one that will get him home to Memphis. He does not stay to see the sights or attend fancy receptions."[20] He was uncomfortable in the places he visited. In China, for instance, an aide indicated that he took along peanut butter and jelly in order to avoid most of the native foods.

A technocrat at heart, Hackett did enjoy functioning in his administrative role. He was a career governmental employee who had been involved in government service since he had left Memphis State University. He arrived at the mayor's office by 7:00 A.M. and sometimes did not return home until 10:00 in the evening.[21] As he put it, "I love this job. I feel so comfortable in it, so right in it, that sometimes it sort of scares me."[22] He characterized himself as an administrator and public servant, and after his defeat asked if anyone was interested in hiring "an honest, hard-working administrator."[23]

His chief administrative officer, James Broughton, ended up being more of an assistant than an operations manager. Hackett tended to micromanage departments and special projects. One of his administrators noted that she received weekly phone calls from the mayor about the progress of a particular project; moreover, the mayor was notorious for driving around the city in the evenings, spot-checking city operations and listening to citizens.

Specific examples abound. According to Broughton, "[H]e'd call me at 9 at night and tell me about a situation in a southeast Memphis park and then half a hour later he'd be in North Memphis wanting to know why we couldn't get a sweeper on some street."[24] Or, on one well-publicized occasion, he paid a surprise visit to a police station in the Orange Mound area, only to find a number of officers sitting around watching television. Shortly thereafter, the mayor banned televisions in all police stations.[25]

Hackett's administrative style emanated from his work in the Mayor's Action Center. As director, he would ride on garbage trucks and go into the fields to obtain firsthand knowledge of agencies. He said that the job "helped [him] relate to the everyday problems of services."[26] His work in the center helped him understand the nuts and bolts of city government.

There was also a darker side to the Hackett administrative style. He could be ruthless and made great demands upon his division directors. He was, for instance, relatively quick to replace division directors when they did not meet his administrative requirements or when he wanted to shake up city services. According to an interview with a staff member, Hackett told his directors that if they did not abide by their budget limits he would immediately dismiss them. In addition, some people did not trust his word. One of his city hall staff members called him a man lacking in integrity. There was also an incident in which neighborhood leaders believed he had agreed to terminate plans for an expressway through their neighborhood (Sam Cooper Boulevard) and then denied that he had made the statement.

Overall, however, his was essentially a scandal-free administration; further, he exhibited a loyalty to his directors and his close campaign supporters. After his 1991 loss, for example, he returned that loyalty by taking supporters to various Memphis State sporting events. At budget time, the raises for his administrators regularly exceeded those of public employees. And he occasionally kept a terminated administrator on the payroll until that administrator was able to find another job.

On the other hand, Hackett had a relatively difficult time interacting with the thirteen-member city council. Oscar Edmonds, a conservative Democrat, was his closest ally, and Andy Alissandratos shared Hackett's penchant for a fiscally conservative city. He also enjoyed regular support from Bill Davis and Bob James. But that was about the extent of his reliable support. Hackett had opposed the election of councilperson Mary Rose McCormick. Moreover, he seemed to have negative relations with council moderates, such as Barbara Sonnenburg and Florence Leffler. Black city council members, such as Kenneth Whalum, James Ford, and Shep Wilbun, had a distant relationship with him as well. Whalum asserted that "the Mayor's major strength is his ability to control. The Mayor's major weakness is his inability to share governance."[27] Ford was a frequent foe, too, while Wilbun increasingly accused Hackett of misusing Housing and Community Development funds.

Hackett presented major projects to the council, but he was not inclined to trade votes with them.[28] He also was able to circumvent their will. When the council opposed his downtown trolley project, for instance, he asked private companies to pay the cost of purchasing and restoring the trolley cars. As another example, initial funds for his "drug czar" came not from the city council but from a private donor.

This negative relationship with the city council had a peculiar effect on local government. While Hackett enjoyed considerable popularity, the council was among the most unpopular of local institutions. Citizens, for example, voted against referenda that would have given the council more power or that would have raised council members' salaries. Overall, the public clearly sided with the mayor.

Public Policies

To this point we have painted a picture of a man whose politics was somewhat more moderate than the conservative white majority that elected and revered him. An insular "man-of-the-people," he was an enthusiastic administrator and a reluctant, although quite successful, politician.

We will next examine his achievements and failures in public policy;

and, in the process, we will see his brand of conservatism in action. Specifically, we will examine tax policy, economic development projects, and "people" programs.

In general, Hackett did not change basic city services dramatically. An examination of service categories, for example, shows that their funding levels remained essentially the same over the course of his years in office. Nevertheless, he was quite successful at holding the line on new taxes and at stimulating the local economy.

A conservative at heart, Dick Hackett was very proud of his ability to maintain a stable tax rate. He noted that, whereas other cities were experiencing fiscal distress, "we're hiring new workers, getting things done and holding the line on taxes at the same time."[29] In a Rotary Club debate with Dr. Herenton during the 1991 campaign, Hackett emphasized that the city had been fiscally conservative, yet had "not reduced services or laid off employees."[30] And he had accomplished these goals without increasing city debt.[31] He felt that his knowledge of the mechanics of the city bureaucracy allowed him to control and even reduce the cost of delivering public services. When many thought that a 1992 tax increase was inevitable, he argued that there were still inefficiencies in the bureaucracy that could be reduced.[32]

Hackett was also sensitive to problems with the city's tax structure. During a Rotary Club debate, for example, he supported a less regressive tax arrangement and cited the sales tax on food and prescription drugs as a glaring example of this regressivity. He further indicated a willingness to tax those from Mississippi and Arkansas who were working in Memphis, and he specifically mentioned a similar tax that Memphians had to pay in Mississippi.[33]

The record shows that Hackett did indeed limit the growth of both taxes and fees. The sole tax increase was a 1985 hike in the property tax. Nevertheless, he benefited from a .75 percent increase in the sales tax passed just before he took office, as well as from the revenues generated by the city's 8.75 percent sales tax during the economic growth years of the 1980s. For example, the total revenue produced by the sales tax consistently increased until the last years of the Hackett administration. Consequently, when he increased fees such as the garbage collection fees, zoo admissions, court charges, and sewer fees, the percent of city income from fees actually decreased—from 13.8 percent in 1982 to 12.4 percent in 1990—thanks to the surge in sales tax receipts.[34]

Overall, Memphis had a low tax burden compared to most other cities. Although the sales tax was very high, there was no income tax in Tennessee, no payroll tax in Memphis, and the property tax was low. An average 2,600-square-foot house in Milwaukee, for example, had a property tax burden of $5,426, while a similar house in Memphis had a tax burden of only $1,630.[35] A recent article in the *Commercial Appeal* indicated that Memphis was in the lower third of cities in state and local taxes, and it was at the bottom when compared to cities in the South.[36] *Money* magazine ran a survey of the fifty largest metropolitan areas and found that Memphis was twelfth from the bottom in terms of tax burden.[37]

Nonetheless, fiscal problems still developed. For example, the Hackett administration had a revenue shortfall in four of its last five years. This shortfall reduced the city's cash reserve fund from $32,000,000 dollars in 1987 to $15,000,000 by 1990.[38] A decline in sales tax revenues and the mayor's unwillingness to increase property tax rates meant the city would have to spend more than it took in if services were to be maintained at existing levels. There were limits to what the mayor could save simply by increasing bureaucratic efficiency.

There were also underlying problems over which the Hackett administration had little control. As with most cities, Memphis experienced a loss of population, in this case beginning in 1970. And that loss affected the city's tax base, in particular because it was the more affluent who were moving out.

Historically, Memphis had been able to increase revenues through annexation. Yet, as discussed at length in chapter 5 below, changes in state annexation law meant that only limited annexation would take place during the Hackett administration. Meanwhile, there was little new construction occurring in the city; thus, there were few new sources of tax revenue.

Nevertheless, it was in fiscal policy that the Hackett administration received its highest marks. His administration was able to stabilize property taxes and to continue delivering public services at a time when the city was losing middle-income and upper-income taxpayers. In addition, the city was not forced, as a number of other cities were, to borrow from its bond fund to pay for operating expenses. Overall, the city lived within its means during the Hackett administration and did not suffer significant financial distress. In particular, it enjoyed a high bond rating, a primary indicator of fiscal health. Bond-rating companies, for example, continued to rank Memphis very high in the second tier of American cities. This ranking held even as the city launched large public construction projects like the Pyramid and trolley system, as well as major renovations of city streets, the Pink Palace Museum, the Memphis Zoo, the Brooks Art Museum, and Liberty Bowl Stadium.

Hackett played an important role in the city's economic development. His philosophy was simple, reflecting his ideologically conservative world view: he believed that social problems could be solved by creating jobs in the private sector. Government's role was to promote business and help focus business attention on public problems. He did not differentiate as to whether the jobs would be for the middle class, those outside of Memphis, or for low-income Memphians. Any job creation, in Hackett's view, was good for Memphis.

In order to create jobs, his more immediate goals were both to attract new companies and to retain existing ones. A variety of strategies were employed in order to achieve these goals. For example, he pursued businesses directly—through public-private partnerships—and indirectly—by improving the city's amenities and by renovating its downtown area, which was designed to boost tourism and make Memphis a more attractive place to do business.

His primary goal was to attract companies to Memphis. Coors, Nike, and Williams Sonoma were but a few of the companies attracted to the city during the Hackett years. And, most notably, International Paper moved its corporate headquarters from New York City to Memphis in 1986, as Memphis outbid other Sunbelt cities such as Dallas, Charlotte, and Jacksonville.[39]

The other side of the strategy was to keep companies from leaving Memphis. Hackett had little control over the loss of large Firestone and International Harvester plants, both of which announced their closings before he took office. He also could not dissuade Holiday Inn from moving its corporate headquarters to Atlanta, where a foreign holding company wanted to consolidate its North American operations. Yet, when St. Jude received an offer to move to St. Louis, Hackett orchestrated a forty-four-million-dollar package that would help keep the hospital in Memphis.[40] Hackett called this successful public and private effort the "turning point of the maturing of Memphis."[41]

Such public-private partnerships would become a mainstay in Hackett's economic development strategy. The Chamber of Commerce, for instance, could call on him at virtually any time to meet with the executives from prospective companies. He had monthly breakfast meetings with the business community, besides regularly visiting local firms.[42] Early in his administration, he was himself a member of the Chamber of Commerce and even invited business groups to attend the city's directors' meetings.[43]

Indirectly, he also attempted to lure and retain businesses by improving the city's amenities. These efforts included aiding the Brooks Art Museum, expanding Tom Lee Park along the Mississippi River waterfront, adding Japanese Gardens at the Goldsmith Gardens, beautifying interstate highway exchanges, and capital improvements at the Pink Palace Museum. However, three of the most prominent examples were improvements at the Memphis Zoo, the development of the Wonders Series, and expansion of the Liberty Bowl football stadium.

The Memphis Zoo was among the most attended of Memphis tourist attractions, yet it had an aging capital facility. Hackett reached an understanding with the private Memphis Zoological Society whereby the city agreed to provide two dollars for each dollar contributed privately. The society had already increased attendance through improvements, including an open-air Cat Country exhibit and an impressive new entrance facade.

The "Wonders Series" idea began with the Ramses exhibit. Ramses II was an Egyptian pharaoh who had built numerous monuments to himself. Playing on the connection between Memphis and the ancient city of Memphis in Egypt, the city managed to arrange for a Ramses exhibit to visit. Ramses was a huge success, as tourists flocked to Memphis; and other tourist attractions, such as Graceland and the zoo, enjoyed their highest admissions ever. In addition, other local businesses also benefited. The sales manager of Graham Lighting noted that "we have people in the showroom every week who are from out-of-town in Memphis for Ramses"[44] The final count was 674,395 visitors to the Ramses exhibit, many of them from out of town. The $1,000,000 profit was primarily used to subsidize low-income housing in the Smoky City area of Memphis.

Soon after Ramses, Hackett planned an annual series of similar exhibits, and these came to be known as the "Wonders Series." As seed money, he received a $500,000 gift from grain dealer Ned Cook to pay for initial expenses in developing this idea. The series began with an exhibit of the Russian art of Catherine the Great and attracted comparable exhibits in subsequent years.

Hackett followed a similar strategy with the city's attempt to gain a National Football League franchise. Hackett supported Memphis's NFL application by expanding the city's Liberty Bowl football stadium, which aided the efforts of businessmen Fred Smith and later William Dunavant. Hackett played a crucial role, noting, "I had to take some pretty hard blows to make that happen. If I would have wavered anywhere during that process, that stadium wouldn't be under construction today."[45]

Lastly, Hackett sought to continue the renovation of downtown Memphis. Downtown had lost its role as a center of commerce and business, particularly after 1970, as shopping malls grew in the suburbs. The deterioration of downtown was seen as hurting the city's potential for attracting tourists.

The first new tourism project built downtown was the convention center in 1974. Next, the city converted Main Street into a pedestrian mall constructed with paving blocks. In 1981 the Peabody Hotel was reopened, and the Mud Island museum and river walk recreation area opened in 1982. These were all projects encouraged by the coalition of Mayor Chandler and downtown business interests.

In return, for example, the Convention and Visitors Bureau indicated that Memphis tourist attractions had three million visitors in 1991.[46] Two years later, Memphis tourism officials estimated that tourism was a $1.5 billion industry that produced 32,000 jobs and resulted in $120 million in state and local taxes.[47] Even if these figures were exaggerated, they still suggested that tourism had become big business in Memphis.

Dick Hackett was an avid supporter of downtown development. He argued that the money spent by tourists circulated throughout the entire community.[48] At the Rotary Club debate with Herenton during the 1991 campaign, Hackett claimed he was "protecting inner-city Memphis" by working for these projects.

Not surprisingly, then, he played a significant role in subsequent efforts. These included providing funds to rehabilitate some Beale Street establishments in 1983, building the Crowne Plaza convention center hotel, building the A. W. Willis Bridge to Mud Island in 1987, and creating the National Civil Rights Museum in 1991. Such projects cost government more than $250 million during his administration, not including the interest costs and operating subsidies.[49]

Two of the largest projects were the Pyramid and the downtown trolley. The Pyramid is a twenty-two-thousand-seat arena constructed in downtown Memphis. After it was decided that expanding the existing Mid-South Coliseum would not be cost effective, the county and city mayors appointed a committee that ultimately recommended a downtown arena. After eighteen months of political gridlock, Federal Express, Holiday Inn, Malone and Hyde, and First Tennessee Bank contributed a total of three hundred thousand dollars to develop a plan for what became known as the Pyramid Arena, again playing on Memphis's Egyptian connection. The entire project was to cost no more than thirty million dollars when completed. Hackett then played a crucial role in marshaling the plan through the city council against intense opposition. He especially liked the design, seeing it as a signature for the city, as well as its downtown location next to the convention center.[50]

Enter Sidney Shlenker, an entrepreneur who owned the Denver Nuggets NBA basketball franchise at the time and had been the manager of the Houston Astrodome when it opened. Shlenker characterized the Pyramid as "the first unique building in America since the Astrodome," and he wanted complete control of the building so that he could develop a variety of enterprises within its walls.[51] He proposed a host of "Disney-quality" attractions, including a rock-and-roll museum based around Dick Clark's memorabilia and a rock-and-roll stage, where visiting would-be rock-and-roll stars could perform to an imaginary audience. Besides a number of shops, there was to be a Hard Rock Cafe, an Egyptian museum, an inclinator to take visitors to the top of the Pyramid, and the College Football Hall of Fame, which was to be relocated to Memphis.

In order to gain control of the project, Shlenker agreed to pay $1.5 million a year to the city and county in order to help repay the bonds used for construction. In addition, he agreed to take over Mud Island, a theme park across from the Pyramid, by absorbing the $2 million subsidy the city annually provided to that publicly built facility.

Shlenker's dreams turned to dust, however, when he had to declare bankruptcy. He was unable to gain the construction financing for the attractions, though he seemed to have received an offer of permanent financing from the TIAA insurance fund. He also squabbled with one of his local partners and was reported to have spent project money frivolously. Wildly popular when he came to town, Shlenker left in disgrace and became a political liability to Hackett. In addition, the final price of the Pyramid rose to $56 million; and now, without Sidney Shlenker, most all of this tab would once again have to be met by the city and county governments.

Another controversial project was the reconstruction of the Main Street mall. Built in 1976, the mall was deteriorating quickly due to poor design. Hackett was able to obtain some federal transportation funds for reconstruction projects. In the end, however, he had to scale down to a trolley project in order to get city council funding. Further, he had to eliminate the portion of the trolley that was to run along the riverfront, settling instead for a run from South Main Street at one end of downtown to the Pyramid at the other. He also had to promise to obtain private-sector funding for the trolley cars. Although much of the private funding did not materialize, the trolley still opened in 1993.

Though an artistic success, the trolley pointed up a flaw in the Hackett vision for downtown. Despite putting vast sums into public projects such as the Pyramid and trolley, the private sector remained reluctant to invest in a renovated downtown area. Thus, most of the Main Street stores remained in awful shape. One of them actually collapsed during construction of the trolley, while another collapsed once the trolley began operating. The *Memphis Flyer* put the paradox in perspective, noting that "the sad truth is the trolley may offer a $32 million ride through a landscape of orange sawhorse hazard barricades and boarded up ruins."[52]

Mayor Hackett concentrated his attention on limiting taxes and developing the private sector. He did not place anywhere near the same emphasis on governmental "people" projects. This lack of emphasis is reflected in the areas of housing, neighborhood development, mass transportation, and education.

Hackett's record in the housing field was less than impressive. The Memphis Housing Authority, for instance, was in near total disarray during the latter part of his tenure. Although the housing authority was quasi-independent, Hackett did orchestrate the appointment of its director, but then did little to clean up the mess that developed subsequently.

Cary Woods, director of the housing authority, had been under fire for poor administration: there were large numbers of vacant apartments and a number of procedural questions that remained unanswered. In August of 1991, for example, the U. S. Department of Housing and Urban Development criticized the housing authority for ineligible expenditures made by board members, for lack of compliance with federal requirements, for disregard of personnel policies in hiring and firing, for a decline in service delivery, for the presence of vacant units, and for overstaffing.[53]

Amidst the mayoral campaign, then, Hackett hired Otis Higgs Jr. to review the situation. Higgs studied the housing authority and issued his report in January of 1992, after the election. In that final report, he would call for the resignation of Woods, labeling the authority the "laughing stock of public housing authorities in Tennessee." He also referred to a "lack of leadership, loss of grant funds, inability to create loyalty among top staff, and gross mismanagement."[54]

Ironically, Hackett had called for the firing of Lawrence Wade, a black director of the housing authority, in 1984 for many of the same reasons. Housing authority workmen had refurbished Wade's personal and business properties; further, the housing authority had violated bidding requirements and provided poor service to tenants. Nevertheless, a number of black political leaders had rallied to the defense of the embattled director.[55] In that light, to have called for the replacement of Woods might well have been incendiary during what had already become a racially charged campaign.

Another area in which the city impacts on housing is through its Community Development Bloc Grant program. These bloc grants provide yearly funds from the federal government for a variety of purposes, including housing, social services, capital improvements, streets, and parks. The Hackett strategy was to tout a small number of visible projects and to claim that the attention focused on these projects reflected a concern about housing policy in general. Estival Place, for example, was a program for homeless families administered by a private social agency, the Memphis Inter-Faith Association (MIFA). The city contributed construction and operating funds for this program, which then successfully provided free housing, counseling, education, job training, and day care facilities for about twenty homeless families. In addition, these bloc grants provided funds to demolish dilapidated housing in Smoky City, the inner-city neighborhood that also had received monies generated by the Ramses exhibit in the Wonders Series.[56] Both of these projects were impressive, but they barely scratched the surface of the city's intense housing problems, and they did not constitute a strategy or plan.

In addition, the city's Division of Housing and Community Development had a reputation for being inflexible and unable to move money into projects at an expeditious rate. Interviews with housing professionals indicated long waiting periods even when funds were allocated. More damaging yet, an audit by the U.S. Department of Housing and Urban Development (HUD) identified $39 million stockpiled and unspent by the agency. It took years to accumulate these funds given that the 1991–92 bloc grant was $13,283,000. HUD had to order the city to spend the funds since its reserve was not allowed to exceed 1.5 times the yearly allocation.[57]

The city's own documentation filed in October of 1991 demonstrated its vast and ignored housing needs. There were 2,300 homeowners on the city hardship list for rehabilitation assistance, yet there were only funds to help 20 percent of that total and the waiting list was frozen. Meanwhile, there was a need to rehabilitate 7,740 homes and 15,480 rental units.[58] Few low-income homes were being constructed, and the Memphis Housing Authority had a waiting list of 8,800 families. In addition, a study by the Enterprise Foundation noted that there were 18,000 vacant properties in the city. The foundation also found that a typical low-income family spent over 50 percent of its income on housing.[59]

On the other hand, there were successes in housing policy for the middle class. The Hackett administration, for instance, provided the infrastructure needed for the Mud Island housing development opposite the downtown area. Moreover, Hackett supported and worked for state legal changes that allowed the city to reclaim the old expressway corridor land in Midtown and to entice the middle class to rebuild housing in the area. Such efforts appeared geared primarily toward increasing the city's tax base.

Apparently sensing his political liabilities in this area, the mayor generated an eleventh-hour pledge. Slightly more than two weeks before the 1991 election, he promised that a five-year housing program would be his top priority if reelected. The goal would be to stimulate private-sector construction of 10,000 low- and moderate-income housing units, including both single-family homes and apartments.[60]

In addition to his troubles in coming up with an effective housing policy, Hackett lacked a policy for dealing with code enforcement throughout Memphis. Code enforcement involves applying city laws designed to require citizens to maintain their property. For example, according to city codes, a citizen may not dump trash and garbage in his or her backyard since doing so will attract rats. Likewise, the city cannot allow a house to deteriorate since it would be a danger to the resident and it would affect both the liability and property value of the surrounding neighborhood. Code enforcement was problematic during the Hackett administration, although there were a number of dedicated and experienced people in the city's housing bureaucracy. Houses in need of demolition were left standing, and they became havens for drug users and a blight to their inner-city communities. Inspectors visited houses about which citizens complained, but then took no action.

The system was a bureaucratic nightmare since five different agencies were involved in enforcing codes, and no agency bore final responsibility for enforcement. The laws among these agencies could produce conflicting instructions from different inspectors. Inner-city ghettoes continued to deteriorate, while central-city neighborhoods with sound housing began to witness incipient signs of deterioration as well. And, as housing problems increased in these neighborhoods, the property tax base decreased and middle-class residents continued their flight to the suburbs.[61]

While his record on housing and code enforcement was uneven at best, Hackett and others in his administration were very fond of road construction projects. Hackett viewed these projects as a form of economic development. He was especially aggressive in supporting transportation that would allow suburbanites to be whisked to and from the Pyramid as quickly as possible. He was also interested in highway construction, but not in mass transit, even though a number of highway projects threatened inner-city neighborhoods, historical sites, and environmentally sensitive areas. The Hackett administration conceived the "Second Street connector," for example, which was to move traffic to and from the Pyramid and connect with Interstate 40, allowing suburbanites to reach their homes quickly. Yet, the connector would displace low-income black residents and destroy historic housing that was architecturally significant.

In addition, Hackett strongly supported the extension of Sam Cooper Boulevard. It was to connect to the nub of the expressway, which had been terminated in 1960s near Overton Park, east of downtown. His administration initially proposed removing businesses and homes and developing an intricate interchange to deliver traffic to North Parkway, a city street that leads directly to the Pyramid. North Parkway is one of the most scenic streets in the city and bisects some of Memphis's most beautiful and functional central-city neighborhoods. The extension itself had a lot in common with the Second Street connector plan, as it would run adjacent to an African-American low-income area. Hackett met with citizens who opposed the extension and told them that the project was "dead in the water." Later, he retracted his statement.[62]

The expansion of Interstates 40 and 240 was another inner-city project related to the ill-fated Overton Park expressway. The state had connected I-40 to the I-240 beltway going north of Memphis, and it had accomplished this connection by using a single sharply banked and dangerous lane. In 1988, that turn ultimately resulted in an accident in which a propane truck exploded and flew into some adjacent housing. Rather than fixing the interchange, however, the state of Tennessee proposed widening the expressway through a low-income black neighborhood. It is not known whether Hackett directly supported the project, but it is unlikely that it could have continued without his assent.

Finally, Hackett sided with developers when he and the city council supported the extension of Kirby Parkway through a bottomland hardwood forest in a forest preserve called Shelby Farms. Although the parkway was ultimately routed away from the forest, it was still slated to run through the Shelby Farms Park.

These transportation projects reflected Hackett's support for developers, even if such support turned out to be at the expense of people and the environment. It is striking that among his various transportation projects, only one, the Nonaconah Parkway in southeast Memphis, did not harm the environment or go through low-income black areas.

Education was another "people" issue that did not appear to have a high priority in Hackett's administration. While discussing education at the 1991 Rotary Club debate, Hackett said that "there is not . . . a more important issue when it comes to being able to move this city forward, to be able to grow jobs in our city."[63] He argued that he had played a role in supporting education through the sales tax increase in 1982. Several times during his administration, Hackett had called himself the "education mayor." Nonetheless, education was not adequately addressed by the city of Memphis, and the mayor did not play a leadership role. The Memphis Board of Education, which was dependent on city funding, seldom had its fiscal needs met. Councilperson Barbara Sonnenburg noted that only 9 percent of the city budget was going to education, proving that it was a low priority.[64]

Among other things, more than three-quarters of the city's public school students are black, while the mayor and the majority-white city council were not elected by black votes. Hackett also did not have a good working relationship with the school superintendent, Dr. W. W. Herenton. He said, "I have to have confidence in the administration of any operation before I will ask for money," and he noted that he looked forward to working with a new superintendent.[65] When Hackett did offer to have the city government take over maintenance of the schools in 1987, he was rebuffed by the school board.

• • •

Dick Hackett was a transitional figure in Memphis politics. His relatively moderate approach to racial issues helped prepare the city for black governance. He was particularly effective in economic development policy, helping the city overcome its backwater image. Hackett was far less successful in the area of people projects. After nine years in office, the best he could promise was that if elected his top priority would be to meet the needs of inner-city housing.[66] In adopting these priorities, he had left himself vulnerable to an opponent who could effectively rally those most in need of public services.

3 Black Politics

What Negroes have in mind is to fight until hell freezes over and, if necessary, skate across the ice to freedom. I don't want to be white. I just want to be free. . . .

—George Lee, July 31, 1959

Since 1870, Memphis has had a population that has been at least 37 percent African American (see figure 2). This has been true despite black migration out of the area and despite repeated annexations of predominantly white suburbs.[1]

Given the size and residential segregation of that black community, it has long possessed a degree of social and economic independence, generating an array of black businesspersons, professionals, and ministers.[2] A number of pragmatic black leaders, willing to seize whatever political opportunities were available to them, have come from this elite group of the black community.[3] As is not uncommon, however, those leaders have often struggled among themselves, dividing the black community. In addition, unlike in most other cities, African Americans have not had a sizable group of white liberals with whom they could align in a reliable long-term coalition. As Harry Holloway put it, "The lack of continuing coalition ties with a particular segment of the white community means that Negroes really are on their own [in Memphis]."[4]

Meanwhile, at the other end of the socioeconomic spectrum, Memphis has been a magnet for many black sharecroppers and farm laborers. These have tended to be individuals who were either driven from the land by mechanization or were simply weary of their agricultural peonage. They were then attracted to Memphis by the lure of economic opportunities. Yet, for the most part, the city's economy has offered these African Americans only low-wage positions. As we demonstrate below, this has left Memphis with arguably the poorest black underclass of any large United States city. Consequently, black Memphians have ended up disproportionately poor, disillusioned, and militant, as well as suspicious of political leaders, including many of their own black leaders.[5]

In expressing this suspicion, George Lee put it this way: "The type of leadership these dark times demand is the aggressive and two-fisted kind that will contend, contend, contend. . . . [We must] banish, ostracize and destroy the type of leadership and that kind of doctrine that stands against the Negro in his effort to find himself. . . . We are too far behind to seek the palm and the olive branch."[6]

The Herenton campaign succeeded in uniting the various elite and mass groups under the banner of an uncompromising black political crusade. For the Memphis African-American community, his election marked a high point in a political struggle that had spanned generations.

Economic Setting

The Memphis economy has long been based largely on commerce and services, as opposed to manufacturing. As one of the earliest regional transportation hubs, for instance, it prospered as a market for cotton and slave trading. And, even after the Civil War, it remained a viable cotton market, as it had not been damaged nearly as much during the war as had a number of its southern counterparts.

The yellow fever epidemics of the 1870s posed a major setback, however. Conditions were so bleak and the city's finances so devastated that a number of the remaining white elites convinced the state legislature to repeal the city's charter. Those town fathers, now with nearly complete political control, set out to construct a reliable city infrastructure. By the turn of the century, they had done so. Most impressively, the city had developed both an artesian well for its drinking water and a sanitation system.

Meanwhile, although the boll weevil was wreaking havoc on the cotton crops, Memphis rebounded in the first two decades of the twentieth century by developing a more diversified local economy. It became the largest hardwood lumber market in the world; further, its invested industrial capital soared from a mere $10 million in 1899 to $467 million by 1920. Among the manufacturers locating in Memphis were giants such as Ford and Firestone. This industrialization reached its peak during World War II.

In the post–World War II period, the Memphis economy quickly returned to its commercial and service orientation. By the summer of 1993, for instance, ten of the metropolitan area's fifteen largest employers were governmental entities. Only eight institutions employed more than 5,000 workers. Federal Express was the largest at 18,831, while five of the others were governmental agencies and two were regional hospitals. Of the top forty, employing more than 1,200 workers apiece, only five were manufacturers, with Cleo (a company that made gift wrapping and cards) the largest at 2,200 employees.[7]

Blacks and the Local Economy

The size and segregation of the city's black population has required the black community to develop its own economic institutions. For example, these circumstances created a need for black doctors, lawyers, and teachers, as well as for black groceries, barbershops, hair salons, funeral parlors, and even banks.[8] Beale Street, the black commercial center in its Jim Crow heyday, was lined with real estate and banking offices, dry goods and clothing stores, theaters, saloons, and gambling joints.[9]

Bert Roddy founded the city's first black grocery chain and subsequently organized the Supreme Liberty Life Insurance Company. Included in his effort was an attempt to build on W. E. B. Du Bois's socialist notion of developing community cooperative businesses,[10] in this case Roddy's "Citizens' Coop" grocery stores.[11] Thomas H. Hayes, as another example, was a successful grocer who also started the T. H. Hayes and Sons Funeral Home, the longest continuously running black business in Memphis. Other prominent black businessmen included James Clouston, Clarence Gilliss, Phillip Nicholson, David Woodruff, and N. J. Ford.

Robert Church Sr. was the best-known entrepreneur. A former slave, he arrived in Memphis in 1863; by the time of his death in 1912, he had amassed more than a million dollars worth of real estate and other holdings. He was most likely the nation's first black millionaire.[12] His Solvent Savings Bank was the first black-owned bank in the city's history, and his donations of Church Park and the adjacent Church Auditorium provided major focal points for black social and cultural life, especially during the Jim Crow period.[13]

More recently, despite desegregation, a number of black businesses have continued to develop and prosper. By the 1980s, there were more than 3,000 black-owned enterprises, with gross receipts of approximately $150 million. Among the largest were Pat Carter Pontiac, Tri-State Bank, and Universal Life Insurance Company. Fewer than 1 percent were manufacturers, however, leaving the overwhelming majority operating in the lower-paying commerce and service sectors.[14]

Over time, these businesses provided blacks with goods, services, and employment that were not always accessible in the city at large. They also generated a number of black leaders who have been quite active in the city's political arena. However, black business success failed to trickle down to sizable portions of the African-American community as a whole.

Even in the city's brief period of industrialization, the white community's discriminatory union and employer practices left black workers "overwhelmingly concentrated in jobs that entailed hardly any responsibility, skill or prestige, [and] wages and salaries that were at best marginal."[15] Black menial labor was such a bargain that the Tennessee state legislature passed "emigrant agent codes" in 1917, making it illegal for outsiders to come into the state in order to recruit away black workers.[16] Meanwhile, of the black women working outside the home, 82 percent were domestics or laundresses, while another 10 percent were either seamstresses or in semiskilled employment.[17]

As late as 1950, despite the job experiences that had been accumulated during World War II, black men once again found themselves largely in manual labor and service positions, while black women remained largely domestic servants. As a result, black family income was only 44 percent of comparable white family income. Moreover, the figures might have been worse yet had it not been for job opportunities in local branches of federal government agencies.[18]

Even when desegregation efforts and anti-discrimination laws gradually began to dismantle the old Jim Crow system, little would improve for many black Memphians. For one thing, much of the city's job base

Fig. 7. George W. Lee Collecting for the Poor, 1939. Courtesy of The University of Memphis Libraries, Mississippi Valley Collection.

consisted of low-wage, unskilled positions.[19] In addition, desegregation would eliminate the need for many black-owned businesses.

The combined results have been devastating. Whereas blacks made up 58 percent of all Memphis families earning less than a thousand dollars in 1949, that figure had grown to 71 percent by 1969.[20] Nearly a quarter of the inner-city work force made less than two dollars per hour that year (as compared to 8.6 percent in Newark, for instance).[21] Not surprisingly, then, nearly 70 percent of the city's African Americans lived below the federal government's poverty level in 1959.[22] By 1990, despite the federal "War on Poverty," more than a third of the black population was still impoverished; and, as for the intensity of the poverty, six census tracts had a median household income below $5,500, while three zip codes had median household incomes below $6,500.[23]

One of the results of this poverty, mentioned above, has been a tendency for the black working and lower classes to be suspicious of white and black leaders. These economic circumstances also have generated a certain propensity to shun traditional electoral politics, even when viable black candidates were available.

Direct Political Action

Our focus on electoral politics should not obscure the amount of "direct action" that occurred in the streets of Memphis. Even as Booker T. Washington urged the nation's blacks to forgo politics and civil rights demands and instead focus on developing their economic base, a number of this city's African Americans were not prepared to be that patient.[24]

In a representative democracy, it is presumed that elected officials will convene to make public policy in the name of the people. The people's voice is heard through the representatives they choose. At times, however, people may determine it necessary to bypass those indirect channels. Instead, they take to the streets to change things themselves. Such politics is referred to as "direct action."

A number of Memphis blacks resisted the day-to-day degradations of Jim Crow. In 1881, for example, prominent musician and schoolteacher Julia Hooks was arrested for her vociferous protest over not being seated in a theater's white section. And, beyond protest, Mary Morrison was arrested for resisting streetcar segregation in 1905, a huge rally followed in Church Park and several thousand dollars were raised for her legal defense.[25]

There were also forms of even more direct resistance. The following incidents occurred in the years 1915 and 1916 alone. Thomas Brooks killed two white attackers.[26] When white men tried to physically remove Charley Parks and John Knox from their trolley seats, Parks stabbed one,[27] while Knox ended up in a gun battle with another.[28] A white trolley conductor was stabbed when he tried to collect extra fare from a black rider.[29] Ambush shootings and arson took place on occasion.[30] And, at times, lower-class blacks resorted to "physical means" in order to resist the brutality of local white police officers.[31]

The record of black resistance continued into the modern civil rights era. In 1960, a sizable number of student sit-ins occurred, and boycotts were launched against downtown retailers. Harry Holloway estimates that there were more boycotts and sit-ins in Memphis than in any other city in the nation.[32] In response, the city's Committee on Community Relations helped usher in gradual desegregation before the Civil Rights

Act of 1964. In addition, public protests against police brutality began in the nineteenth century and continued into the 1990s.[33]

In addition, a labor movement began early in the twentieth century.[34] Prominent black union leaders included Clarence Coe at Firestone, Thomas Watkins of the dock workers, and George Holloway of the auto workers. As an example of their success, the CIO was able to organize Firestone in the 1940s; soon, carpenters, longshoremen, and laundry workers were unionizing as well. At the same time, waiters, busboys, and elevator operators were engaging in wildcat walkouts.[35] More recently, a major sanitation workers' strike occurred in 1968, while the police, firefighters, and teachers walked the picket lines ten years later.

The 1968 strike by black sanitation workers is probably the best known. It began with a sewer worker's grievance over an incident of differential treatment by race. It then accelerated when two blacks were accidentally crushed to death in a garbage compactor. Mayor Loeb's hard-line reaction allowed black leaders to turn the event into a major civil rights struggle. The full-blown strike, ultimately involving eleven hundred workers and lasting sixty-five days, was led by AFSCME local no. 1733 and included support from the NAACP, prominent black ministers such as James Lawson and Martin Luther King Jr., and a group of young "black-power" militants calling themselves "the Invaders."[36]

Mass violence reared its head as the sanitation strike progressed. On March 28, for instance, one of the rallies became unruly when windows were smashed and rocks thrown. The police response left one dead and sixty-two injured, and soon four thousand members of the national guard were called in to restore order. Then, following the assassination of Reverend King, the city exploded into days of looting, burning, sniping, and other forms of mass unrest, leaving the city "traumatized and divided."[37]

Among elite blacks, there had long been avenues available for some degree of direct action. Fraternal and benevolent associations had arisen after emancipation and played active political roles.[38] In the late nineteenth century, educator Ida B. Wells led protests against segregation and lynchings and even aired these grievances internationally. In particular, she aimed her message at British cotton buyers. "Political leagues" and "civic welfare groups" lobbied on behalf of black interests.[39] And, in 1917, businessmen such as Robert Church Jr., Bert Roddy, and W. H. Bentley founded the first Memphis branch of the relatively militant NAACP, following the lynching of Ell Persons. Subsequently, led by individuals such as Jesse Turner and Maxine Smith, the NAACP would be at the forefront of much of the city's black resistance. Besides leading protests, the association filed federal lawsuits against numerous public segregation practices.[40]

Not only did leading activists have to face pressure from the majority culture and its laws and restrictions, but they also had to face internal struggles between different groups within the civil rights community. As an example of the cross pressures faced by elite activists, consider the case of Benjamin Bell. In 1943, Bell was chosen as the chief executive officer of the Community Welfare League (CWL), which had recently become affiliated with the National Urban League (NUL). Attempting to move the local organization more into line with national NUL priorities, he pressed the call for black civil rights in Memphis. This led to a drop in CWL's private contributions, and soon Bell was replaced by the more accomodationist Reverend James McDaniel, whose posture was then criticized by the NUL.[41]

Such economic pressure did not deter subsequent assertions of black power, however. The 1960s, in particular, marked a time when "the politics of moderation was replaced by the politics of race."[42] By the 1970s, John and Harold Ford came to symbolize this militancy as they stood up to the city's white leadership. In 1974, for example, city council member John Ford was cheered by many in the black community when he publicly told a fellow white councilperson to "go to hell."[43] Or, on election night 1991, Congressman Harold Ford also was applauded when he challenged the election board's tallying of absentee ballots in a fiery televised tirade. In responding to the latter incident, a prominent white leader referred to Ford as "the embodiment of evil."[44]

Electoral Politics

> I am told that I should vote as an American and not as a Negro. Well, I love America as much as anyone, and I would like to weigh [all the issues]. . . . However, I'm too busy trying to be free . . . to concern myself with such questions. When I vote, I must concern myself with what is good for Negroes.
>
> —Anonymous black Louisiana lawyer, quoted in Margaret Price, *The Negro Voter in the South*

Focusing on the electoral arena, more than three hundred "free Negroes" were voting in Memphis as early as 1850, while the state of Tennessee enfranchised all of its black citizens in 1867.[45] By 1875, a coalition of blacks, Irish, and Italians dominated Memphis politics. Led by the likes of militant saloon keeper Ed Shaw and the more conciliatory Hezekiah Henley, African Americans held seats on both the elected city council and school board, as well as positions such as wharf master and coal inspector.[46]

Shaw, a Republican—as were most Memphis blacks for nearly a century[47]—became the first African American elected to public office in West Tennessee. Yet, within six months of his 1869 election to the Shelby County Board of Commissioners, that body was abolished, and no black would hold local office until H. S. Prim was elected to the Memphis City Council in 1872. A year later, that council would contain three blacks—Shaw, Joseph Clouston, and Turner Hunt. Then, in 1874, Clouston and Hunt were joined on the council by J. Thomas, J. D. Waters, G. E. Page, and Jacob Moon.

Yet, amidst the ravages of the yellow fever epidemic, the city's charter was revoked in 1879, and the city became the Shelby County "taxing district" until 1893. Among other things, this reorganization allowed the creation of an entirely new governing structure. One of the nation's first commission forms of government was developed; some of its members were chosen by the governor and local judges, while the rest were elected. This time, however, officials would be elected at-large. The end result, regardless of its stated economic rationale, was a commission government comprised almost exclusively of wealthy whites.[48] As Joseph Cartwright puts it, "[T]his conveniently destroyed the democratic representation of blacks in the city government, thereby offering comfort to those white citizens who were concerned about the rapid demographic change that seemed to threaten white ascendancy."[49]

The city's charter was renewed in 1893, but only after the state had imposed a poll tax, which had the effect of restricting black voting participation.[50] Thus, although a few blacks did serve on the Taxing District Commission and later in elected Republican Party positions,[51] no African American would even seek elective city office from 1888 until 1951.

In the interim, three major players in particular, Robert Church Jr., George W. Lee, and O. Z. Evers, continued the struggle to gain political representation. Among other things, Church helped organize and then led the Lincoln Republican League of West Tennessee, a branch of the national Lincoln League. The league was integral in teaching blacks how to register and vote.[52] Lee led a local Lincoln League that also engaged in rallying black Republicans. His group was made up mostly of businessmen and ministers, although as many as sixteen hundred African Americans would rally in Church Park to nominate a black Republican slate of candidates.[53] Evers, on the other hand, headed a small group of independents, calling themselves the Unity League. Despite their differences, such groups were able to unite behind candidates viewed as most supportive of black interests. Consequently, this loose coalition of black Democrats, Republicans, and independents, liberals, and conservatives led Harry Holloway to characterize black politics in Memphis as "pragmatic" and "independent."[54]

This pragmatism was particularly noticeable in the willingness of blacks to cross party lines in order to support a preferred candidate.

Fig. 8. George W. Lee (far right) and Fellow Republicans. Courtesy of Memphis/ Shelby County Archives, Memphis/Shelby County Public Library and Information Center.

Such partisan crossover included Republican leaders who endorsed and worked for candidates in the Democratic Party's primary elections.[55] As George Lee put it, "Freedom is non-partisan, and the battle for freedom needs to be fought."[56]

In addition, Memphis black voters have been far more willing than their white counterparts to cross racial lines. Thus, they have voted for a number of whites even when black candidates were available.[57] As William Brink and Louis Harris concluded, "Fundamentally, this is one vote for one issue: civil rights."[58]

As discussed in chapter 1, Boss Crump was clearly the most powerful political figure during this 1888–1951 interim. In his 1909 mayoral campaign, for instance, Crump promised to rid Memphis of its "easy riders, pimps and gamblers."[59] Yet, in response, apparently reflecting the degree of independence that permeated the black community, W. C. Handy composed the following song:

> Mr. Crump don't 'low no easy riders here.
> Mr. Crump don't 'low it—ain't goin' have it here.
> We don't care, what Mr. Crump don't 'low.
> We gonna bar'l house anyhow.
> Mr. Crump can go and catch his-self some air.[60]

As the Crump machine developed, a selected number of blacks had their poll taxes paid and were marshaled to the polls. The black community received a share of the city's largesse in return for delivering what became a critical voting bloc.[61] Thus, as early as the 1930s, Memphis blacks did not face the "white primaries" and other voting obstructions that would continue to plague a South mired in Jim Crow laws and traditions. As Paul Lewinsohn put it, "The only place in the South where the Negro had by 1930 made a real breach in the white primary system was Memphis."[62] He attributes this "to the outright strength of the Negro population, under very skillful [Negro] leadership."[63]

Memphis blacks, for example, formed a "Colored Citizens Association" early in the century, and newspaperman Harry Pace became its first president. Later, Robert Church Jr. formed the "West Tennessee Civic and Political League," with George Lee as its first president. And, in 1938, the *Memphis World* newspaper sponsored the election of a symbolic "Mayor of Beale Street," and Matthew Thornton was elected. Throughout, leaders such as Pace, Lee, Thornton, J. B. Martin, and especially Robert Church Sr. and Robert Church Jr. rallied black voters and brokered black political support for patronage benefits. Although these leaders were Republicans, as were many of the businessmen and professionals in the black leadership elite, they were able to work effectively with white political leaders—especially while the large majority of blacks remained loyal to the "Party of Lincoln."[64]

Boss Crump's rewards took many forms. Besides the traditional money, jobs, services, and fixed parking tickets, they included the naming of city monuments for well-known local blacks. For example, T. O. Fuller Park was named for a humanitarian minister; the Foote Homes housing project for attorney Will Foote; and Tom Lee Park for the black man who rescued more than thirty people from the Mississippi River when their steamer capsized in 1925.[65] Nevertheless, blacks were not allowed to rise to positions of authority within the party structure or the bureaucracy; moreover, once Crump had fully cemented his position, fewer blacks were registered and fewer rewards were forthcoming.[66]

Before problems with Boss Crump emerged, however, a combination of Crump's efforts and Franklin Roosevelt's emerging New Deal electoral coalition lured many blacks from their traditional allegiances to the Republican Party. At that point, Dr. Joseph E. Walker organized the Shelby County Democratic Club as an independent political base for black Memphians. Although the Democratic Club would remain organizationally separate from the Crump machine, Walker worked with Crump until the two had a falling out over the issue of social segregation. The flash points included the previously mentioned visit by civil rights activist A. Philip Randolph and segregated seating for a Marian Anderson concert. Such developments drove Walker into the camp of a number of white "reformers" who emerged around the successful machine-challenging Senatorial bid of Estes Kefauver. Meanwhile, the independent nature of the Democratic Club made it difficult to raise money and to provide the patronage necessary to hold the organization together. Yet, the club persisted, and, by the 1960s, Holloway would describe it as an "effective, aggressive, mass-based organization."[67]

In 1951, Walker challenged the machine himself by running for the school board. In the course of the campaign, he and George Lee mounted the first of many aggressive voter registration drives within the black community. Although Walker was soundly defeated, he was the first black candidate in decades to seek public office, and black voter registration nearly tripled in 1951 alone. Then, after Crump died in 1954, the poll tax was eliminated, registration drives continued in earnest, and the percentage of registered blacks tripled again over the course of the 1950s, leaving more than 60 percent of the city's African Americans registered by 1960.[68] By 1963, as blacks struggled for the right to vote across the South, black Memphians were already registered at the same rate as white Memphians, participating at quite possibly the highest rate for blacks anywhere in the South.[69]

Meanwhile, it is important to note that a "second reconstruction" was developing. The nation had become more attuned to issues of justice and democracy following World War II, and it had been jolted out of its complacency by civil rights marches and urban unrest. The United States Supreme Court responded with decisions such as *Smith* v. *Allwright* and *Brown* v. *Board of Education,* while the Congress added the Twenty-Fourth Amendment, the 1957 and 1964 Civil Rights Acts, the 1965 Voting Rights Act, and the 1968 Fair Housing Act. These national events would provide a significant context for emerging racial assertiveness in Memphis.[70]

In addition, none of this should be seen as understating the political role played by local black churches. While ministers like Sutton Griggs and Thomas Fuller eschewed politics in favor of reaching quiet accommodation with wealthy whites,[71] others were more political. In 1955, as just one isolated example, dozens of churchmen representing virtually every black denomination came together to form the "Ministers and Citizens League." Their ranks included people like Henry Bunton, W. H. Brewster, and A. E. Campbell. As David Tucker notes, they adopted a two-thousand-dollar registration budget, hired three full-time secretaries, and pledged themselves to utilizing other resources at their disposal in order to increase black voter registration. The black ministers used the pulpit to preach the need to register, they held mass meetings, and they even drove unregistered voters to the courthouse.[72]

That same year, 1955, Joseph E. Walker's Democratic group endorsed Edmund Orgill's successful candidacy for mayor, and he won in no small part because of black votes. However, the city commission thwarted Orgill's subsequent attempt to name Walker to the city hospital board.[73] Meanwhile, black minister Roy Love ran for the school board. He finished fifth in his race for one of four school board seats; apparently because of this "close call," the election rules were quickly changed so that candidates would have to run for specific seats instead of allowing the top vote getters to gain the seats that were available. Despite that setback, as Melton points out:

> The *Memphis World* noted that in the 1955 local elections black voters had demonstrated awareness of their power. Furthermore, the death knell had been sounded for the "back door leader" or "the self-appointed spokesman" who ingratiated himself to the white power structure in exchange for recognition of his "influence" in the minority community. Likewise, the "shake a hand" leader who acquiesced to white liberals or "friends of the Negro" simply for personal satisfaction without real benefits would obtain little respect in the future.[74]

When S. A. Wilbun, a black man, ran for the state legislature in 1958, he did well in the black community and managed to attract a number of white votes. But even more important, his campaign manager, Harvard-educated lawyer Russell Sugarmon Jr., soon succeeded in creating at least a temporary precinct-level political organization for the Shelby County Democratic Club. With the death of J. E. Walker that same year, the organization was now in the hands of aggressive young leaders, such as Sugarmon, Benjamin Hooks, and A. W. Willis. They would begin to interview white candidates prior to endorsing them, and, in the process, they could strike bargains on behalf of the black community.[75] At the same time, this renewed assertiveness and the practice of black "single-shot voting" in multimember district elections also began to worry many whites.[76]

In 1959, Russell Sugarmon ran for a seat on the city commission and led a field of black candidates, prompting the "Citizens' Leadership Council" to form in order to bring together black Republicans, Democrats, and independents to support Sugarmon and his "Volunteer Ticket." They raised twenty thousand dollars and enlisted some twelve hundred precinct workers.[77]

Not surprisingly, this rather quickly became a very racially divisive election. While prominent African Americans, such as Martin Luther King Jr. and Mahalia Jackson, appeared to help rally the black vote, the white Citizens for Progress ran under the banner "Keep Memphis Down in Dixie."[78] Meanwhile, the *Commercial Appeal* editorialized that "at this juncture, it would not be well for the Negro citizens or for community tranquility to elect a Negro Public Works Commissioner or Judge of the Juvenile Court."[79]

Although all black candidates were defeated, Sugarmon had made a strong run for the city commission. In addition, each of the Volunteer candidates finished second, and nearly two-thirds of black voters were now registered. Sugarmon concluded, "We won everything but the election."[80]

A black man had never won an election of any kind since Reconstruction. Lucius Wallace, elected in 1887, had been the last black elected for nearly three-quarters of a century. Finally, in 1960, Jesse Turner won a seat on the Democratic Executive Committee.

In addition, white candidates were now routinely being interviewed by a small bipartisan group of black leaders in order to assess the candidates' positions on issues important to the black community. In 1963, for example, these black leaders openly opposed Sheriff M. A. Hinds's mayoral bid, claiming Hinds had served under Crump as the "head of the Gestapo to keep the Negroes in their place."[81] The interview process also allowed bargains to be struck. In 1960, for instance, Sugarmon's organization displayed its pragmatism and independence by striking a votes-for-patronage deal with a conservative segregationist Democrat, Paul Barrett.[82]

By the mid-1960s, the city of Memphis had a voting-age population that was approximately 34 percent black, and two-thirds of them were registered. Odell Horton had received a federal appointment as an assistant United States attorney, and Benjamin Hooks had been appointed to the criminal court bench by the state's governor.

Nevertheless, the city commission was comprised of five white men, all elected at-large. No African American had ever been a serious candidate for any one of these positions. As H. T. Lockard put it, "There has been no conscientious effort by the Democrats over the years to cultivate any real working relationship with Negroes who are also Democrats. I've been in politics since 1951 and this is the first time I've ever been before a white group on behalf of the Negro people."[83]

In 1964, with the help of a large presidential election turnout, A. W. Willis won a seat in the state legislature and Charles Ware won a constable position—both by plurality votes.[84] Thus, it was not long before a successful effort was launched to create a runoff provision in local elections. Meanwhile, the number of annexations of predominantly white areas continued with vigor. In addition, as Harry Holloway points out, Republican "election challenges" focused on registrations in the black community, obviously intimidating some legitimately registered blacks. Sometimes extra field wages would be offered on election day, with the field hands being brought back too late to vote.[85]

Fig. 9. Jesse Turner Walks the Picket Line, 1963. Courtesy of The University of Memphis Libraries, Mississippi Valley Collection.

By 1965, the city's entire governmental system was coming under heavy scrutiny. Although for somewhat different reasons, many blacks and whites had become dissatisfied with the commission arrangement. The "Program of Progress" grew out of this discontent, and it would soon usher in a new governmental structure.

Program of Progress (POP)

In 1965, a reporter for the *Commercial Appeal,* Jack Morris, began a series of articles entitled "Managing the Metropolis." The basic theme running through most of the articles was that cities such as Dallas and Atlanta had outpaced Memphis in terms of highway construction, renewal projects, and civic projects. Memphis's failures could be traced back to its commission form of government. It was time for leaders in the city to step forward and create change, beginning with the creation of a mayor-council governmental form.

Soon after his series ran, a number of citizens began organizing, many of them holdovers from the earlier Kefauver reform movement. There were eight sponsors of the first meeting of the Program of Progress in November of 1965, and Dr. Vasco Smith was the only African American among them. Meetings were open to the public, and press accounts described the attendees as a "mixed" group, suggesting both racial and residential diversity. In addition, any citizen could become a member of the POP, but it required a twenty-five-dollar donation. A new charter would be drawn up by an elected board of POP directors, and the members would vote on its passage. Once it passed the membership, the charter would then be presented to the city commission to be placed on the next city ballot.

The POP chose twenty-five directors, six of whom were black (Smith, Reverend Alexander Gladney, H. T. Lockard, Russell Sugarmon Jr., Jesse Turner, and A. W. Willis). They then broke down into ten committees, and, although no African American was chosen to chair any of the committees, blacks did comprise approximately one-fifth of the committee memberships. On the floor of the full body, blacks made 12 percent of the motions and 67 percent passed, while whites made 88 percent of the motions and 82 percent passed.

At a crucial juncture, it was proposed that there be a combination of district and at-large city council seats with no reference to the size of the council or to the proportion of members elected at-large or by districts. Black directors Turner, Sugarmon, and Smith opposed at-large seats in a majority white city, and they even requested that their negative votes be put in the record (no other individual votes were ever recorded). Yet, once the decision was reduced to determining the appropriate district/ at-large split, with the exception of Lockard, the African-American directors apparently favored having ten district seats to three at-large seats, compared to the seven-to-six split the white majority ultimately adopted. Thereafter, the POP charter revision passed its referendum vote by a three-to-two margin (57,957 to 39,350), with indications of three-to-one support in the African-American community.

Overall, there was considerable African-American participation in the POP process, and there was no clear pattern of intent to discriminate on the part of the whites involved. On the other hand, the process was not exonerated from discrimination, either. African Americans were numerically underrepresented at virtually every stage, and there was clear evidence of interracial disagreements, particularly concerning the question of district versus at-large city council seats. Lastly, the fact that black wards ultimately voted for the POP charter compromise by a three-to-one margin should not necessarily be read as overwhelming support for this particular alternative. They had struck about the best compromise they were going to get, and it was certainly better than the existing system.

Electoral Politics under the Mayor-Council System

The city now had a mayor-council system. And, in 1967, despite much advice to the contrary, A. W. Willis launched a mayoral bid. His candidacy ended up splitting the black community, as a variety of more gradualist ministers and community leaders disagreed with the NAACP's inclination to press for the election of a black mayor at this time. In the end, a majority of blacks ended up voting for a white liberal, William Ingram. Willis failed to make the runoff, and Ingram was then defeated by Henry Loeb.[86] Nevertheless, seven of thirteen council members were now being elected by districts, and African Americans Fred Davis, James Netters, and J. O. Patterson won three of the thirteen city council seats that year.

In 1972, Patterson became Tennessee's first black major party candidate for the United States House of Representatives since Ed Shaw had run as a Republican a century earlier. Then, in 1974, Harold Ford became the first and only black Tennessean ever elected to Congress, defeating four-term incumbent Dan Kuykendall to win a House seat by 774 votes out of the 135,000 votes cast.[87]

After his election, Ford developed a reputation for having the most effective political operation in Memphis. Besides personally paying overdue rents, distributing food at Christmas, contributing to church bazaars, giving graduation presents, and so on, his local Congressional staff was quite proficient at helping constituents through the maze of federal and local bureaucracies. In addition, his Congressional seniority and consequent committee assignments put him in a position to bring federal funds to Memphis. The word was that "Harold delivers," and his "deliveries" were extensively chronicled both in his newsletters and in the *Tri-State Defender*. Such service helped build a core of very loyal supporters.

In addition, the Congressman, his staff, and a small group of loyalists regularly composed and distributed a sample ballot endorsing a variety of candidacies. Such endorsements, which often appeared to require a financial contribution to the Congressman's campaign fund, are believed to have generated a sizable number of votes for the endorsed candidates.[88]

Factionalism

> Blacks appear to have united from time to time, but factionalism appears
> to come to the forefront on local issues.
>
> —Charles Williams Jr., "Two Black Communities in Memphis, Tennessee"

Despite devices like the Ford ballot, it has not been uncommon for black leaders to split—especially in recent years over which mayoral candidate to support. These splits have been based on things like partisanship,

Fig. 10. O. Z. Evers (right) on the Campaign Trail with William Ingram, 1967. Courtesy of The University of Memphis Libraries, Mississippi Valley Collection.

gender, intergenerational rivalries, and personalities. Such disunity has diluted the influence of the black community. This has been particularly problematic in a city where whites long managed to remain a majority, where much of the black population has remained exceptionally poor and difficult to mobilize, and where white allies have been few and far between.[89]

In 1975 and again in 1979, Otis Higgs became the first serious black candidate for mayor when he ran against incumbent Wyeth Chandler. Higgs, a lifelong Memphian, put together an integrated campaign team and ran on an accomodationist platform that stressed his personal attributes, economic development, and improved race relations. As he put it, "My goal is to merge into the American society. I'm proud to be black. I don't want to be white. But I want to merge into total society and have my qualifications and my abilities measured by the same yardstick that all men are measured by. . . ."[90]

His approach won him unprecedented white support, including between 8 and 11 percent of the white vote over the course of four elections.[91] He also garnered virtually all of the black votes cast. However, at least in part because he was viewed as having crossed the line and become too accommodating to whites, he became a victim of the "racial reflexivity" phenomenon. In the end, his candidacy simply did not generate enough excitement in the black community. As a result, there was not enough black turnout to overcome Chandler's incumbency, campaign funds, and endorsements, besides the fact that whites held a clear majority of eligible voters. Even at the leadership level, Charles Williams concludes, "[V]arious local black leaders (politicians, educators, public service workers, labor leaders, and many black ministers) could not agree on Higgs's candidacy."[92]

In a 1982 special election after Chandler left office, a long-standing rivalry between then acting mayor J. O. Patterson and the Ford family did not help. At least in part due to this split, Patterson lost the mayorship to Dick Hackett. Internal divisions had once again proven to be a significant electoral problem.

In 1983, black candidates Higgs, John Ford, and D'Army Bailey split the African-American vote, despite Harold Ford's black unity efforts and a highly successful voter registration drive.[93] This split helped allow the incumbent, Hackett, to win his first full term.

Then, in 1987, black candidates Minerva Johnican and Teddy Withers competed for votes in the black community. Unable to establish their

Fig. 11. Otis Higgs Jr. Concedes on Election Night, 1975. Courtesy of The University of Memphis Libraries, Mississippi Valley Collection.

viability, both lost badly to Hackett, who got a record 18 percent of the black vote. Meanwhile, John Ford's ballot had endorsed white Republican Bill Gibbons.[94]

Following the 1987 election, black union leader James Smith called for a leadership summit before the next mayoral election. As he stated, "I think the leadership of this community—the black leadership—is going to have to sit down and come up with a consensus candidate."[95] Election Commissioner O. C. Pleasant concurred, stating that "[a] strong black candidate who is able to excite the electorate will be able to take that [black] support from Hackett. The one that does that is going to be the next Mayor."[96]

• • •

Despite a host of social, economic and political obstacles, African Americans have continued to be a sizable and assertive political force in the city of Memphis. Nevertheless, they have had difficulty maintaining internal cohesion; further, unlike minority citizens in most other large United States cities, Memphis blacks simply have not had a reliable white liberal contingent with which to align in a long-term coalition. Whites, whether liberal or conservative, have been disinclined to support a black candidate for citywide office unless that candidate projects such a moderate image as to dampen enthusiasm in the African-American community. Such a "point of racial reflexivity" poses an ongoing interracial paradox, whether it occurs in Memphis or any other city in the United States.

4 Dr. W. W. Herenton

With the number of eligible voters split almost evenly along racial lines, the tradition of racial division in Memphis voting, and the black community's difficulties in agreeing on a single black candidate, it was going to be an uphill battle for an African American to win the mayoral election in 1991. Even if consensus could be reached on a single black candidate, the relatively low socioeconomic position of much of the city's African-American population would make it very difficult to galvanize the kind of registration and turnout that would be necessary to defeat a reasonably popular white incumbent—a man who only four years earlier had actually garnered a record number of black crossover votes to easily secure his second reelection. In addition, Mayor Dick Hackett's popularity meant appeals to the white community were likely to be less successful than usual; and, in an atmosphere of "racial reflexivity," such appeals would most likely make it even more difficult to arouse the necessary unity and enthusiasm in the black community.

Herenton's Personal Background

Willie Wilbert Herenton was born to Ruby Lee Herenton, a laundry worker, on April 23, 1940.[1] He grew up in a two-bedroom apartment along with his only sibling, Dorothy Elizabeth, his grandmother, his mother, and his stepfather, Joe Harris, who worked for a trucking firm. His father, Willie Witherspoon, lived a few blocks away and would get together with the young Herenton when he could break away from his work, first as a drugstore delivery man and later as an employee of Firestone Tire and Rubber Company.

In 1965, W. W. Herenton married Ida Jones, sister of local State Representative Rufus Jones. Ida Jones had been a fellow student of Herenton's at LeMoyne College and subsequently worked as a teacher in the Memphis public schools, as had Herenton. They divorced in 1988, and Jones ultimately moved to Chicago. In the interim, they had three children, Rodney, Andrea, and Errol. At the time of the 1991 mayoral election, Errol lived and worked in Memphis, Andrea was a student at Spelman College, and Rodney was attending Harvard Business School.[2]

In his own childhood, Herenton was raised amidst considerable squalor and violence in a racially segregated neighborhood. His family, for instance, shared an outdoor privy with residents in five other apartments. In addition, crime was commonplace, and one had to fight to survive on the mean streets surrounding Barton and Crump. Recalling his first neighborhood fight, Herenton notes that "I came into the house crying and my grandmother threw me back out there. She said, 'Boy, don't come back in here. If somebody hits you, you hit them back.' I learned the struggle and survival in a ghetto neighborhood very early. . . ."[3]

As for race, Herenton recalls, "I went to segregated schools, rode the back of the bus. I remember going to Goldsmith's and drinking out of the 'colored only' water fountains."[4] He concludes that "a lot of times you [had] to work harder than your [white] counterpart in order to excel. But . . . I never believed that simply because I was black I was inferior. I *never* believed that."[5] Through ability, hard work, religious faith, and under the watchful eye of a strong and loving mother and grandmother, Herenton managed to overcome his environment.

At approximately the age of nine, he took his first job as a newspaper carrier for the *Memphis World*, an African-American newspaper. The neighborhood was dangerous enough, however, that his mother would accompany him when he made his weekly collection rounds. It was not long before Herenton distinguished himself in his very first employment, winning a new sweater for having the highest newspaper sales.

When his stepfather bought him a bike, he mounted a basket on the rear and began working as a delivery boy for a neighborhood grocery store. He then worked his way up to a higher-paying position with the Hogue and Knott grocery store on Third Street.

Generous from an early age, he saved much of his money to buy gifts for a number of the special people in his life. For example, his first gift to his mother was a fourteen-piece punch bowl set that she still proudly possessed when he was elected mayor of the city some forty years later.

As for his demeanor, his mother recalls that as a child he was "quiet, meek and humble, but he was mischievous like [any] average child."[6] In terms of discipline, she notes that "[t]he last whipping I tried to give Willie, he was about seven or eight years old, and he grabbed the belt from me, and I didn't want him to know that he was about to get the best of me. So the next time he did something, I had [his] stepfather to whip him. He gave him one whipping, and he didn't have to whip him ever any more."[7]

A product of the segregated Memphis city schools, Herenton attended LaRose Elementary School and Booker T. Washington High School. He readily admits that he was not an outstanding student. He rarely brought home any schoolwork, and he would tease his sister about her efforts in school. Nevertheless, he passed his classes and graduated from high school in 1958.

A gifted athlete, the six-foot, six-inch Herenton played college basketball even though he had not played in high school. His coach, Jerry Johnson, persuaded him to try out for the team after spotting him playing in a physical education class and being impressed with his rebounding and tenacious defense. By his junior year he was a starter. Yet, according to Herenton, as a kid he had always looked at basketball as a "sissy game," for his real athletic love was boxing.[8]

He had an early desire to emulate great boxers such as Jack Johnson, Sugar Ray Robinson, and Joe Louis. This led him into Golden Gloves boxing. Thus, after work and school, he would walk miles to practice at a local gym. By age eleven, he was boxing competitively for the local YMCA, and he reached the Tri-State semifinals in his very first year. A tall and lanky youth, nicknamed "slim" by coach Tom Harris, he was flyweight (112-pound) champion at age thirteen. By the time he was eighteen, he had won a number of AAU titles, the Kentucky Golden Gloves, and had been Tri-State boxing champion on four different occasions and in four different weight classifications. Talk of his "fancy dukes" led to the nickname "Duke," which a number of close friends still call him. He was offered boxing scholarships to several universities, including a four-year boxing scholarship to the University of Wisconsin; instead, he decided that he would move to Chicago in hopes of becoming a professional boxer.

His mother feared for his safety in the ring, and she urged him to pursue his education. He was torn; but, before he left Memphis, an eye-opening incident helped him make up his mind. As a way of earning money for his trip to Chicago, he had applied for a job at a local furniture factory. Once at the factory, however, he witnessed a group of older job-seeking black men being cruelly degraded as they were turned away at the plant gate. In those unskilled men he saw himself if his boxing dreams did not materialize. He soon abandoned his Chicago plans and enrolled at all-black LeMoyne College, at the time the only local college that would accept African-American students.

As a student at this small liberal arts college, he struggled his first year and ended up on academic probation. Thereafter, however, he began to take his education more seriously, and his grades improved. While at LeMoyne, he made the decision to pursue a career in teaching. The opportunity to teach in segregated schools made it one of the only professional careers realistically open to talented and aspiring African Americans. Upon graduation, at the age of twenty-three, he began his career as a fifth-grade teacher at Shannon Elementary School.

It took only one year of classroom teaching for Herenton to realize that what he really wanted was to become a school principal. With Memphis State University now desegregated, he was able to enter its graduate program, where he earned his master's degree. Then, at age twenty-eight, he was hired at Bethel Grove Elementary School as the youngest principal in the history of the Memphis public schools and the first black to head a predominantly white school.

Yet, he was not advancing as a "go along to get along" type of person. He was a fighter, and he was prepared to fight for more than his own personal advancement. Thus, in 1969, for instance, he was the only principal to participate in the "Black Monday" protest marches.[9] On Mondays, a sizable number of black students would boycott classes and march. These protests were designed to call attention to what were seen as racially discriminatory hiring and promotion practices in the Memphis school system. As Herenton put it, "I believed so strongly in fairness, I put my job on the line."[10]

Meanwhile, he was popular with most of the teachers who worked for him. They described his administrative style as incorporating "relaxed, non-demanding ways and [an] open-door policy without favoritism."[11] Yet, viewed by many as a hard-working loner, his quiet and serious demeanor masked a warmth that only those closest to him came to appreciate.

After two years as principal at Bethel, he had even higher aspirations. He attained his doctorate from Southern Illinois University, writing a dissertation entitled "A Historical Study of Desegregation in the Memphis City Schools." Later, he was chosen over a hundred other applicants to win a Rockefeller Foundation fellowship to a program designed to cultivate minorities for high-level administrative positions in urban public school systems. As the first trainee ever from the South, he spent a full year working in the Baltimore and Washington, D.C., schools.

When he returned to Memphis, he was initially appointed to be the coordinator of a school system evaluation team. He then became the first African American to be appointed as a deputy superintendent. In point of fact, his position was deputy superintendent for instruction, essentially the number-two position in the hierarchy of the Memphis public schools. Thereafter, in December of 1978, he was finally appointed superintendent in his own right, but the appointment was not achieved without a struggle.

Race and the Board of Education

The previous time the school district had chosen a superintendent, a national consulting firm had been retained to assist in making the choice. This time, however, the process would be different. Instead of a national consulting office, a committee of twelve local community and education leaders conducted the search. From a pool of forty-two candidates, they recommended six finalists to the board. Herenton, it turned out, was the only candidate who received the unanimous approval of the committee. Retired Palm Beach, Florida, superintendent Dr. Joseph Carroll received eleven votes, while Grosse Pointe, Michigan, superintendent Dr. William Coats received ten. The others received progressively fewer committee-member votes, but in the committee's minutes it was carefully noted that "these data cannot be used to show ranking among the [candidates]."[12]

A highly regarded deputy superintendent, Herenton appeared to be a logical choice for the top position. As a matter of fact, many viewed Herenton as Superintendent John Freeman's hand-chosen and groomed successor. The school board, on the other hand, had other thoughts. In what Herenton described as unfortunately a "very astute observation," his twelve-year-old son had warned him that "you won't get that job. The white man will get it."[13]

In a decision process that had clear racial overtones, Herenton was subjected to an interview that black school board member Maxine Smith described as "what amounted almost to jeers and taunts by some who didn't want him there."[14] The board then offered the position to Coats, even though he had never administered a school system larger than fifteen thousand students, while the Memphis system had more than seven times that many.

Herenton refused to comment publicly, maintaining the "cool dignity" that journalists Cornell Christian, Michael Kelley, and others have described as his trademark, even as the black community responded with a furious barrage of "demonstrations, angry speeches, and heated confrontations at Board meetings."[15] According to the *Press-Scimitar,* the final vote of the school board "brought a wave of fury from the black community, with many charging that the selection was racially motivated."[16] Of the six white school board members, five had cast their votes for Coats, and the sixth for another white candidate. All three black board members had voted for Herenton. In particular, suspicion arose over an alleged strategy meeting between four white board members at the home of one of those members.[17]

George Brown Jr. was one of the three African Americans on the school board at the time. And, according to Brown, "[T]he only time I've ever walked a picket line was when the Board selected Coats. . . . I don't think the vote was [against Willie] so much as it was [the board's] inability to come to grips with the fact that we had in our presence an outstanding educator who was black."[18]

In the end, amidst this considerable racial turmoil, Coats withdrew. At that point, three of the board's white members changed their votes to Herenton, giving him a board majority. He then accepted the job, describing it "not so much as . . . a personal challenge, but [as] a collective challenge for [all] black people."[19]

White board member James Blackburn, who ended up as a pivotal swing vote in the final decision, recalls Herenton's remarkable rapport with "people who are out of power and don't have any money." He also noted that "occasionally he calls on these people and they show up for meetings and pack the hall."[20]

According to white board member Barbara Sonnenburg, those three school board members changed their votes "because of what might happen in the city."[21] School Board President Mal Mauney lamented that the decision to offer the job to Herenton amounted to little more than "the willingness to give into intimidation . . . to subvert the will of the majority."[22]

Years later, Herenton characterized those events somewhat differently, stating that "[t]he Memphis Board of Education which was predominantly White, could not come to grips with having a chief executive officer who was African American. . . . So racism reared its ugly head, but I was determined. The African American community expressed its outrage and we turned that event around. . . ."[23]

Dr. Herenton, at the age of thirty-eight, had been chosen to head a two-hundred-million-dollar school system, then the eighteenth largest in the nation. It was also a system rife with problems. Most pressing was the fact that court-ordered school busing had contributed to the flight of some twenty thousand students to private schools. Most of those who had departed were white, which left the city schools with approximately 75 percent black students.[24]

Confronting Fear and Developing Innovations

> The job that I hold is more than a position for Willie Herenton. The position that I hold is an embodiment of the aspirations and expectations of a lot of black folks. If I succeed, my race succeeds. If I fail, then my race fails.
>
> —Dr. Herenton, 1980

A central theme was to reassure city residents that there was quality education occurring in the city's schools. Beyond that, he argued that "[y]ou can send your children to a private school and allow them to be educated in a sterile, antiseptic environment," or students could be sent to a public school, where they could get both "academic quality plus the experiences of functioning in the real world . . . a total education."[27]

But success would require more than image alone. As a primary educational device, he introduced the concept of "optional schools." Optional schools were actually high-quality specialized programs located within select public schools scattered across the city.[28] Although first priority went to children living in the particular district and meeting the program's qualifications, remaining seats were open to any qualifying area student on a first come-first served basis. Not only did this arrangement provide an additional high-quality educational opportunity for talented local students, but also such a "magnet school" arrangement, with flexible racial quotas in each optional school, significantly reduced the need for mandatory school busing.

Further, he introduced tougher promotion standards for all students, whether inside or outside the optional schools. At the same time, he initiated a "Focused Instructional Program," which was designed to provide deprived inner-city students in elementary schools with extra help learning basic skills.

Among other initiatives at the administrative end, he arranged for his top managers to receive advanced management training from the American Management Association. His leadership style was largely to appoint strong people beneath him, to be sure they were sufficiently trained, and then to give them the freedom they needed to operate.

Consistent with his basic administrative approach, another identifying mark of the "Herenton Plan" was an attempt to change the basic orientation of many of the school system's principals. According to Herenton, who had once been a principal himself, principals spent too much time implementing and not enough time planning and leading. As he put it,

> [W]hile a principal is a manager, his or her major responsibility is to improve instruction in the school. Which means they must know the curriculum; they must keep up with the recent trends in teaching methodologies, strategies, research on teaching. . . . Not simply to count textbooks, to see to the children being fed. . . . All that's important, but the improvement of instruction must be in the forefront.
>
> I think we have clearly established the expectation that principals will spend a great deal of their time in the classrooms, working with teachers and students. Not sitting in offices drinking coffee.[29]

As for funding, Herenton was able to tap a well of support he had built up over time with the private business sector, both inside and outside the city. He had served on the boards of corporations, including Holiday Inn, First Tennessee Bank, and Methodist Health Systems, as well as being active in national organizations, such as the American Association of School Administrators and the Association of Curriculum Development. These involvements left him with invaluable connections. For example, Herenton initiated the "adopt-a-school" program, whereby local businesses could provide monetary and other types of assistance to a particular school of their choice. In time, all of the city's public schools were "adopted," and the adoption program was given the first national Private Sector Initiative Award by President Ronald Reagan. Herenton also was reasonably successful at acquiring grants from private corporations such as IBM and both the Ford and Rockefeller Foundations.[30]

What were the tangible results of Herenton's considerable efforts? To begin with, no matter how it was measured, there was no clearly identifiable reduction in the city's high school dropout rate of approximately 25 to 30 percent. Nevertheless, that rate was still well below those found in large cities such as New York, Chicago, Cleveland, Milwaukee, and Detroit.[31] For those remaining in school, however, there was some overall improvement in college-entrance examination scores.[32] For example, when Herenton first took office in 1979, the average American College Testing (ACT) score was 14.3 compared to a national average of 18.5. By the time he left the post, those numbers had improved to 17.9, compared to a national average of 20.6.[33] And, when compared to other large cities with comparable rates of poverty, Memphis fared better yet. Compared to the largest fifty city school districts in 1988, for example, Memphis rated second in average Scholastic Aptitude Test (SAT) scores and eighteenth in average ACT scores, ahead of cities such as St. Louis, New Orleans, and Chicago.[34]

When all of the city's students were accounted for, and not just those taking the pre-collegiate ACT and SAT entrance exams, Memphis showed marked improvement. In terms of statewide and national achievement test scores, the city still lagged behind state and national averages but showed steady improvement, especially in the primary grades.[35]

As for racial mix, approximately 75 percent of the students in the city school system were black when Herenton took office. That figure grew to nearly 80 percent by the time he left. Nevertheless, there are still those who credit his policies, especially the optional schools program, with at least slowing the tide of white flight. According to the *Commercial Appeal*'s Jimmie Covington, these schools have been "credited with retaining many white students who otherwise might have attended private schools."[36]

Superintendent Herenton received a variety of personal awards for his educational leadership throughout his career. For example, on three different occasions the *Executive Educator* magazine named him as one of the top one hundred school administrators in North America. And, in 1987, Greater Memphis State, Incorporated, named him Educator of the Year.

In addition, he received honorary doctorates from local Rhodes College and Christian Brothers University. LeMoyne Owen College named him Alumnus of the Year in 1976, while another alma mater, Memphis State University, chose him to receive its Distinguished Alumnus Award in 1989. In 1987, he was chosen Humanitarian of the Year by the Memphis chapter of the National Conference of Christians and Jews; and, in 1988, the Horatio Alger Association picked him to be one of ten recipients of the 1988 Horatio Alger Award.

His successes prompted Governor Ned McWherter to offer him the position of state commissioner of education, an appointment Herenton declined. The awards also led him to be courted by school systems across the country. For example, he was a strong candidate for the superintendent's position in Chicago, a finalist for that post in New York City, and he was chosen over fifty-five other applicants to be superintendent in Atlanta. However, in the end, Dr. Herenton declined the Atlanta position and decided to remain in Memphis, where many supporters had petitioned him to stay.

Nevertheless, all was not peace and harmony. As Herenton himself put it, "I didn't accept this job to sit in that chair and accept the status quo. And I'm not the type of manager who will avoid critical or complex issues."[37] He rather quickly became embroiled in heated debates with parents, politicians, teachers, school administrators, and religious groups over issues such as his ban on compulsory prayer and organized Bible reading; his support for the Family Life Curriculum, which included elements of sex education; the closing of a number of under-utilized neighborhood schools; his plans for competency tests for teachers; his assertion that services and programs were higher priorities than teacher salaries; his rapid replacement of a number of well-entrenched high-level administrators; and his seemingly endless complaint that the politicians never provided him with adequate funding.

To be sure, his budgetary proposals were not always readily accepted. In February of 1989, for instance, Herenton initiated his own comprehensive reform plan. Fully implemented, the superintendent's plan would have added $12 million per year to the school district's $320 million annual budget. It included "an early childhood education program, eight 'de-regulated' pilot schools, a computer-based instructional management system, a new multicultural education program, and more staff development."[38] Except for a small portion of the deregulated school project, however, the school board refused to include these changes in its annual budget.

This refusal was similar to others, since the board rarely included in its yearly budget any of the new programs proposed by the superintendent in his annual "needs assessment."[39] In addition, the city council never did fully fund even the school board's pared-down budgetary requests. Such refusals on the part of the board and city council were a source of ongoing consternation for the reform-minded Herenton.

Thus, although the school system's operating budget doubled in "current dollars"[40] over the course of Herenton's twelve years as superintendent, at times he still accused those legislative bodies, composed predominantly of white members, of not being inclined to spend money on a school system that had come to be nearly 80 percent black. As part of his criticism, he cited such things as local government's penchant for funding economic development and beautification projects ahead of things like providing simple air-conditioning for the public schools.[41] As a matter of fact, when Herenton announced his resignation in October of 1990 (to take effect in June of 1991), he cited as a primary reason that he simply felt the schools would never get adequate funding from city and county officials as long as he was superintendent.[42]

One of the superintendent's highest-profile confrontations occurred when he challenged Mayor Wyeth Chandler. It revolved around Herenton's accusation that the mayor had contributed to the city council's decision to lower the property tax rate received by the schools. In the course of the well-publicized exchange, Chandler implied that Herenton did not seem capable of running the system within a reasonable budget. Herenton responded by impugning the mayor's level of intelligence and refusing to apologize for his remarks.

Not too surprisingly, criticism mounted. One of the most common general criticisms was that Herenton had created a top-heavy, over-bureaucratized system, even though, in fact, the number of administrators actually appears to have declined over the course of his tenure as superintendent.[43] In addition, as *Memphis Magazine* editor Larry Conley put it, many also complained about the superintendent's own "bureaucratic high handedness." And Conley concludes that "walking the tightrope of public controversy . . . made Willie Herenton one of the city's most prominent targets."[44]

The OCI Report

In January of 1989, a group of Memphis business leaders hired a California consulting firm to analyze school system operations in Memphis. Among other things, the group's final report recommended that Superintendent Herenton become more of a "strong, active, present leader, not just a policy-maker and direction-setter." Both the initiation of the report and its findings were a blow to the superintendent, as he had generally enjoyed a good working relationship with much of the city's corporate hierarchy.[45]

Such criticisms appeared to culminate when the school board split along racial lines in voting to hire a five-member North Carolina evaluation team, Organization Consultants, Inc. (OCI), to investigate the school system's personnel process and to make recommendations for improvement. African-American board member Carl Johnson put it bluntly when he stated, "I don't like the word racism. But what precipitated this whole process was pure and simple racism."[46]

The investigation included personal interviews with 350 school system employees, as well as interviews with board members, with Herenton, and with some twenty to thirty people who had requested that they be interviewed.[47] There was then a follow-up questionnaire mailed to all school employees, 56 percent of whom responded. The study culminated in a relatively critical report submitted in September of 1989.

Overall, the final eighty-one-page report characterized the system's personnel policies as being "in shambles" and the entire district as being "seriously flawed and at risk." Among other things, the report concluded that "[w]ithout any doubt, and to an unusual and disquieting degree, the schools of Memphis have been organized and administered on a personal and political basis rather than upon the impersonal one which seeks the answer but to one question, 'What is best for the children of the city?'"[48] More specifically, it also concluded that there was too much favoritism in promotion decisions, morale was low, discipline lax, and employees lacked faith in the school system's leadership. Further, the report criticized Herenton for delegating too much, accusing him of "failing to effectively manage the working relationships of certain of his key staff members" and urging him to be "much more circumspect in his social relations with . . . employees." Specifically, it urged him to pay closer attention to problems in the personnel process, besides recommending a handful of new personnel policies and procedures.[49]

Following that report, the board and Herenton clashed again, this time over the creation of additional oversight committees. And, as had been the case throughout much of this most recent controversy, protesters—the bulk of whom were black and rallying to the support of the beleaguered superintendent—often filled the school board auditorium. Nevertheless, despite losing the battle over the oversight committees, Herenton subsequently embraced most of the final OCI report and initiated new personnel policies designed to allow employees more formal avenues for airing complaints and for seeking job openings. Yet, for all intents and purposes, he continued to stand by his management team and his basic management style. He also continued to question the motives of his critics. "The Memphis city school system has undergone more scrutiny than any public organization in this city. Now it's interesting to raise the question as to why. Could it be that this is the only institution that's headed by a chief executive who happens to be black?"[50] Two of Herenton's most vocal critics, City Councilman Jimmy Moore and County Commissioner Pete Sisson, summarily dismissed his suggestion of racial undertones as being "absolutely ridiculous."[51]

Probably the primary single catalyst for the Organization Consultants investigation was the allegation raised by a disgruntled city schoolteacher. Her name was Mahnaz Bahrmand.

The Mahnaz Bahrmand Controversy

In 1988, the same year Herenton and his wife officially divorced, city schoolteacher Mahnaz Bahrmand filed six-million-dollars' worth of lawsuits against Herenton and the Memphis School Board. In the suits, Bahrmand, a thirty-four-year-old math teacher at Bellevue Junior High School, alleged that Superintendent Herenton had initiated an intimate affair with her by promising her a job promotion. Specifically, she filed suit the day after Herenton changed his mind and decided not to recommend her to the board for the position of multicultural curriculum coordinator. Now, she was alleging "fraud, outrageous conduct, and gender discrimination." An early allegation of "breach of promise to marry" was later dropped, although she continued to claim to have had two abortions and a miscarriage over the course of the affair.[52]

As the controversy swirled, the rumors surrounding it grew in proportion. For example, there were allegations that a sex-for-advancement arrangement permeated the entire school system. County Commissioner Pete Sisson called for an independent investigation, claiming that he had received numerous complaints about improprieties in the school system's personnel process.[53] He also asserted that "the information that I have uncovered . . . shows that [Herenton] cannot be the role model the students . . . deserve."[54] Soon, both Sisson and City Councilman Jimmy Moore were calling for Superintendent Herenton's resignation, while school board member Dr. Tom Gill implied that Herenton ought to "take a strong look" at the possibility of resigning.[55]

Over the course of this turmoil, Herenton received what he characterized as a number of "horrible letters." For example, one writer sent him a condom with an admonition that he should learn to use it. Another scrawled the following on the envelope: "Open Letter to a Wicked, Immoral, Irresponsible Superintendent of Memphis City Schools." A third actually mailed him some dried human feces. And, beyond these, he received direct death threats, although he declined subsequent offers of police protection.[56]

At the height of the ordeal, Herenton addressed the congregation of Mt. Vernon Baptist Church. In his address, he apologized for the embarrassment he may have caused them. As he stated, "I have a conscience and I have integrity that I have to stand by, and all that I ask [is] your forgiveness."[57] According to Pastor James Netters, "The church stood by him 100 percent."[58]

Although Herenton admitted having had a personal relationship with Bahrmand, he labeled her legal accusations "frivolous and without merit."[59] He also characterized them as "a calculated attempt to discredit me."[60] In addition, he concluded that the firestorm that had followed these accusations was "all about politics, race, power, jealousy, envy, even bigotry."[61] Beyond that, he argued that "what people do in their private lives, in terms of the relationships they establish, is their own business," and he bemoaned the fact that "there are a hell of a lot of ignorant and narrow-minded people in Memphis."[62] He added that "I haven't contemplated for one moment resigning. I see no reason to resign."[63]

Little specific evidence of any sort of illicit promises ever material-
ized. In fact, two police detectives investigating Herenton for the
New York superintendent's job ultimately filed a report that dismissed
Bahrmand's charges as groundless.[64] In September of 1989, the job discrimination portion of the suit was "dismissed with prejudice" in chan-
cery court, meaning it could not be refiled. Meanwhile, the fraud and
outrageous conduct accusations were also dismissed in circuit court.

Herenton and Bahrmand then reached an out-of-court settlement and
all outstanding lawsuits were dropped. The contents of that private settlement have never been revealed. All Herenton would state publicly was
that "I'm very pleased the parties have resolved their differences and
can move on with their personal and professional lives."[65]

The Emerging Candidacy

> God moved on my heart that my people were in bondage, and in the real
> sense, the city of Memphis was in bondage.
>
> —Dr. Herenton, 1992

Prior to the 1983 mayoral election, Herenton told the Memphis *Press-
Scimitar* that "I'm not ruling out a bid for elective office." Further, he
also stated that "I've always known that if I wanted to be Mayor, I could
win an election, but it wasn't something I wanted to do."[66] According to
Maxine Smith, a lot of people simply "ordained him Mayor back in those
wonder years. . . ."[67]

His constituency of support was broad. For example, according to
Ron Terry, the chairman and chief executive of First Tennessee Bank,
Herenton had "two natural constituencies." One was his "broad base of
solid black citizenry" and the other "the business community." Accord-
ing to Terry, "I don't believe there is a [black] man other than Willie
Herenton who could [win] this time."[68]

Yet, the then popular school superintendent chose to watch and wait.
And, before he ever officially threw his hat in the mayoral ring, the
late 1980s storm of controversy swept down on him, tarnishing his good
name. By his own estimates, "prior to the personal lawsuit and some
other controversies during the last two years of my tenure [as superin-

tendent], I would have gathered comfortably, 20 percent of the white vote."[69] Nevertheless, through it all, Herenton never lost his faith.

As an active member of Mt. Vernon Baptist Church, under the pastorship of Reverend Netters, Herenton practiced his deep and enduring Christian beliefs. As Herenton put it, "I have a very strong belief in God. I believe He has blessed me to overcome many obstacles, many trials and tribulations. . . . I feel that God has placed me on this earth to serve a purpose. And hopefully that purpose is to improve mankind to whatever degree God enables me to."[70]

Interestingly enough, it was in the pulpit of the Clayburn Ball Temple AME Church, on the winter night of January 21, 1991, that the mayoral "crusade" took its first major public step. While speaking to a crowd gathered to commemorate Dr. Martin Luther King Jr. on the anniversary of King's birthday, W. W. Herenton spontaneously challenged Congressman Harold Ford to help him bring the city's black community together. In particular, he called for a black summit meeting in order to unite the black community behind a single ticket for the upcoming city elections.

From that point on, the momentum of events just seemed to carry him, and, before long, he was right in the middle of it all. Although Herenton had never run for any elective office prior to his run for mayor, he had always believed that he could win elective office if he made the decision to seek it, whether it be to the United States Congress, to city mayor, or to whatever. He was confident in himself and in the support he had in the black community.

Despite his public disclaimers, a number of people close to him had the sense he had long wanted to be the city's mayor. In particular, Herenton confidant Eddie Walsh notes that Herenton had grown very frustrated with the city government's unwillingness to provide the kind of financial support he was convinced the school system required, and he had become equally frustrated by what he saw as the news media's unnecessary magnification of the Bahrmand story. These events left him torn. W. W. Herenton, the private man, wanted out of this unfair public arena, while W. W. Herenton, the fighter, was not inclined to call it quits.

Yet, it was precisely the Bahrmand controversy that led Walsh to initially counsel against a mayoral run at this time. Maxine Smith also counseled against it, "because I didn't want to see him hurt again."[71] Even Herenton's own mother was initially opposed to his running.[72] Nevertheless, there was a strong core of supporters who had been weighing the race for months, and they had concluded it was viable. Soon Walsh, Smith, and Herenton's mother were on the bandwagon.

As for his final decision to seek the mayor's office in 1991, Herenton explained it this way. Describing Memphis as a "backwards river boat town,"[73] he stated,

> I did not run against Dick Hackett. I ran against old-line, tradi-
> tional Memphis, which Dick Hackett symbolized. . . . I've always
> had deep regrets that [Memphis] could never realize [its] full po-
> tential because of our preoccupation with race and maintaining the
> status quo. How can a city grow when a majority of its citizens are
> underskilled, undereducated, and not included in the mainstream
> of life? I just knew we were never going to make progress if we
> kept the same leadership and the Old South mentality.[74]

He then concluded by claiming that "I felt I was prepared to be Mayor, more so than any other person of my race in this city. I also felt that I had the ability, if anyone could, to bring Memphis together and move forward."[75]

• • •

Dr. W. W. Herenton possessed a number of characteristics that made him both a viable consensus candidate in the black community as well as a potentially charismatic crusade leader. He was a native Memphian who had overcome the hardships and mean streets of the ghetto to obtain a doctorate and become the city's first African-American superintendent of schools. The school board position gave him considerable name rec-ognition; moreover, surviving the many attacks of white critics in the public and especially in the press had made him a hero of sorts in the city's African-American community. He was enterprising and a fighter by nature, definitely a "stand up" type of individual. Politically, he was an outsider, not clearly identified with any of the politicians who had engaged in the various divisive intracommunity battles of the past. School system associates provided a potential army of volunteers, an as-set that would be particularly valuable at the two black unity confer-ences that were held to choose a single consensus black candidate for this election. And, finally, his deep religious faith gave him strength and allowed him to draw on numerous religious themes and metaphors in leading the crusade.

Actually, in many other settings, his position as head of a large city school board might well have been a major impediment. With nearly insurmountable challenges and never enough money, such school systems almost inevitably end up damaging the reputations of those in charge. When it is time to place blame, such administrators are the most visible and likely targets. Thus, such a high-profile, difficult position is prone to becoming a political dead end. However, in the milieu of "racial reflexivity," white attacks on a black superintendent are likely to be seen, at least in part, as racial attacks, which led many in the black community to rally to Herenton's support.

In addition, Superintendent Herenton was accused of personal indiscretions. Under normal circumstances, even allegations of that nature could well sink a mayoral candidacy, especially the candidacy of a political newcomer who did not already have an existing political track record or a wealth of ongoing political relationships to provide a shield. Yet, in the atmosphere of racial reflexivity, these accusations were both more damning in the already resistant white community and viewed as just that much more race mongering in much of the already defensive African-American community.

The next few chapters will frame and chronicle the ensuing mayoral campaign, a campaign that ultimately pitted W. W. Herenton against incumbent mayor Dick Hackett. Chapter 5 sets the context in terms of the evolution of the city's demography, electoral history, and election-related law. Chapter 6 describes the Hackett campaign. Chapter 7 traces the emergence of the Herenton bid, as well as the campaign he ran in the general election, culminating in his victory.

5 The Electoral Context

The general developments in the Memphis black and white communities described in the previous chapters helped set the stage for the historic events of 1991. This chapter will focus empirical attention on three of the contextual circumstances that had a direct bearing on the 1991 mayoral election. First, Memphis voting history reveals a pattern of overwhelming white electoral success amidst high levels of racial solidarity. Second, however, an examination of demographic changes indicates that, as of 1991, there were finally as many black as white voters in the city. The key for Herenton would be getting those black voters registered and then inspiring a higher than normal turnout rate. Last, there were changes in two election-related laws that had long contributed to the white domination of the city's elective offices.

Historical Voting Patterns

Historical voting patterns provide a context for understanding what takes place in a specific election. In this section we will examine two significant trends in Memphis election history: racial polarization and racial bloc voting.

In Memphis, the traditional political culture allowed whites to unify behind white candidates in citywide elections. With the help of election-related laws that this majority had established over time, virtually all victorious candidates continued to be white even after viable black challengers began to emerge.

Memphis mayoral elections have featured white and black candidates since 1967, and continuously since 1975. Figure 12 shows the percent of the vote received by the single leading white and black candidates respectively. White candidates lead the voting in all elections except 1982 and 1991. In 1982 the white candidate's vote dropped below the black vote because there were two popular white candidates who split the white vote. Nevertheless, the top white candidate subsequently triumphed in the runoff election that followed.[1]

In 1975 and 1979, black challenger W. Otis Higgs opposed white incumbent Wyeth Chandler. Both elections required a runoff since Mayor Chandler had white challengers in each, leaving him only a plurality winner in these two general elections. Higgs's best showing was in the 1979 runoff, in which he received 47 percent of the total vote compared to Chandler's 53 percent.[2]

Mayor Chandler resigned in 1982, and Dick Hackett then became the candidate of white conservative Memphians. In his first run for the mayor's office, his opponent, city council member Michael Cody, received 26 percent of the vote in the general election, while Hackett re-

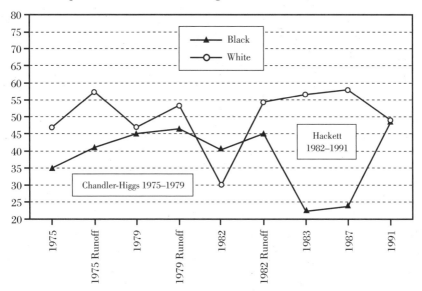

Fig. 12. Vote for Black and White Candidates, 1975–1991.

ceived 30 percent. It was only because of the stiff challenge from Cody that Figure 12 shows a dip in the vote for the white candidate in the general election.

The 1983 and 1987 elections show the strength of the Hackett political organization in mobilizing the white political culture. Before Hackett solidified his hold on the mayor's office, black candidate Otis Higgs had been making steady gains in 1975 and 1979. Some had speculated that black victory was near if only the black community continued to choose a strong candidate who could make appeals to the white community. Figure 12 shows that Hackett, as an incumbent mayor, took an election process that was competitive between blacks and whites and won impressive majorities in both the 1983 and 1987 general elections.

Again, our concept of racial reflexivity helps explain a frequent phenomenon found in Memphis politics. Many mayoral elections have included a black-supported candidate, a white conservative candidate, and a moderate candidate trying to attract votes from moderate blacks and white liberals. The white population's identification with the conservative candidates has been mirrored by black support for the opposite candidates. Chapter 1 indicated that, before 1975, black voters supported white candidates such as Turner and Ingram. Beginning with the 1975 mayoral election, however, black candidates carried the electoral torch for the black community. Afterwards, however, the middle ground would become even lonelier whether the racially moderate candidate was white or black. Memphis simply did not have the number of white liberals found in many other United States cities, and neither racial community appeared generally willing to move from its polarized moorings in order to support a middle-of-the-road alternative.

The pattern of white victories was equally rigid in other citywide races. Before 1991, only two black candidates had won citywide victory in a multitude of elections that included city council, the school board, and city judgeships. Further, both of these citywide victories were anomalies. Minerva Johnican won a city council seat in 1983 by creating a coalition with white Republican women as political repayment for helping a Republican woman get elected to the state legislature. Then, in 1990, Earnestine Hunt won a city court position in a very low turnout, off-year election.

Racial polarization and racial bloc voting were manifestations of the city's traditional political culture, and they allowed whites to consistently

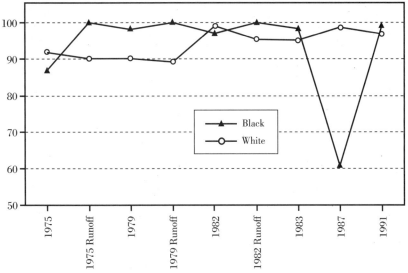

Fig. 13. Racial Polarization in Mayoral Elections, 1975–1991.

win election after election. The outward manifestations of racial reflexivity were readily apparent here.

Polarization

Racial polarization refers to the percentage of votes cast by all the voters of a racial group for the various candidates of that race (e.g., black votes for any of the black candidates). Polarization helps us understand the extent to which the two racial groups aggregate their votes and select candidates along racial lines.[3]

As Figure 13 suggests, racial polarization has typically ranged from 90 to 99 percent in both the black and white communities. The one exception was 1987 when blacks crossed over to vote for the incumbent white mayor, Dick Hackett, and the John Ford–endorsed white Republican, Bill Gibbons.[4] Even in this election, however, more than 60 percent of African Americans still voted for one of two obviously futile black candidacies. White polarization was lower in the 1970s, given the accommodationist candidacy of Otis Higgs, although it increased markedly beginning with the 1982 election. These polarization scores were consistently higher than those typically found in the mayoral elections of other cities.[5]

One of the contributing factors may well have been the city's nonpartisan system of electing candidates for local offices. In a partisan system, voters can identify candidates by political party designation. Those parties assume certain agendas and often attract a variety of demographic groups, regardless of a particular candidate's race. Thus, Democrats might attract lower- and moderate-income whites and blacks.

Memphis, on the other hand, has a system of nonpartisan elections. The nonpartisan system came to fruition as part of a reform movement in America. Proponents of this system argued that municipal decisions on policy do not lend themselves to a Republican or Democratic perspective. According to this view, picking up the garbage, protecting citizens against crime, and determining zoning in the community are not partisan issues, but rather questions of efficiency in administration. Therefore, political leaders are best able to make these businesslike decisions when they are unencumbered by political party concerns.

Without partisan cues, citizens look for other ways to evaluate candidates. Sometimes, those cues revolve around personal characteristics of the candidates. Candidates who are charismatic or whose names are already well known are more apt to receive support from the voters in a nonpartisan system. Social cues such as the race of the candidate are also more apt to play a role as citizens try to sort out the voting alternatives.

A second factor clearly had to do with the Memphis political culture described in chapters 1 and 3. That culture has led to social, economic, and political polarization between the city's whites and blacks. Because Memphis seemed to have reached the threshold of racial reflexivity, candidates tended to focus their campaigns toward their own racial group, and voting continued to be racially polarized.

Bloc Voting

Bloc voting refers to the level of cohesiveness of blacks and whites in voting for the leading candidate of their own racial group. It is expressed as the percent of citizens of one race who voted for the leading candidate of that racial group.[6]

Bloc voting can be very complex since it relates to the number of viable candidates emerging from a particular racial group. Thus, if two viable black candidates split the black vote, it would lower the level of bloc voting among black voters. Bloc voting also relates to the quality of

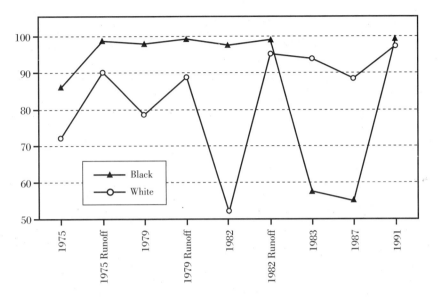

Fig. 14. Racial Bloc Voting in Mayoral Elections, 1975–1991.

the candidates of a racial group. If the black candidate is unknown, then blacks may be less inclined to vote as a bloc for that black candidate. In addition, strategy can play a role. If a black candidate has little chance of winning, a black candidate may not appear on the ballot. If there are no blacks on the ballot, most blacks will be more apt to vote for a white candidate. Nonetheless, the degree to which a racial group succeeds in unifying itself behind a single candidate is still important when studying the impact of race on electoral politics.

These illustrations are equally applicable to white bloc voting, although whites have been more likely to have viable candidates on the ballot since they have been in the majority during virtually all of the historical period being examined. In the white community from 1975 to 1987, bloc voting was less important in the general election than in the runoff. Because of the white community's majority status, at least one white candidate was apt to get into a runoff even if there was a split in the white vote during the general election.

Figure 14 describes mayoral bloc voting from 1975 through 1991. Except for the 1982 runoff between two strong white candidates, Hackett and Cody, the dominant white candidate received the consistent support of white voters. This ranged from 72 percent to 97 percent, with an average of 83 percent for all nine elections. In addition, white bloc voting in mayoral elections increased through the years. In 1975 it was only 72 percent, while it was 95 percent for the 1982 runoff and 97 percent for the 1991 mayoral election. Whites demonstrated lower levels of bloc voting in those years in which the white plurality candidate had a viable white challenger. In 1975, for instance, Judge Turner received 16 percent of the total vote. Michael Cody received 26 percent in 1982, while Republican Bill Gibbons received 15 percent in 1987.[7]

Figure 14 also describes bloc voting among African Americans. Bloc voting in the general elections was consistently high, except in 1983 and 1987. It averaged 96 percent for the elections not including 1983 and 1987, while it averaged 88 percent for all nine elections. In 1983, only 1 percent of the city's African Americans crossed racial lines to vote for Dick Hackett. However, these data suggest that the existence of two strong black candidates, John Ford and Otis Higgs, split the black vote and thus negatively affected black cohesion.

The only time that Hackett received more than 1 percent of the black vote was in 1987 when his black crossover reached a high of 13 percent.[8] These data suggest that besides the weaknesses of that year's two black candidates, Johnican and Withers, Hackett's more racially moderate politics and policies may have been responsible for attracting some black voters as well.

Lastly, let us compare the level of bloc voting in the white and black communities. Figure 14 suggested that in the 1970s, African-American bloc voting was higher than white bloc voting. For example, in the 1979 runoff between Higgs and Chandler, the former received 97 percent of the black vote and the latter received 79 percent of the white vote. Thus, there was a larger white crossover vote for the black candidate. In the 1980s and 1990s, however, bloc voting was much higher in the white community, and it dropped in the black community for the 1983 and 1987 Hackett elections. Nonetheless, polarization and bloc voting were high in both communities in 1982 and 1991, both of which were years that Hackett ran.

Demography

Historical voting patterns suggest a consistency over time. Until the

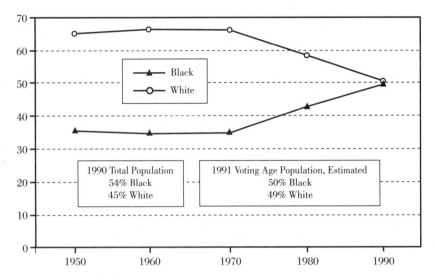

Fig. 15. Voting-Age Population by Race, 1950–1990.

1990s, only one black candidate was elected in a citywide election. In looking at mayoral races in which there was a black candidate, blacks have voted overwhelmingly for fellow blacks, and whites have voted overwhelmingly for whites, in a process labeled polarization. Whites were also able to vote as a bloc to divert enough votes to one candidate to assure the election of a white, even in cases in which there were two or more strong white candidates.

The ability of whites to assure victory through bloc voting and the inability of blacks to do the same was due in large part to demography. Simply put, historically there have been significantly more whites in Memphis and that has translated into substantially higher levels of white voter registration and voter turnout in city elections. Then, by the 1990s, for a variety of reasons, the city's population demographics began to change in significant ways.

Population Change

United States Census Bureau figures indicated that the 1990 population of Memphis was 610,337, making it the nation's fifteenth largest city. Blacks made up 54 percent of that total, whites 45 percent, and "others" 1 percent. However, when examining only the voting-age population and interpolating those figures to 1991, blacks outnumbered whites by only a 50 percent to 49 percent margin.[9]

Figure 15 places the above figures into historical perspective.[10] From 1950 to 1970, the voting-age population leveled off at approximately 65 percent white and 35 percent black. Yet, sometime between 1971 and 1980, blacks began to increase their percentage of total eligible voters. By the 1991 election, the black voting population was larger than that of whites.

There are at least two reasons for these recent population changes. The 1990 census showed that approximately 75,000 whites, or 20 percent of the white population, had moved out of the city over the course of the 1980s.[11] Much of this movement was to the suburbs and adjacent unincorporated areas, and it came about because of higher taxes, higher crime, and other social problems, including those stemming from court-ordered school busing in the city, and also because of greater housing availability and closer proximity to jobs in the outlying areas.[12] Further, the black population has experienced some movement into the areas surrounding the city.

However, this exodus has been counterbalanced by a much higher birth rate in the black community. This combination of white flight and black births, which increased the proportion of blacks in the city, can be seen by examining age groups. In the fifteen-year-old to nineteen-year-old group, some of whom voted for the first time in 1991, blacks were a majority with 68 percent of the population. In the sixty-year-old to sixty-four-year-old group, many without the means to move out, whites were a majority with 61 percent of that population.

Several contextual factors described next indicate how this population change has influenced the registration and turnout of black and white Memphians.

Registration and Turnout

Memphians have very high overall voter registration and turnout rates. Local newspapers report the rates to be among the highest in the nation.[13] A Shelby County election commissioner stated, "I don't think there is any metropolitan area with more eligible voters registered."[14]

Our search of the literature did not provide any data for registration or turnout by city. Thus, we conducted our own study of eighteen large

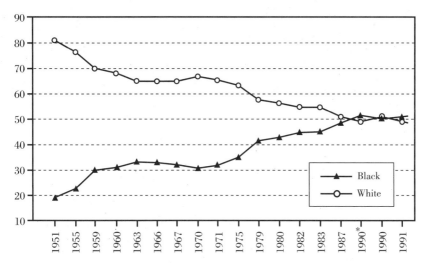

Fig. 16. Voter Registration by Race, 1951–1991.

American cities, obtaining information from election commissions concerning their latest mayoral elections. These cities were primarily in the East, Midwest, and South.[15] Our study confirmed the conventional wisdom. Memphis had a registration rate of 84 percent, which contrasted with 77 percent for the next closest city. The mean for the 18 cities examined was 67 percent. In addition, Memphis had a turnout rate of 55 percent, which contrasted with 41 percent for the next closest city and an eighteen-city mean of 31 percent.[16]

We then compared black and white registration in Memphis. Figure 16 provides "total" data for the percentage of those registered who were either black or white.[17] We selected 1951 as a starting point because it was the beginning of continuously recorded registration in Memphis. These data are also early enough to provide perspective on registration changes in the African-American community.

Figure 16 reveals a general narrowing of the racial gap in registration until blacks finally reached parity around 1987. More specifically, the data in Figure 16 reflect six different historical periods.

Stage one occurred before actual registration data were available and refers to the pre-1951 Crump era. The Crump machine played a major role in increasing black registration rates beyond those of many cities, since it depended upon the black community for substantial numbers of votes. Black registrants included many city employees (e.g., teachers) who were dependent upon Crump for their jobs. Ward heelers, who were city employees or ran businesses dependent on city licensing, were actively involved in registration. For example, those ward heelers paid the poll taxes and then retained the receipt until election day when they instructed blacks how to vote.[18] Although the operatives running the Crump machine took care not to register more blacks than they anticipated needing, an interview conducted by James Jalenak estimated a typical year's registration to have ranged between three and eight thousand blacks.[19] Although reformers viewed such procedures as unsavory, many African Americans did register and thus developed familiarity with the process and a habit of political participation.

Stage two reflects the post-Crump era from 1951 to 1955. During this period, black registration increased to approximately twenty thousand and was roughly 20 percent of the "total" registration. By this time Crump had lost his influence as age and illness took its toll on the great manipulator. Jalenak suggests that the growth of labor unions and "closing the Beale street dives" actually had begun to limit Crump's influence much earlier.[20] The year 1951 saw the beginning of independent black registration drives. In 1951, for instance, George Lee and H. H. Gilliam conducted a registration drive as part of the effort to elect a black to the school board. Although their incipient efforts were not successful enough to swing the election, the endeavor itself reflected a movement beginning to stir within the black community.[21]

Stage three occurred from 1959 to 1971, with black registration rates reaching approximately one-third of total registration. This was the transitional period that included the civil rights movement and the local assassination of Dr. Martin Luther King Jr. In 1959, Memphis was "Deep South in character. . . . [T]he Negro had made little progress toward social equality in Memphis; the city schools, the municipal public transportation facilities, restaurants, hotels, and lunch counters were completely segregated."[22] Yet, legal desegregation took place soon thereafter and essentially was completed by the end of the sanitation strike in 1969. This period of activism marked the prelude to much more competitive black electoral participation.

Stage four occurred from 1971 to 1983. Black registration, as a result of many successful voter registration drives, grew from 36 percent to 45 percent of total Memphis registration. For example, in 1983, the *Tri-*

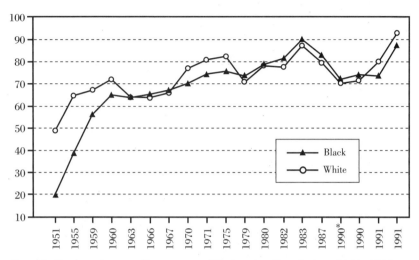

Fig. 17. Registration as a Percentage of Voting-Age Population, 1951–1991.

State Defender reported an effort to add thirty thousand new black voters. Organizers included Congressman Harold Ford and his two brothers James and John, county commissioners, state legislators, the local executive director of the American Federation of State, County and Municipal Employees, and O. C. Pleasant, chairperson of the election commission.[23]

Stage five, which runs from 1987 to the present, was the period of virtual black and white registration parity. This led to the 50 to 49 percent registration advantage blacks held over whites on the eve of the 1991 mayoral election. In actual numbers, rather than percentages, however, blacks simply had been maintaining their number of registrants, while the number of white registrants had been decreasing.

It is also important to examine the "component data" in order to contrast the registration and turnout rates within the black and white communities.[24] Figure 17 provides a needed perspective by showing the percentage of black and white registrations as a percentage of their respective voting-age populations.

Figure 17 shows that there was a substantial registration-rate increase within the African-American community from 1951 to 1960, beginning with 20 percent and increasing to 65 percent. The variation between blacks and whites also changed from a 29 percent difference in 1951 to an 8 percent difference by 1960.

Beginning with 1963, Figure 17 indicates that the two racial groups tracked each other. From 1979, the two lines are almost identical. Utilizing standard estimation procedures, it would be fair to conclude that blacks and whites registered at roughly the same rates from 1979 to 1991.

There are at least five factors, peculiar to Memphis, that have contributed to these registration rates. Memphis blacks have a history of registration that dates to the Crump political machine in the 1930s and 1940s. Thus, there was a long tradition of political activity, albeit one that did not provide blacks with much political influence. Second, Memphis appeared to have few legal impediments to registration, especially once the poll tax was eliminated in the 1950s. Third, Memphis citizens have been allowed to register in a variety of ways besides visiting the election commission. Registration can take place by mailing in a form; further, candidates and political groups may collect registration forms and file them with the election commission. Fourth, black candidates have relied on registration drives as a tool for gaining votes. Having access to very limited funds for political advertising, African-American candidates instead have depended on grassroots efforts, including strong registration and turnout efforts. Finally, the high visibility and intensity of local elections have helped maintain high registration in both the white and black communities.

Again, however, these registration rates mask the underlying changes occurring in the population as a whole. Because there have been increasingly more blacks than whites in the city, identical registration rates have meant that blacks gradually have become an increasingly larger proportion of the total electorate.

Turnout trends also constitute an important contextual factor for understanding the 1991 mayoral election. There is extensive literature nationally on variations in white and black turnout. Margaret Conway, for instance, suggests that in national elections blacks vote in lower percentages than whites. She reports a range of black turnout from 34 to 42 percent in various national elections. For whites in the same years, the range was 64 to 66 percent.[25] And, as indicated in the introduction, this differentiation does appear to hold in the urban South as well.

Frank Parker did find a relationship between the number of black candidates and black turnout.[26] Nevertheless, he still notes a consistent gap in black electoral participation when compared to white rates. Given the lower registration and turnout rates of blacks, he describes a "65 percent rule" in order for black candidates to be elected. His standard is that 65 percent of the total population or 60 percent of the voting-age population must be black for most citywide black candidates to begin to be successful.[27]

A number of factors are presented to help explain this lower turnout in the nation's black communities. First, as a group, blacks find their occupations and income levels requiring them to spend more time working, leaving less discretionary time for political participation.[28] As expressed by Memphis political leader Minerva Johnican, blacks are "thinking about survival, not civic duty."[29] A related demographic explanation is age, since younger citizens vote at markedly lower rates. As demonstrated earlier, in Memphis the black community is considerably younger than the white community. Another explanation is that political rules such as at-large elections and runoffs have disadvantaged black candidates, causing some African Americans to view elections as futile from the outset. Finally, there is a migration theory of turnout. Jalenak suggests that in 1960, for instance, 70 percent of black Memphians came from the rural areas of Mississippi, Arkansas, and Tennessee. He characterizes blacks from the rural South as having less "political consciousness" and thus being less inclined to participate.[30]

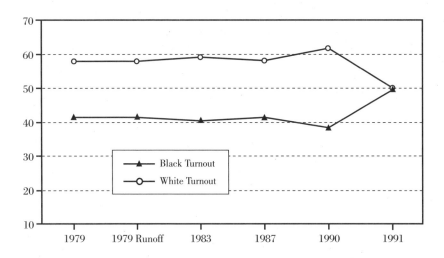

Fig. 18. Voter Turnout by Race, 1979–1991.

Did all of this translate into lower black turnout rates in Memphis? To answer that question, we analyzed the city's turnout rates over time. Unfortunately, unlike the registration data that were at least available from 1951 to 1991, the election commission has only collected voter turnout data since 1979.

We first examined the "total" turnout data by race.[31] Figure 18 shows that white voters have consistently outnumbered black voters by some 15 to 20 percent from 1979 to 1990.[32] Quite dramatically in 1991, black and white turnout came together, with the black share increasing and the white share decreasing.

There are several things to note about these results. Historically, the turnout difference between blacks and whites has been approximately 15 percent. The turnout data are much different from the registration data, however. Black and white shares of the total number registered steadily came together from 1979 to 1991, even to the extent that black registrants came to outnumber whites. By contrast, the turnout gap remained about the same from 1979 to the 1990s despite decreases in the registration gap.

We next examined turnout "component" data.[33] Figure 19 displays the turnout rate of each racial group's voting-age population from the 1979 mayoral race to the 1991 mayoral race. These figures show a gap in black

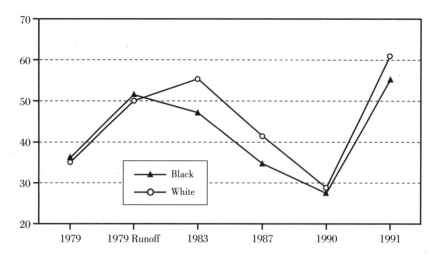

Fig. 19. Turnout as a Percentage of Voting-Age Population, 1979–1991.

turnout for 1983 and 1987, similar to that expected by the political scientists who have analyzed voter turnout. However, black and white turnout rates were the same in 1979 and in 1990, while white turnout was only slightly higher in 1991.

Figure 19 also shows, however, that black turnout reached historically high levels in 1991. There are a number of reasons why black turnout was so high. To begin with, a strong African-American candidate had an opportunity to win the election. Many articles appeared in the local newspapers describing the majority status of the black population, high registration rates, and the removal of the runoff requirement, which is discussed at length below. In addition, as described in detail in chapter 7, the black community came together in an unprecedented way behind a charismatic candidate who ran a nearly flawless campaign.

Election-Related Institutions

The change in demographics that increased black registration and turnout would not have occurred and would not have been enough for a Herenton victory without significant change in key election-related institutions that had historically supported white domination of elective office. These institutions included annexation policy, the runoff, and at-large electoral rules. We will also examine two events, a charter commission and a federal lawsuit, which first created and then changed two of these institutional arrangements.

Annexation

The annexation of surrounding areas has long been a significant component in the racial politics of Memphis. After a long history of liberal annexation policy under a permissive state law, a change in that law slowed the city's ability to continue to annex its surrounding areas in the 1980s.[34] Table 2 shows the impact of annexation on the city's circumference and population.

Memphis was ceded its city charter in 1826 and began to annex in 1832. By 1849, its land area had been increased sixfold to approximately three square miles. It added some twelve square miles in 1899 alone, leaving it with more than sixteen square miles and one hundred thousand residents. It added more than twenty square miles in 1929, more

Table 2
Area and Population Growth, 1826–1991

Year	Square Miles	Population
1826	<1	500
1850	3	8,841
1900	17	102,320
1950	104	396,000
1960	128	487,524
1970	217	623,988
1980	264	646,356
1990	256[a]	618,682

[a]All Measures are "dry land," with reduction over the course of the 1980s apparently due to Wolf River encroachment on land previously categorized as dry.

than forty-six in 1947, and more than eighteen in 1950. Then, between 1951 and 1967, the city added approximately sixty-one square miles and fifty-four thousand people. The largest of these were the additions of Frayser in 1958 and Parkway Village–Oakhaven in 1965. Whitehaven was annexed in 1969, while both Raleigh and a sizable segment of east Memphis were added in the 1970s.[35]

The city's official rationale for annexation has been twofold. First, annexed areas are often near the city boundary and have a taxing potential that will exceed the cost of providing city services. Thus, Memphis can recapture part of the tax base that has moved outside its city limits. In some cases, the city already extended public services, including utilities, with the intention of eventual annexation. Second, annexation takes place because there is a threat that other municipalities may annex the area or that the citizens may attempt to incorporate into their own separate municipality. Most, though not all, of the existing municipalities surrounding Memphis have developed reservation agreements with the city, defining which municipality will eventually annex which of the remaining unincorporated areas.[36]

As the annexed populations generally have been disproportionately white, however, annexation also has contributed significantly to the city's remaining majority white. As David Tucker put it, "[S]o long as the city continued to annex fleeing white suburbanites back into Memphis, the black population . . . would surely fall short of a voting majority."[37]

As one might expect, then, the politics of annexation generally has split the city council along racial lines. African-American city council members have consistently opposed these annexations, and they unanimously opposed both the most recent Hickory Hill and Cordova annexation resolutions. In 1982, black council members and mayoral candidate J. O. Patterson called for a limited freeze on annexation because it could negatively affect the African-American proportion of total registered voters.[38] In addition, city council member Minerva Johnican commented in 1986, during the Hickory Hills annexation debate, that it was unfair for the city to take on new responsibilities. She argued that the city had not fulfilled promises to improve Boxtown, a black area annexed eighteen years earlier.[39] Despite such opposition, however, the most recent *Memphis Polls* have shown considerable popular support for annexation. In fact, support was greater among African Americans than among whites.[40]

Nevertheless, annexation has become more difficult because state law now gives targeted areas more tools with which to fight the annexation. Originally, Tennessee cities could only annex by state legislation. A 1955 state law allowed localities to annex by local ordinance under certain conditions; then a 1974 amendment to that law restricted that discretion.[41]

The 1955 state law allowed annexation by municipal ordinance, although it required a plan indicating the cost and timing of services in the annexed area. In any challenges, the burden of proof rested with the challengers to show that they would not sufficiently benefit from the move. No jury trial option was available.

Then, in 1974, the state legislature allowed for a jury option and shifted the burden of proof. Now, when challenged, the burden of proof would rest with the city to convince a jury that the annexation was necessary for the health and safety of both the city and the annexed area.[42]

Tennessee's new annexation rulings were tested when Memphis set out to acquire Cordova and Hickory Hills. In September of 1981, the Memphis City Council passed the "Memphis 2000 Plan," which outlined prospective annexations for the remainder of the twentieth century. Under this plan, the city attempted to annex a 7.5-square-mile tract in the Cordova area located directly east of Memphis. In addition, the city also moved to annex Hickory Hills, a densely populated and heavily developed region located southeast of the city limits. This was an area that already included some 37,000 people on approximately 14.3 square miles. These moves, and subsequent countermoves, had a direct effect on the 1991 election.

Cordova citizens filed four petitions for independent incorporation, beginning in 1979. Before these efforts, the Memphis City Council had said that it would not annex any of the Cordova area for ten years as long as there were no incorporation efforts or attempts by other municipalities to annex any of this area. Nevertheless, residents of this prosperous east Shelby County enclave proceeded toward incorporation because they feared eventual absorption into Memphis.

In response, the city filed its final annexation petition in 1984. It called for the absorption of a 7.5-square-mile Cordova corridor near Walnut Grove and Germantown Roads. The residents of the area brought a suit won by Memphis in a jury trial. The city also prevailed in an appeal to the State Supreme Court that rendered a decision in 1990. According to the court, the annexation was reasonable since Cordova citizens would now pay for city services they had been receiving, cleaner air would result in the region because of emissions testing, and services such as fire, police, and schools would improve.

The Hickory Hills area posed a much different set of circumstances. Hickory Hills was more densely populated than Cordova and had extensive commercial economic development, including a large shopping mall and a major national distribution center. Studies of annexation began in 1975, and by 1982 the city made it known that it would eventually annex the area because of its lucrative tax base. Formal annexation proceedings commenced in 1987. A city report estimated that the population of 37,000 residents would produce a $13-million surplus to the city treasury within five years of annexation.[43] Hickory Area Residents for Tomorrow (HART) and attorneys representing Hickory Hills business interests legally contested the annexation. According to HART attorney Dan Norwood, the move had clear racial undertones: "The city of Memphis annexed [the African-American] Boxtown area over 20 years ago, yet many of those residents still do not have running water. It is an outrage that the city of Memphis would attempt to annex Hickory Hills while not fulfilling the promises made to Boxtown. It has been my contention that the city has been part of a conspiracy to dilute the voting strength of Memphis blacks as well as ignoring their public needs."[44]

The suit then proceeded to bog down in a lengthy discovery process. Yet, even if the city had prevailed in the local courts before the 1991 mayoral election, annexation of Hickory Hills would most probably not have been completed until after 1995, given the likelihood of a protracted appeals process.

We examined the annexations of both Cordova and Hickory Hills in terms of their impact on voter registration by race. The city finally absorbed Cordova in 1990, one year before the 1991 mayoral election. The area contained approximately 1 percent of the city's total registered voters, of whom 97 percent were white and 3 percent black. This meant adding 4,662 more white than black registered voters. Meanwhile, if Hickory Hills had been added, its registrants would have been 5 percent of total city registrants. At the time of the 1991 election, 85 percent of the Hickory Hills voters were white, which would have meant adding 14,259 more white than black registrants to the city's voting rolls.

Annexation, as a contextual factor, then, had an impact on the 1991 election. With the previous annexation law, the city would long ago have absorbed Hickory Hills and its multitude of white voters. Besides being a large area, Hickory Hills was growing very quickly. At the time of the 1987 annexation, the area had an estimated 37,000 residents. By the 1990 census, the population had increased to 46,000 residents. As we will suggest in chapter 8, these additional white votes would have been far more than enough to sway the mayoral election to the white incumbent.

Election Law

Two important decisions had been significantly affecting Memphis's electoral process since the mid-1960s. These were the decisions by a charter commission to adopt a runoff provision and a mixed district/at-large council. These two moves, along with the city's annexation policies, created institutional arrangements that made it difficult for blacks to win elections.

A city commission had governed Memphis from 1910 to 1967. It was a five-person body that included a separately elected mayor and four commissioners. The commissioners, like the school board members, were chosen at-large in a citywide multimember district. In other words, the top vote getters were elected.

In 1965, as discussed at length in chapter 3, citizens began organizing through a charter commission called the Program of Progress (POP). Two key electoral institutions ultimately created were a runoff for citywide races and at-large voting for six city council seats. At-large elections required office holders to be elected citywide, instead of from a particular district. Runoffs also required that the winner have attained at least a simple majority (more than 50 percent) of the votes cast. If that percentage was not achieved in the first election, then a runoff election was to be held between the top two vote getters.

The runoff meant that since they were a minority of the population, blacks could not hope to win citywide races given the traditional level of white polarization and bloc voting. Without a runoff, blacks could have run single candidates in races in which there were several white candidates and, by giving a candidate a plurality of the vote, had some reasonable possibility of winning. In 1982, for instance, J. O. Patterson outpolled both Dick Hackett and Mike Cody by a plurality in the general election, only to lose to Hackett in the subsequent runoff.[45]

The history of the runoff shows that it had indeed been initially proposed as a device to limit black officeholders. In 1959, for instance, African-American Russell Sugarmon declared his candidacy for a city commission seat already contested by four white candidates. The prospect of Sugarmon being elected by a plurality prompted Commissioner Henry Loeb to petition Governor Buford Ellington to call a special session of the state legislature to pass a runoff provision for Memphis.[46] Ellington declined, as would the state legislature on two other occasions.

Seven years later Lucius Burch, who subsequently founded the progressive Memphis Committee on Community Relations (MCCR), argued that "[w]hether he's a member of your race or mine or any other, a candidate shouldn't be elected if the majority of the community doesn't want him."[47] Nevertheless, the POP directors voted not to put a runoff provision in their city charter proposal. Clearly, this was due largely to strong opposition from the African-American members within the POP.[48]

In the end, three white state legislators petitioned the all-white city commission to place the runoff on the ballot. On May 17, 1966, the *Press-Scimitar* reported that the three legislators presented the proposed ordinance to the city commission "backed by petitions and newspaper ballots from between 1500 and 1600 citizens supporting them."[49] The runoff was placed on the August ballot and won by four-to-one margin (29,419 to 7,453).

At-large electoral schemes also make it difficult for members of a racial minority to win elections in a racially polarized city. If offices require a citywide majority, a white majority voting in a bloc can control these elections. This was the case in Memphis, where only two blacks were elected in citywide races from 1967 through 1990. Consequently, the school board and city council remained safely in white hands.

Historically, the city's African-American leadership had opposed at-large schemes. In 1961–62, for example, opposition to the proposed city-county consolidation effort related to the consolidated government's proposed at-large council. Then, in 1966, black POP director Dr. Vasco Smith responded that "[w]e don't stand a ghost of a chance in this town when it comes to running at-large. Officials elected at-large think of what's good for all the people or what's best for Memphis as what's best for only 61 percent of the people. They forget about the 39 percent who are Negro."[50]

Yet, as described in chapter 3, the directorship of the POP voted to accept a combination of district and at-large seats for the city council.[51] Thereafter, it was unanimously decided that there would be a total of thirteen council seats, and the white majority ultimately voted to have six of those be elected at-large. In October of 1966, the new electoral system was easily adopted by popular referendum.

Following an act of the state legislature in 1883, school board members were all elected at-large. In 1970, after blacks boycotted the schools to demand more board and administrative representation, the system was changed. Thereafter, seven members were to be elected by districts and only two at-large.[52]

The Voting Rights Lawsuit

The institutional combination of liberal annexation policy, a runoff election, and at-large elections for six city council seats held sway in Memphis from 1967 to 1990. Then, as in many other small and large southern cities, the Voting Rights Act was used to challenge such arrangements.

In Memphis, this challenge occurred in the form of three separate legal efforts. In 1988 local political activist Dr. Talib-Karim Muhammad and his attorney, Margaret Carey, sued to overturn several electoral requirements. Muhammad claimed that the at-large districts and the runoff requirement were racially discriminatory. In 1990, attorney W. Otis Higgs, representing a broad-based group of blacks called Citizens for Equal Representation, filed a second suit that also challenged the election system. Both suits were proceeding slowly, and the city devoted limited resources to its defense.

The surprise for the city came in February of 1991 when the United States Department of Justice filed a separate suit under the Voting Rights Act of 1965. Specifically, a 1982 amendment to the Voting Rights Act had allowed election processes to be challenged based solely on their discriminatory *results,* even if there was no evidence of discriminatory intent.[53] Following a string of federal court decisions overturning various at-large and runoff schemes, the U.S. Justice Department charged that the city's electoral arrangements diluted the vote of black Memphians and prevented them from winning communitywide elections.

Specifically, the Justice Department made three claims against the city of Memphis. In at-large elections, the white majority has voted as a bloc consistently to defeat the candidates of the black community.[54] It also charged that the runoff eliminated "the possibility that black candidates could win elections by a plurality vote." Finally, the government charged that the electoral system in conjunction with annexation "ensured the effectiveness of such devices by maintaining an effective white electoral majority in the city." Consequently, it proposed blocking all subsequent at-large elections, runoffs, and annexations until racially neutral alternatives could be found.[55]

The suit had some interesting political implications. Mayor Hackett had endorsed George Bush in the 1988 presidential election and had been considered for an appointment by the Bush administration. Thus, such an action by the Bush administration's Justice Department appeared to shock Hackett, who increased the city's legal defense efforts. Moreover, the suit itself operated in an ambiguous legal context since the city had now become majority black in population.

Hackett seemed willing to compromise on the at-large requirement. The city council, on the other hand, was more rigid since some white members would have lost their seats in a district arrangement.[56] City council members defended the philosophical basis of the at-large positions, which were seen as providing a communitywide interest on the council rather than the more parochial interests of specific districts.[57] An important hearing in this ongoing suit took place in August of 1991. At that hearing, the United States Department of Justice successfully argued that the intention of establishing the runoff was to thwart black office seekers. Federal District Judge Jerome Turner then enjoined the city from using the runoff in the 1991 city elections.

Overall, then, the institutional context no longer posed as significant a threat to black success in the 1991 mayoral or city council elections. The 1991 mayoral election would take place with only a single election and the possibility of plurality victor. The at-large arrangement for city council seats remained for the 1991 election, although there would be no runoffs. Further, annexation of the predominately white Hickory Hills area was on hold, raising serious questions about the city's ability to annex in the future.

• • •

This contextual analysis further demonstrates the importance of the black and white historical trends discussed in the chapters above. Given the size of the African-American population in Memphis, as well as its relatively high rates of registration and turnout, it was peculiar that black candidates had not been more successful in citywide races well before 1991. Instead, a combination of racial polarization, bloc voting, annexation practices, and election rules had combined to counter these demographic resources. In the end, it took a change in the annexation laws, a partially successful federal lawsuit, and a historic mayoral campaign to finally elect the city's first African-American mayor.

Part **II**

The Election of 1991

6 The Hackett Campaign

Mayor Dick Hackett had become the standard-bearer for the dominant white political culture. Moreover, he had already been elected on three separate occasions, in each instance by a larger majority than the time before. Four years earlier, he had attracted far more black votes than any white candidate had received since black mayoral alternatives became available in 1975. In addition, he continued to ride a wave of popularity, especially in the white community.

Yet, there were also potential problems. With the city unable to continue aggressive annexation, there were now approximately as many eligible black voters as white voters. The black community succeeded in uniting behind a single black mayoral candidate. In addition, nine years in office had left the incumbent mayor with at least a few political liabilities. For example, the Pyramid project had become a bit of an embarrassment as Sidney Shlenker's scheme floundered; Holiday Inn had just decided to move its headquarters to Atlanta; and a variety of social services, especially public housing, appeared to be badly maintained.

Insiders were well aware that this was likely to be a much closer election than recent history may have suggested. The challenge for Hackett would be to shore up confidence in his administration by stressing both his accomplishments and his vision for the future. As his base was predominantly white, his primary goal would have to be to register and turn out white voters. Yet, he would need to do that without further unifying the increasingly large black community by appearing to be racially exclusive or antagonistic in his approach.

This chapter will discuss the Hackett campaign during the 1991 mayoral election. Most of the public electioneering occurred between September and early October. We will speculate about Hackett's personal motivations in pursuing the campaign and then examine his campaign strategies.

Hackett's Personal Motivations

Richard Hackett was well aware of the changing racial composition of the city. Thus, he had quietly stated earlier that he did not intend to seek a third full term in 1991. The *Commercial Appeal*, for example, had reported as early as 1986 that Hackett planned to "get out of politics" after the 1987 election.[1] In 1989, he reiterated his intention, telling a group of one of the author's students that he had chosen not to run due to the demographic changes in Memphis.

Nevertheless, in an interview following the 1991 election, Hackett explained his change of mind. In general, he had reached the conclusion that he had an obligation to run for the position. Supporters had lobbied him relentlessly to seek another term, and he honestly believed that he had a chance to win. Among other things, he was proud of his record of appointing black city administrators, and he thought that the black community would appreciate that effort. He also argued that if any other white had run for the position, the city might well have been subjected to a verbal "blood bath" between the black and white candidates. He did not want that to occur.[2]

A number of election watchers subsequently rationalized his defeat by suggesting that he had approached the campaign in a halfhearted way because he never expected to win. We categorically reject that assessment. Our interview with Hackett revealed how badly he felt about the defeat.[3] Moreover, he was anxious enough about the election that he phoned a local pollster on election eve to inquire about whether he could rest easily that night.[4] The *Commercial Appeal* also indicated that his wife arrived in tears at campaign headquarters just after midnight on election night.[5]

The mayor's campaign workers had in fact been quite confident that he would win. Dr. John Bakke of Memphis State University conducted three independent polls for television station WREG. His polling results had consistently indicated that Hackett was ahead; and, until the final weekend, it appeared that he stood to benefit from a substantial black crossover vote.[6] Consequently, several of his campaign workers believed that the election was "in the bag." Hackett himself noted that he had fewer volunteers during this election since his supporters thought that he would win. To counter that excessive confidence, he continued to put pressure on his campaign workers to make a maximum effort until the end.[7] An incident involving some campaign signs demonstrates this determination. Campaign workers had installed signs facing against traffic on a major thoroughfare. Hackett had been traveling the street and noticed the problem. He then called a campaign volunteer at home on a Saturday evening and insisted that he reverse the signs at once.

Hackett indicated that he himself had worked harder in this election than in any of his previous ones. He stated that he had "worked like a dog" for "seven nights and seven days a week for five months." He recounted that he lost "25–30 pounds during the campaign."[8] A report on WMC-TV revealed, for instance, that he had not slept on election eve as he took care of final details for the campaign's election-day efforts.[9]

The candidate clearly believed that he had a chance to win, even though he did not have the certainty that had accompanied his previous elections. One campaign worker related that just after midnight on election night the Hackett staff had been reasonably certain that he would win when the election commission finished counting the absentee ballots. After that scenario failed to materialize, Hackett still emphasized that he had not lost by 142 votes. Instead, he had come within 142 votes of winning.[10]

The Campaign

As the campaign approached, there was much to do. First, a general campaign strategy had to be designed. Most important, Hackett had to decide whether or not to engage his opponent directly. Beyond that, volunteers had to be organized, and money had to be raised. In addition, potential supporters had to be registered, and registered supporters galvanized.

The decision to conduct a low-profile "Rose Garden" campaign was made early. Instead of openly engaging the challenger and running the risk of racially dividing the city and spurring even more black participation, the decision was made to ignore Herenton and any attacks he might make. Instead, Hackett would focus his efforts on small backyard get-togethers in which he would attempt to reinforce his long-standing base of support. In addition, by not attacking Herenton, it was hoped that the mayor's moderate record on racial issues might continue to allow him a reasonable number of black crossover votes.

The "Rose Garden Strategy" takes its name from presidential politics in which an incumbent does not directly engage his opponent, but instead remains in the White House Rose Garden, looking and acting presidential. The incumbent has the advantage of being better known, and the strategy deprives the challenger of additional public recognition that direct engagement with an incumbent would bring.

Mayor Dick Hackett engaged in a municipal version of this strategy, visibly spending much of his time running the city. Dr. Bakke referred to it as a "peek-a-boo approach,"[11] while Larry Sabato, a nationally recognized expert on elections, described it as a classic incumbent strategy.[12] In our interview, Hackett characterized his strategy as continuing as mayor and doing the work of the city.[13]

As the incumbent, Hackett could make public appearances without appearing to be acting in an overtly political manner. On September 9, for instance, he attended a luncheon honoring Memphis Inter-Faith Association (MIFA) senior volunteers. On September 11 he spoke to the Memphis Restaurant Association and thanked it for its efforts in feeding the hungry. On September 13 he honored a local historian by declaring "Eleanor Hughes Day" in Memphis. Shortly thereafter, he spoke at the dedication of Estival Place, a homeless program that the city had helped fund.[14]

As part of this Rose Garden strategy, Hackett chose not to engage Herenton directly. Early in the campaign he did not even mention Herenton by name, instead referring to him as "the consensus candidate" if he referred to him at all.[15] On August 29, in a report on WMC-TV, anchorman Joe Birch noted that "voters are wondering, where's the campaign."[16] The lack of engagement included Hackett's unwillingness to make joint appearances with his opponent. Meanwhile, Herenton repeatedly challenged Hackett to debate. On one occasion, Herenton said, "I cannot understand why he would not discuss his record or his vision for Memphis in the future." Hackett's response was that his "track record [was] well established. I don't see much left to be gained by a debate or public fight."[17]

There were two appearances of the candidates that came about as close to a debate as there would be. Shelby County Interfaith (SCI), a religious group that mobilizes citizens to deal with community problems, invited the candidates to appear jointly to discuss their reaction to SCI's agenda for the city. Herenton appeared as scheduled. Hackett initially turned the group down with a statement that he "applaud[ed] SCI and [was] excited to work with them."[18] He later made a surprise appearance and addressed the gathering; however, the two candidates did not share the same stage.

The Rotary Club also invited Hackett to make a joint appearance with Herenton, and he finally consented very late in the campaign. Though the forum was limited to Rotary Club members and their guests, WMC televised the October 1 session. It was in fact a joint appearance, however, and not in any way a debate. Both Hackett and Herenton made carefully prepared speeches and responded to a limited number of questions forwarded to a moderator from the audience. Hackett stressed his record in economic development, while Herenton emphasized his vision for a greater Memphis and the need for an aggressive urban agenda. There were no direct exchanges between the candidates, and neither candidate set out any ideas that had not been presented previously in the media.

Probably the closest Hackett came to directly responding to a Herenton remark occurred in mid-September. On a number of occasions, Herenton had accused Memphis of being "mean spirited" in its toleration of problems such as homelessness, poverty, and inadequate livable housing. Thus, on September 10, Hackett indirectly responded by referring to Memphis as a "kind-spirited, generous city."[19] The following day, he also characterized it as "very caring, a very sharing, a very high-spirited city."[20] Less than a week later, at a Universal Life Insurance breakfast, Herenton then qualified his remarks, noting that he had only been referring to the Hackett administration and not the city's residents.[21]

Meanwhile, Hackett undertook to campaign in the least visible way possible. He visited hundreds of private homes where small groups of neighbors came together. Although the attendees were primarily white, there were a few racially mixed audiences. Hackett noted that he had used this forum in past elections, but not to the same extent.[22] Democrats Jimmy Farris and Peggy Pearson coordinated this portion of the campaign, and in September they held as many as four per day.[23] The process developed almost invisibly, however, and the *Commercial Appeal* only mentioned a few of these get-togethers as they occurred: a gathering on September 12 at the home of Vincent and Connie Smith; a September 27 get-together at the Cordova home of Amber and Phillip Northcross; a September 30 reception by Robert Crawford; and two backyard receptions on October 1.[24] In general, these sessions were controlled, friendly, and out of sight. The typical format was for Hackett to begin with a few informal remarks. Attendees would then have an opportunity to ask him questions. Thereafter, a hat would be passed to collect monetary contributions, and then Hackett would be off to the next gathering.

Hackett also spoke at other well-orchestrated sessions. These included the League of Women Voters, Optimist Club, Al Chymia Shrine, Fox Meadows Optimist Club, Mental Health Providers, and Kirby Woods Baptist Church. He appeared at some shopping centers and bowling alleys.[25] Then, in a departure from the other events in his campaign, he appeared on a call-in show on a black radio station, WDIA.[26]

Organization

As the candidate circulated from one carefully chosen meeting to the next, there was much to be done behind the scenes. A campaign staff had to be assembled; a campaign headquarters had to be established; money had to be raised; voters had to be registered; and on and on. Even campaigns with Rose Garden profiles involve endless attention to detail.

William "Bill" Boyd coordinated the campaign's fieldwork as well as establishing the campaign headquarters. Political insiders considered him a brilliant campaign tactician. The Hackett campaign employed him, and filings at the election commission show that he received $30,375 as compensation.

The primary headquarters was located at Poplar Plaza in Midtown. Key campaign activities coordinated through the headquarters were voter registration, sign crews, the manning of phone banks used to contact voters, and arranging rides to the polls on election day.[27] The campaign paid two staff members $4,200 and $3,300 respectively to work in each headquarters. Hackett reported that a hard core of approximately one hundred supporters worked almost every day, while a few thousand worked occasionally.[28]

Hackett's political appointees, roughly two hundred in number, were a helpful group of campaign workers. They included the directors and assistant directors of departments, employees in the mayor's office, and members of agencies in the mayor's executive office. These appointees did all the typical campaign tasks, from putting up signs and registering voters at shopping centers to phoning voters and working the precincts on election day.

The greatest amount of work came from a core set of directors who were either politically astute or had been with Hackett for some time. The most deeply involved administrators were Director of Finance John Pontius, Director of General Services Danny Lemond, Chief Administrative Officer Greg Duckett, and Director of Emergency Services Jeff Crenshaw.

Most of the Hackett-appointed city employees with whom we spoke were willing participants in the campaign. At the very least, they believed that their jobs were at stake and therefore participating in the campaign was in their self-interest. One of these individuals had a unique campaign theme: "Even if you do not like Hackett, vote for me, my job is at stake with this election." We did, however, find one employee who felt somewhat compromised. He saw himself involved in a nonpolitical position and did not want to electioneer for either candidate. He indicated that his participation "was expected," although there was no explicit pressure. As long as these workers did not campaign during working hours, it was legally proper for Hackett to ask his political appointees to participate in the election. After all, they served at the will and pleasure of the mayor.

On the other hand, there were about fifty-three hundred city workers who enjoyed civil service protection. The city charter stated clearly that such employees were allowed to vote and to state their opinions privately and through groups, but they could not participate actively in the campaign.[29] There were no accusations or indications that this rule had been violated. In fact, Hackett was very sensitive on this issue. In 1987, for instance, he had sternly chastised a deputy fire chief for his activities in recruiting fire fighters to work in that campaign.[30]

Although Hackett made the major campaign decisions and was involved in the day-to-day work of the campaign, he did depend upon a number of confidants. The titular heads of the campaign were his white co-chairmen, Jeff Sanford, and black co-chairman, George Jones. These appointments were symbolic and attempted to convey the integrated nature of the campaign. They followed in the tradition of two previous co-chairmen, Downing Pryor and A. W. Willis, who had since died.

Sanford owned a public-relations consulting firm and had been a member of the Memphis City Council from 1977 to 1983, chairing it in 1980. On the council he was one of the centrists who had at times supported Hackett's programs. He had since developed a personal friendship with the mayor. Jones was a black businessman who operated a number of McDonald's restaurants in the city, including the one at the airport. He had no previous involvement in campaigns. He was on the board of the Chamber of Commerce, and Hackett had previously appointed him to the park commission.

Another important member of the campaign staff was Paul Gurley, an accountant who had been with Hackett since his first campaign for county clerk. Gurley began campaigning in the 1970s, working for fellow Jaycees who were seeking public office. He also worked on Otis Higgs's campaign for criminal court judge. He met Hackett when both were working on the 1979 Chandler campaign. Gurley went to work for the city after the 1982 election, and he was Hackett's chief strategist in working with the city council.

Greg Duckett was the most active African American in the Hackett campaign. He attended meetings with black audiences to explain the impact of Hackett's programs on the black community, and he was the contact person with some of the black city employees. Duckett had joined the city in 1987 as director of Public Services, a department he worked to abolish. He then served as director of Housing and Community Development from 1988 to 1991, at which point Hackett appointed him to be his chief administrative officer—the top appointed position in the city. Duckett was politically astute, knowledgeable about bureaucratic politics, and highly talented. He had a law degree from Memphis State University, had worked for Senator Al Gore from 1985 to 1987, and was deputy director of Gore's 1988 presidential primary campaign. He worked for the Clinton transition team in 1992 and subsequently became a vice-president at Baptist Hospital.

Bill Boyd, as previously indicated, coordinated the campaign's field operations. He had been with Hackett throughout his career. He worked with him on Chandler's campaigns and was a veteran of Hackett campaigns going back to the 1978 county clerk's race. Boyd, like Hackett, had worked for the city under Chandler; Boyd was Chandler's director of Public Services. He had also won two elections as county assessor, although his tenure in that office had come to be seriously marred by controversy.

Fund Raising

James McGehee and Thomas Farnsworth Jr. were co-chairpersons of the important and effective finance committee. McGehee was a real estate consultant who had once owned a mortgage banking company. He had been a confidant of Mayor Chandler and had worked in three of Hackett's political races. Hackett had subsequently appointed him to serve on the airport authority. Farnsworth owned a real estate investment company and had served on the airport authority.

Farnsworth and McGehee were superb fund-raisers. They started the process in November of 1990 with a thousand-dollar-a-plate dinner at the Memphis Country Club, raising more than two hundred and fifty thousand dollars. In addition to business leaders, the guests at this appreciation dinner included county mayor William Morris, Democratic Tennessee governor Ned McWherter, and Democratic U. S. Representative John Tanner. McGehee indicated that the early event was held to raise money and to show business support for the work of the mayor.[31] Promotional material for the event read: "We think you will agree that over the years [Dick Hackett] has served as Mayor, Memphis has enjoyed a period of unparalleled growth and prosperity."[32]

Fund raising continued into the campaign with events at the Summit Club, the Orpheum Theater, and in private homes.[33] By the end, Hackett had raised well over seven hundred thousand dollars. The McGehee-Farnsworth team had been able to elicit donations at a rate unparalleled in previous Memphis elections.

Overall, the Hackett contributions were relatively large. For example, only 7 percent of Hackett's funds came in contributions under a hundred dollars, while more than 40 percent of Herenton funds came in those amounts. This pattern suggests that the Hackett contributors were people of more substantial means than the Herenton contributors.

To verify that conclusion, we used the *City Directory* to determine the occupations of the individuals who provided contributions of one hundred dollars or more.[34] Figure 20 displays the data on the percentage of contributions by type of occupation. For each occupation we subtracted

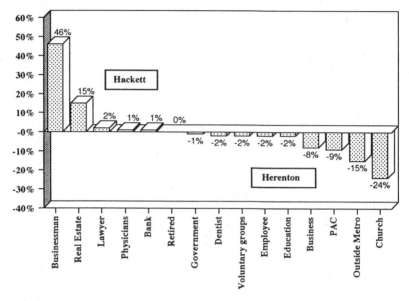

Fig. 20. Sources of Mayoral Campaign Contributions, 1991.

the percent of those in the occupational category who contributed to Herenton from the percent who contributed to Hackett.

Not only did Hackett receive the bulk of his funds from businessmen, but businessmen were by far the most one-sided in their contributions. Hackett raised 46 percent more from businessmen, and 15 percent more from those in real estate and development. Other categories did not reflect large differences between the candidates, although Hackett did receive more funds than Herenton from lawyers, physicians, and bankers. He also received 3 percent more money from the Memphis suburbs.

The list of Hackett contributors reads like a Who's Who of Memphis business, including a number of the historically prominent family names noted in chapter 1. Some of the larger contributors are displayed in the following list:

1) Principals of the prospective NFL ownership group contributed $22,000: Billy Dunavant, a cotton merchant, provided $12,000; while Paul Tutor Jones, a Wall Street financier, gave $10,000.

2) The homegrown companies discussed in chapter 1 made sizable contributions, including Federal Express Political Action Committee ($10,000), First Tennessee Bank Political Action Commit-

tee ($7,500), Malone and Hyde ($8,000), National Bank of Commerce Political Action Committee ($5,000).

3) Downtown business interests provided considerable funds: the Belz family, which owns a downtown hotel and has considerable real estate holdings, contributed $7,000; principals in Morgan Keegan, a financial investment firm in downtown Memphis, gave a total of $8,500; a principal of Alfred's Restaurant on Beale Street gave $1,000, realtor Meredith McCullar contributed $1,000, Charlie Vergos of the Rendezvous Restaurant gave $500, and the owner of Captain Bilbo's Restaurant gave $600.

4) Owners and employees of Dobbs automobile sales and leasing contributed a total of $20,000.

5) Hackett finance committee chairpersons Farnsworth and McGehee provided $11,200 and $5,000 respectively. Delos Walker, whose company ran the media campaign for Hackett, gave $2,000.

6) Many other prominent Memphians made contributions: Dr. John Shea, an eye surgeon ($7,000); William Clark, who once owned an office building called Clark Tower ($7,000); Ira Lipman, owner of a large security firm ($6,000); the Boyle family, involved in real estate development ($4,500); the Fogelman family, another family with real estate concerns ($3,000); the Seesel family, owners of grocery stores ($3,000); a principal of Lichterman Shoes ($2,000); the Mallory family ($2,000); Fred Gattas, owner of a local catalogue store ($1,500); Samuel Hollis of Federal Compress ($1,500); the president of Blue Cross and Blue Shield ($1,000); William Wolbrecht, a Hackett appointee on the park commission ($1,000); Robert Snowden ($800).

7) St. Jude Hospital principals who had worked with Hackett to keep the research hospital in Memphis also contributed, including the chairman of the board, Richard Shadyac ($250), and medical chief Dr. Joseph Simone ($1,500).

8) A philanthropist of the arts, Morrie Moss, contributed $6,000. Former businessman and philanthropist Sam Cooper gave $7,000. Clarence Day, a local philanthropist and a businessman with holdings in lumber, provided $1,000.

9) Republicans made contributions to Hackett: Bill Gibbons's political action committee gave $500, while Phillip Langdon, local chairman of the Republic Party, provided $150.

10) Companies that worked for the city or depended upon city decisions during the Hackett administrations also provided funds: Browning Farris, a waste disposal company, gave $1,000; principals from Hnedak Bobo, the company that designed the city's trolley system, gave $2,000; principals in the law firm of Heiskell, Donelson, Bearman, Adams, Williams and Kirsch, which fought the city's voting-rights lawsuit, gave $4,250; the Liberty Bowl Festival Association gave $1,000; Sidney Shlenker, of Pyramid fame, gave $1,000; architect Ken Shappley gave $1,000; Jack Snoden, of Graceland, gave $1,000; John and Pat Tigrett, involved with the Pyramid and other civic projects, gave $2,000.
11) Commodity trader Charles McVean provided $5,000. McVean had been involved in an ill-fated scheme to race hackney ponies at the Mid-South Coliseum. McVean also employed city council chairperson Jack Sammons.

Figure 21 provides a comparison of the expenditures made by the two

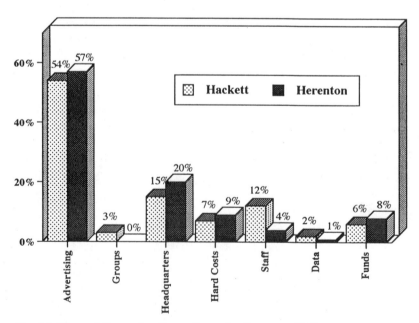

Fig. 21. Mayoral Campaign Expenditures by Category, 1991.

candidates.[35] Advertising costs were the major expenditure item, absorb-
ing a majority of both campaign budgets. Hackett spent his advertising
money through an agency, Walker and Associates, while Herenton spent
his money directly.

Hackett spent 6 percent of his campaign funds on fund raising, the
majority of which was for his 1990 appreciation dinner, while Herenton
spent 8 percent raising money. Hackett, on the other hand, spent 12 percent on staff, compared to Herenton's 4 percent. Herenton spent slightly
more (9 percent) on hard costs, such as mailing, transportation, and fieldwork, than the 7 percent that Hackett spent. Hackett spent 15 percent
on his headquarters, while Herenton spent 20 percent. Spending on data
and external groups was negligible.[36]

Figure 22 shows that Hackett spent $394,634 and Herenton spent
$324,217. Herenton's figure was slightly higher than reported since there
were some expenditures reflected in a later filing. Essentially, it appears
that their expenditures were essentially the same. Taken together, the two
candidates spent a total of approximately $730,000. This translates into
roughly $2.94 for each voter or $1.61 for each city resident of voting age.

A *Commercial Appeal* headline claimed that the amount reflected a
"record spent by Herenton and Hackett," although that is only partially

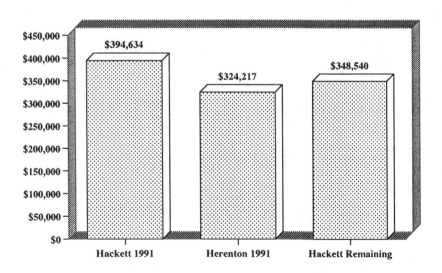

Fig. 22. Mayoral Campaign Expenditures, 1991.

correct.[37] No matter how it was measured, the two candidates did indeed spend more money on this campaign than had been spent on any previous Memphis election. Nonetheless, the amount was certainly not out of line with mayoral races in other large United States cities.

The most interesting aspect of these expenditure figures, however, has to do with the amount left over in the Hackett treasury. Figure 22 shows that Hackett had $348,540 in unspent campaign funds after the election. These funds approximately equaled the amount spent by either Herenton or Hackett during the campaign.[38] Hackett eventually converted the funds to his "Dick Hackett Community Involvement and Scholarship Account." By law, the funds were available for charitable purposes, campaign expenditures, and personal use.

In 1992, for instance, Hackett made contributions of $14,415, or one-third of that year's expenditures, to a variety of community groups. These included MIFA, Ronald McDonald House, Boy's and Girl's Clubs, the Church Health Center, Thanksgiving on Beale, and Christian Brothers High School. He also paid taxes from the fund, made several campaign contributions, retired some outstanding campaign debt, and paid for storing his mayoral memorabilia.

Nevertheless, in an election that ultimately turned on 142 votes, why were more funds not expended on Hackett's 1991 campaign itself? James King, then a Memphis State University political science professor, argued that Hackett could not have spent much more given his low-profile campaign strategy.[39] In our interview, Hackett noted that he had spent more money on this campaign than he had in any of his previous campaigns, including a mailing to every registered voter in the city. He simply did not see much else on which the money could have been profitably spent; further, he did not feel that it was morally right to spend the money frivolously. In addition, he said that his finance committee had raised money with the idea that there would be a runoff election requiring additional funds. He also said unequivocally, "I don't think you can buy an election."[40] Another explanation is that Hackett wanted to use the excess amount as a source of funds for a subsequent election effort. He may have felt that he could not get any more votes expending the funds in 1991, and instead opted to have them available for a county mayoral race some time in the future.

A bitter campaign contributor, on the other hand, responded to the latter explanation as follows. "[Hackett] ought to give very serious consideration to all the people like me who gave him money he didn't spend and the very poor race he ran with our money. . . . He should have spent the money and not put it in his pocket."[41]

Many believed that Hackett had made a mistake in not utilizing more of the available money. Jackson Baker, for example, quoted a Hackett "political operative" who described a potentially valuable usage: "Let's say that on election day he'd spent $50 a head on 40 people to man the telephones and hustle up friendly voters, and another $50 for 200 people to patrol East Memphis and get people to the polls."[42] Given the close margin of the race and Hackett's acknowledgment that he did not have as many volunteers as in past years, such a strategy could well have made a difference.

Voter Registration

Apart from raising lots of money, the Hackett campaign saw the registration process as a key to winning the election, especially given the typically polarized white and black voting patterns in Memphis. In June, at the Hackett headquarters, a receptionist was answering the phone with the phrase, "Good afternoon, voter registration."[43] The campaign set up registration tables at stores and malls until the late September deadline for all registration.

On the surface, the campaign's registration effort was successful. The *Commercial Appeal* reported that the last batch of eligible registrations included 32,000 voters, 25,000 of whom registered as a result of the Hackett campaign. There were a total of 110,000 registration cards submitted during the entire campaign period, with only 5 percent disqualified due to errors.[44]

However, the results show that Hackett was only able to remain even in the percentage of black and white registrants. Registration data from May and October show that whites as a percentage of total registrants were the same 49 percent, even though the total number of registrants increased by 7 percent.

There were a number of reasons why Hackett's registration efforts were not more successful. Registration volunteers reported that they filled out forms for many whites who had moved from the city to the suburban areas outside the city limits. Some of the forms were address changes within the city and not new registrations. In addition, Hackett made it clear to his volunteers that they were not to discriminate against black citizens.[45] Although the Hackett campaign set up its tables in areas with high levels of white traffic, the campaign also registered black citizens at those sites. Hackett estimated that about 25 percent of their cards had been filled out by African Americans.[46]

Issues

With regard to the issues of the campaign, Hackett did not believe that there were any major policy differences between himself and Herenton. By and large, this may have been true, although they did differ on "people" programs. Herenton spoke about his urban agenda and the need for better housing and infrastructure in the inner city, while Hackett ignored the weakest part of his own record, that relating to housing and neighborhoods.

Meanwhile, Hackett's Rotary Club presentation encapsulated his record. His remarks outlined his positions on four of the campaign's key issues. First, he had led the city through a period of unprecedented economic development. Memphis had grown as a distribution center, and events like the Ramses and Catherine the Great exhibits had attracted tourists to the city. Overall, he claimed responsibility for bringing 105,000 new jobs and reducing unemployment by 52 percent.

Second, he pointed out that his sound management of city government had led to seven years without a property tax increase. Mud Island, which had been a drag on city resources, had produced six million dollars through privatization. And he had accomplished all of this with "honesty, integrity and good old fashioned hard work."

Third, he asserted that he should not be held responsible for the city's particularly high homicide rate. Such crime, in Hackett's view, simply could not be deterred by the police. He blamed homicides on the moral breakdown in society and the lack of respect for human life.

Lastly, Hackett argued that he had contributed to racial harmony in the city. Among other things, his had been the most integrated administration in Memphis history.[47]

After the election, Mayor Hackett stated that he was very displeased with the way race played into the 1991 election. He referred to racial politics as one of the unpleasant political realities of Memphis. In the end, as there was much agreement between himself and Herenton, he felt that race wound up being the only real issue in the campaign.[48]

Hackett saw 1991 as an unpleasant time in his life. He said that "I just pray we can put this ugly election behind us."[49] He felt that he had run a clean campaign and had not brought race into it. He even indicated that individuals had offered him unflattering audio and video recordings of Herenton and that he would not talk with the parties involved. In his own words, he "did not sacrifice his principles, God, or beliefs in his campaign."[50] He also had a pragmatic reason for eschewing negative campaigning. He felt that a negative racial campaign would make it more difficult not only to win but subsequently to govern the city. He said that "the more divisive you are during the political process, the harder it is afterward to get everyone back together."[51]

Hackett's moderate racial views would appear to be borne out in his appointment of black directors. In 1991, Mayor Hackett had six African-American directors working in the city's staff. These included Chief Administrative Officer Greg Duckett, City Attorney Monice Hagler, Treasurer Larry Harleson, Housing and Community Director Roland McElrath, Drug Czar Jerry Oliver, and Police Director James Ivy. Previous black directors included Gene Busby and Ed Knight in Personnel and Treasurer Carol Jefferson. Most members of this group were highly regarded for their administrative and/or political skills by insiders at city hall.

Hackett's appointment of African Americans actually went even further. Blacks made up 41 percent of the managers and supervisors in the city, and they constituted 43 percent of all city employees. These data compared favorably to the overall city population, of which 50 percent of those over the age of eighteen were African Americans. In addition, Hackett's task in appointing blacks, especially administrators, was made much more difficult by the fact that there were so few in the city's managerial positions when he first came into office.[52]

Nevertheless, Hackett's appointment of black directors was criticized by some as a political move. As far back as 1982, he had expressed frustration that when he made efforts to reach out to blacks he was criticized for being political, while if he had not done so he would have been criticized for being insensitive. In 1982, for instance, he stated that his efforts at racial harmony would "do zero" for him politically.[53] Herenton's most clever criticism of the appointments was that "the Mayor has practiced discrimination in the sense that if you're white you can't get an appointment in city government."[54]

Hackett had a number of prominent black supporters. For example, George Jones, Minerva Johnican, and James Smith signed Hackett's qualifying petitions.[55] State Representative Alvin King not only endorsed and worked for Hackett, but he was pictured in the newspaper installing a Hackett sign.[56] Bishop Ford of the Church of God in Christ sent a letter to ministers in Memphis telling them that Hackett would do "what is best for the total city and the church," although he remained neutral arguing that "we can't afford to alienate anyone."[57] Hackett also was endorsed by the Shelby County Democratic Club, a relatively small group of African Americans.[58]

Hackett's most prominent black endorsement, however, was from a small group of black ministers who called themselves IPAC, or the Independent Political Action Committee. The newly formed group was concerned about the process by which Herenton was chosen at the People's Convention (which is discussed in the next chapter) and about his performance in the school system. The group also felt that "Hackett had done an exceptional job of appointing blacks" to his administration. This group staffed Hackett's Whitehaven satellite office and worked to obtain crossover votes.

As should come as no surprise in an atmosphere of racial reflexivity, many of the Hackett-appointed directors and black supporters were sharply criticized in the black community. Whether in the pages of the *Tri-State Defender* or in calls to either of the two black radio stations, WDIA or WLOK, these attacks were even vehement at times. After George Jones was named as a Hackett campaign co-chairman, for instance, the *Tri-State Defender* ran a short article in which an unnamed group called for a boycott of all McDonald's restaurants, several of which Jones owned.[59] The leader of IPAC, likewise, reported threats and insults as a result of that group's endorsement.[60]

In May of 1991, as another example, the *Tri-State Defender* responded to the appointment of black directors. An editorial in the paper read, "[O]ne would think that the Mayor's Black appointment binge would be enough to make the most progressive minded Ku Klux Klansman super mad. But not so. Both the Mayor and the Klan are well aware of the new majority population . . . in Memphis."[61] In August another article in the paper reacted bitterly to Hackett's black supporters: "[Y]es, Mayor Hackett, got his Black folks coming out of the woodwork like flies out of a garbage can when the lid is lifted. Why couldn't they have gone into the voting booth and quietly supported Hackett? Why did they have to slap the black community in its face?"[62]

By contrast, black radio station WLOK handled things somewhat differently, at least on one occasion. Bill Adkins, host of a popular call-in show, had allowed callers to make some relatively vicious personal attacks on Hackett. Hackett apparently called the owner of the station to express concern about the extremism of those attacks. The station subsequently dropped the program. Some argued that the station owner had received a loan from the city. However, an article in the *Tri-State Defender* argued that the cancellation was a function of a personality dispute between Adkins and the owner, based on differences in their personal backgrounds. The newspaper reported that the black chief executive of another radio station had complained about the nature of the calls as well.[63]

Media Campaign and Institutional Endorsements

While Hackett's standing was low among the major black media outlets, this did not deter him from launching a sizable media campaign. Walker and Associates, a local firm specializing in campaign consulting and public relations, coordinated the Hackett media campaign. Founded in 1965, Delos Walker's company had offices in Memphis, Little Rock, and Atlanta. He had a total of sixty employees at the three sites and grossed approximately thirty million dollars a year. He ran the campaigns of prominent politicians such as Arkansas Congressman Bill Alexander, United States Senator Dale Bumpers of Arkansas, and Tennessee Congressman Ed Jones. He claimed to have won fifty-seven of sixty-seven campaigns.[64] Campaign filings with the election commission indicated that the firm received $161,515 from the Hackett campaign.

On September 15, the campaign began running television advertisements. The television spots were positive and low key, emphasizing the highlights of the Hackett record.

Announcer: Dick Hackett understands what's important in the development of new jobs.

Hackett: Let me tell you, there is nothing as important to economic development as education.

Announcer: Dick Hackett has led Memphis to more than 91,000 new jobs since 1985. His vision in bringing the Wonder Series to

Memphis is boosting our economy by drawing thousands of tourists to our city right now. Reelect Dick Hackett, Mayor. A steady hand for changing times.

This commercial was confusing. It addressed the Hackett record, but mixed in one of his weakest areas, education, and then did nothing with that reference. It also did not point out the multitude of economic development projects for which Hackett was responsible. In an interview after the election, we asked Hackett about the Walker ads, but he refused to comment. For whatever reason, the question seemed to agitate him.[65]

Most surprising, however, was Hackett's recollection that his campaign did not conduct any polling of Memphis citizens. The Hackett campaign had taken polls in previous elections, though he did not indicate how often. Nonetheless, he did not believe in polls and said that he had not needed polls to tell him what was happening in this race. He expressed great confidence in his own political intuition and said that he had believed all along that it was going be a close race.[66]

Over the course of the campaign, there were a number of endorsements for Hackett. The Republican Party endorsed him, for instance, while the Democratic Party did not endorse either candidate.[67] The mayor also was formally endorsed by unions such as the International Brotherhood of Electrical Workers and the Building and Construction Trade Council. In addition, the sanitation workers, many of whom were black, chose not to make an endorsement. This was viewed as a moral victory for Hackett. The director of the union, James Smith, had even signed a Hackett qualifying petition.[68]

The *Commercial Appeal* endorsed the incumbent mayor. It focused on his public-private partnerships and said that Hackett had "a record of steady, sober accomplishments which has been marked at times by surprising imagination and initiative." It described his honesty, vision, and the promotion of blacks in his administration. The article also discussed Herenton's weaknesses, especially his inability to overcome the unfortunate events in his public and private life.[69]

• • •

The Hackett campaign can be viewed from two perspectives. First, this was a campaign run by a seasoned politician who had held public office

for fifteen years. He conceived a strategy meant to contact his supporters without alerting his opponents. He worked to register his supporters,
raised vast sums of money, and employed a professionally developed
media campaign. Second, even though he succeeded in maintaining support in the white community, he failed in his attempts to attract black
votes. His appointment of blacks to city government was criticized as
little more than a campaign tactic. His use of blacks in the campaign
was met with derision. In his 1987 campaign, Hackett had made inroads
into the black community. In 1991, he had worked harder in that community with far fewer results. One big reason was the campaign of Dr.
W. W. Herenton.

7 The Herenton Campaign

Dr. Willie W. Herenton's triumph and the events that preceded it have been described as much more than a campaign. Some say the *peoples'* victory that motivated a record voter turnout on October 3, 1991, was a miracle *Crusade* which was the fulfillment of a dream deferred—that could no longer be denied.

—Vernon E. Ash, *Dr. W. W. Herenton*

Once again, given racial parity in the number of eligible voters, a long tradition of voting polarization by race, and the black community's recent inability to agree on one black candidate, it looked like another uphill battle if an African American was going to win the mayoral election of 1991. Even if there turned out to be a single black candidate, the relative indigence of much of the city's African-American population would make it very difficult to muster the level of black registration and turnout necessary to defeat a popular white incumbent—an incumbent who had received a record number of black crossover votes four years earlier. In addition, Mayor Hackett's popularity meant there was little hope of successfully appealing to many white voters; and, in an atmosphere of "racial reflexivity," such appeals would most likely just make it that much harder to generate the necessary unity and enthusiasm in the African-American community. To win, a strong, single black candidate would need to emerge and lead an unprecedented black electoral "crusade."

A Unity Movement

Despite the odds, there were some encouraging signs as well. Looked at another way, for the first time there were now enough eligible black voters so that a strong registration drive and turnout could win the election even without white help. With that prospect in mind, the question arose as to who could best galvanize a record voting turnout in the African-American community.

A group of W. W. Herenton's supporters, mostly educators, began meeting regularly on Sunday afternoons in the early fall of 1990. They met at the home of William Hawkins. Besides Hawkins and Herenton, the group included Kenneth Cole, Alan Hammond, Curtis and Logan Mitchell, Halloe Robinson, Hugh Strong, Eddie Walsh, Eldredge Williams, and Roland Woodson, among others. Once the group was convinced that a Herenton candidacy was viable, and Herenton agreed to seek his first elective office, the earliest of campaign strategies began to form.

One reality was crystal clear from Memphis history. There would be no defeating incumbent mayor Dick Hackett if there turned out to be more than one significant black candidate on the 1991 general election ballot. First the black community needed to understand this and dedicate itself to avoiding it. Then, a mechanism needed to be developed for guaranteeing this end result. Finally, for Herenton's supporters, a campaign needed to begin to make certain that the one chosen candidate would be W. W. Herenton.

The Clayburn Challenge

On the wintry night of January 21, 1991, hundreds of people jammed the Clayburn Ball Temple AME Church to commemorate the birth of Dr. Martin Luther King Jr. The event was sponsored by Health Care Workers Local No. 3600 of the American Federation of State, County and Municipal Employees (AFSCME). Nearly a quarter of a century since Dr. King had lost his life attempting to help city workers organize a labor union and have it recognized by Mayor Henry Loeb, this seemed like a very logical site from which to launch an electoral crusade designed to take the next step—to place those very reins of mayoral decision-making power in the hands of an African American for the first time.

The event was being coordinated by a union leader, Lorenzo Banks, a newspaperman, Vernon Ash, and a former state representative, Teddy Withers. W. W. Herenton had been invited as the evening's primary speaker, and he was introduced by Withers.

The situation presented itself, and Herenton seized the opportunity. In the course of his remarks, presented without notes as is his custom, he paused and posed a challenge. With Congressman Harold Ford and a number of other local black leaders in the audience, Herenton challenged Ford to help him bring the black community together. It was time to cease letting internal discord scuttle the chances of electing an African-American, and it was also time to stop allowing "the white power structure . . . to determine who the black candidate is going to be for Mayor."

> Harold Ford, in my opinion, has been a great congressman. And Harold, I want to challenge you publicly, because you are very distinguished, and I consider you to be our most powerful political leader in the black community—and somehow or another I think that Congressman Ford ought to assume the responsibility of bringing us together to help us deal with all this mess that we've got here in the black community.
>
> I know he might have a problem with me putting him on the spot like this, but he has been our leader. . . . We need a black summit meeting right here in Memphis, Tennessee.

Ford, although not officially scheduled to speak at the event, subsequently followed Herenton to the podium and "gladly accepted" the challenge. "It doesn't have to be a Ford, it can be a Chevrolet, it can be anybody, but we must unite this community in October of 1991," Ford remarked.[1]

When he was accused of further polarizing the city by such a call for racial unity, Ford responded, "African Americans need to come together at this time to gain their fair share of the power in this city. Then, they can sit down at the table as equals to Whites. That is when the polarization can end, and we can work together to make this city better for all."[2]

The unity summit concept was not a new approach, at least outside the South. It had been employed successfully in both Newark in 1970 and Chicago in 1983, allowing those racially mixed cities finally to elect their first African-American mayors. What set Memphis apart would be the black community's inability even to unite behind a single unity conference. There turned out to be two separate "unity" conventions, and some prominent black leaders publicly stated reservations about the entire proposition.[3]

On February 7, Councilman Wilbun called a press conference to announce the formation of a grassroots "people's conference," arguing that the nomination process should be as open, public, and inclusive as possible.[4] This conference would ultimately become the "African-American People's Convention Organization," and joining the convention would include a pact that all prospective black mayoral candidates would sign pledging to accept the decision of that convention.[5]

It looked to be an ideal forum for nominating Councilman Wilbun. Besides Wilbun, leaders included Withers and Banks, as well as Del Gill, Henri Brooks, Barbara Cooper, radio talk show host Reverend Bill Adkins, Donald Howery of AFSCME Local No. 3600 and Sidney Chism of Teamsters' Local No. 1196. None of the original core of Herenton supporters were involved, and it appears that the People's Convention organizers were not even aware of the emerging Herenton effort.

One quite prominent black political force glaringly absent from these early planning sessions was Congressman Harold Ford. The People's Convention approach had been designed and was being executed by a group of individuals who were not regularly counted among "the Ford people."

Thus, on March 1, Congressman Ford announced plans for a parallel "leadership summit," loosely modeled after the 1983 Chicago process that ultimately led to the election of Harold Washington. It would bring together 148 black religious, civic, and political leaders. Besides holding community meetings to discuss issues and candidates, ultimately leading to the final leadership summit, the plan was that each leader would also be assigned the position of "captain" to direct voter-registration drives in the 148 lowest registration neighborhoods in the city. Meanwhile, as for his own role, Ford declared that "I am neutral and I will stay neutral."[6]

Besides Herenton, a number of other names were being bantered about in the press as possible black mayoral candidates. These included the executive director of the national NAACP, Benjamin Hooks, a Memphis native who admitted exploring the possibility with his nephew, County Tax Assessor Michael Hooks, who was a potential candidate in his own right.[7] Others often mentioned were Wilbun himself, City Councilman Kenneth Whalum, Public Defender A. C. Wharton, three-time mayoral candidate Judge W. Otis Higgs Jr., black Muslim leader Dr. Talib-Karim Muhammad, and both Congressman Harold Ford and his brother, State Senator John Ford.[8]

The People's Convention

Willie W. Herenton had made his decision. He would seek the office of city mayor. A campaign organization was beginning to take shape, and, as Herenton put it, they would "play to win."[9] As the first step toward achieving that goal, he and his supporters would overwhelm the People's Convention.

On a stormy Saturday morning, April 27, the People's Convention convened at the twelve-thousand-seat Mid-South Coliseum. According to Wilbun's initial proposal, to be a delegate one simply had to be a "registered voter from the African-American community; or if not registered, registration upon arrival . . . will be required."[10]

This proposal immediately generated controversy: did it, in effect, exclude supportive whites? On this question, there seemed to be disagreement, with the final rules being left somewhat ambiguous in this regard.[11] Nevertheless, a city council member, Pat Vander Schaaf, had challenged the legality of a racially exclusive event being held in a public facility.[12] Convention rules committee chairwoman Del Gill responded, "While we are not proactively seeking the participation of European Americans in this process of determining the future of the Memphis African-American community, let me explicitly state that the rules adopted do not exclude anyone from the process on the account of race."[13]

It is estimated that more than four thousand African Americans ultimately attended.[14] Then, according to the convention's rather complex set of twenty-six rules, they were subsequently organized by their respective wards and precincts. At high noon, Teddy Withers convened the entire group.

The convention program included full-page advertisements for four candidates. They were Herenton, Otis Higgs, Dr. Talib-Karim Muhammad, and Shep Wilbun. Of the four, Herenton's ad was the simplest and most direct, showing the long-embattled school superintendent sitting proudly and professionally at his school board desk. Declaring him the "People's Choice for Mayor" and the most qualified candidate, the advertisement stressed his proven leadership ability, managerial skills, integrity, and courage.

From early on, it was quite apparent who would emerge victorious. A sea of red and white Herenton signs flooded the convention floor in a show of support orchestrated by, among others, Reginald French, a prominent member of the city's elite "100 Black Men" organization.

Because the convention had been organized by wards and precincts, the Herenton people organized themselves that way as well, bringing along walkie-talkies and signs to help dominate the proceedings. Most of the voters had not been contacted ahead of time, so the challenge was both to persuade them and marshal them.[15]

The convention first adopted a "People's Platform" to guide the endorsed candidate and subsequent conventions. In its most general terms, it called for the pursuit of authentic socioeconomic progress in Memphis through justice and accountability in government.[16] In addition, those assembled even voted to recall Mayor Hackett for "malfeasance and misfeasance," following a motion made by citizen-activist Cornelia Crenshaw.

After formal nominations of Herenton, Higgs, Wilbun, Muhammad, and Dr. Isaac Richmond, those in attendance finally had the opportunity to vote on a mayoral candidate. It was no contest. W. W. Herenton won on the first ballot, receiving more than 70 percent of the votes cast, the minimum proportion required for nomination.

In a rousing acceptance speech, he emphasized how he had overcome adversity. As school superintendent, "I have been crucified. . . . I have been nailed to the cross." Now that was all behind him. He stood before them triumphant and prepared to be the city's first African-American mayor. They would not be denied. History and God were on their side.[17]

It was a terrific start for Herenton, as he took one giant step closer to becoming the black community's single "unity candidate." In a subsequent letter to Congressman Ford, for example, Dr. Muhammad noted that he had withdrawn his candidacy in support of the People's Convention winner; for all practical purposes, he urged the Congressman to follow suit.[18]

However, there was a potential downside to this show of unity as well. The whole notion of such a racially conscious nomination process stood to alienate many in the city's small contingent of liberal whites, and this problem became exacerbated by the perception that whites were not allowed to attend.[19] In addition, this entire arrangement had circumvented

Congressman Ford and his organization, leaving the Congressman less than pleased as he launched his own parallel "unity summit" process.[20]

The Unity Summit

Not only was the unity summit designed to deliver a consensus on issues, a mayoral candidate, and a leadership structure, but also organizer Ford promised a $250,000 war chest for the ultimate winner. As of late May, he claimed that $75,000 had already been committed.[21] Meanwhile, the summit process was to occur in phases, beginning with "summit workshops" analyzing candidates and issues. The results of those workshops would then be compiled and presented to a group of seven to eight hundred black leaders at the final leadership summit. Decisions as to a final platform and candidate were promised within two weeks of that summit.

Suspicions abounded that the process originally had been designed to culminate in the choice of the Congressman as the unity candidate. There were no clear indications that this was the case, although Herenton and many others were reasonably certain that Harold Ford had always envisioned himself as the first black mayor of Memphis. As a matter of fact, Herenton seems to share the view that Ford had made moves over the years designed to reduce the likelihood of anybody else of stature rising up to challenge his position of power in the Memphis black community.[22] Professor William E. Nelson Jr., a former Memphian, discussed the absence of trust exhibited by a number of the local black leaders, concluding, "They suspect that Harold Ford's process is going to be designed to benefit Harold Ford."[23]

Regardless, Ford had initially announced that the final summit would occur sometime in February. It was now May. Issue workshops had been occurring, although they had apparently been sparsely attended.[24] There was no clearly scheduled date for the culminating Unity Summit session, and there was even some indication from the Congressman that it might not be held after all.[25]

On May 24, a frustrated Herenton lost patience and formally declared that he would be running for mayor regardless of the outcome of the Unity Summit process. In his announcement speech at the Holiday Inn Crown Plaza Hotel, he stated, "We do not have the luxury of waiting anymore. We have given Congressman Ford ample time . . . to be forthright with the summit. We are obliged to launch a campaign, with no disrespect for him."[26] Similar sentiments had already been articulated by the editorial staff of the *Tri-State Defender*.[27]

Finally, the Unity Summit meeting occurred on June 15, one day after Harold Ford officially pulled himself out of the race. This left Herenton and W. Otis Higgs Jr. as the primary remaining candidates. As these two men squared off, Congressman Ford apparently continued to harbor ill feelings toward Dr. Herenton, most recently related to what he perceived as Herenton's legitimization of Wilbun's People's Convention.[28]

Given the considerable confusion about the procedure Ford's final summit would follow, Herenton broached the subject with Ford one evening at the bar of the Peabody Hotel. When Ford talked around the point, Herenton believed Ford was employing a delaying tactic, and that Ford did not want him as the summit's choice. As a matter of fact, Herenton is certain that he was not the choice of the bulk of the established black leadership in the city.[29]

Nevertheless, although they lacked a clear notion of exactly what to expect, the Herenton supporters approached the Unity Summit much as they had the People's Convention. They went all out. To begin with, they had signs and supporters on the various street corners surrounding Bloomfield Baptist Church; and that is what Ford, Higgs, and others saw when they drove up. Once inside, Herenton described Ford as "visibly disturbed," for it was clear that the Herenton supporters packed into Bloomfield had no intention of being turned aside. This effort had already taken on a "movement" quality.[30]

Hattie Jackson, a retiring elementary school principal and longtime Ford supporter, declared from the summit floor that "Dr. Herenton will always be my boss," a declaration that brought a roar of support from the largely pro-Herenton crowd.[31] Teddy Withers had already warned Ford that "[a]nything short of him being with Herenton will definitely appear as a sellout to Dick Hackett."[32] In addition, some of these supporters even carried petitions that threatened to launch a recall effort against the Congressman if Herenton were denied. Reverend Ralph White, pastor of Bloomfield Church, intervened to remind the tension-filled room that the purpose was to achieve unity, and that little would be accomplished by making personal attacks.[33]

No vote was ever taken. There was no doubt who would win. Instead, after Task Force issue reports were read and adopted as a platform of sorts,[34] Ford, Higgs, and Herenton retired to an antechamber and had what Herenton referred to as "a verbal knock down, drag out exchange." In a meeting that lasted approximately one hour, Ford was "told" that he was going to endorse one of them or the other. Actually, Herenton believed that the crowd was quite "serious" and that Ford "would have been lucky to get out of there intact" if he had not gone along. Meanwhile, by Herenton's own account, he also was blunt with Higgs, telling him in no uncertain terms that Higgs could not win a mayoral election because he did not have enough white supporters and the black community just was not that taken with him. An irritated Higgs then left the building by a side door, and Ford returned to the podium to lift Herenton's hand in victory.[35]

Although only Herenton, Wilbun, and Muhammad had signed the People's Convention pact pledging to support its single nominee,[36] momentum built quickly. According to the pact, no other black candidate should attempt to break the unity that had been so painstakingly achieved. Arelya Mitchell, editor of the city's only black newspaper, the *Tri-State Defender,* even threatened that if any such renegade candidacy emerged, "it is up to the Black citizenry to get him or her out—to use Malcolm X's phrase—by any means necessary."[37]

The Kennedy Democratic Club proceeded to follow suit and endorsed Herenton. In addition, club president Charlie Morris called on "every club and organization to support Dr. Herenton in his efforts to become Memphis' first black Mayor."[38]

Although Otis Higgs threatened to continue his own candidacy, he rather quickly decided against that course of action. He publicly withdrew on June 17, only two days after the Unity Summit.[39] Thus, when the August 1 petition deadline came and went, and despite the fact that neither Herenton nor his aides had spoken directly with any of the other prospective candidates, no other black candidate had emerged to split the black vote. In addition, very few black leaders had endorsed the incumbent mayor. The unity process had succeeded, at least to this point.

The General Election Campaign

The official campaign kickoff was set for the Fourth of July, less than three months from the general election. Meanwhile, there was much to do. Strategies had to be designed. Funds had to be raised. Voters had to be registered. Absentee voters had to be marshaled. And, ultimately, voters would have to be delivered to the polls. With every vote likely to be crucial in a race that had the potential of being very close, campaign organization had to be tight and Herenton himself had to be inspirational.

On June 20, over the course of a two-hour private meeting at his Memphis School Board office, Dr. Herenton outlined some of his hopes and fears. An essentially reserved man by nature, he expressed his discomfort at the prospect of all the political glad handing that lay ahead, and he indicated personal disdain for much of the symbolic politics and posturing that are so common to political life. In addition, he wanted very much to keep the campaign on the "high road," discussing issues and not slinging mud. Herenton also feared the possibility of becoming isolated, and thus he invited those around him to challenge him constantly.

Nevertheless, he exuded a quiet confidence as well. Claiming to have a good feel for community sentiment, he believed that there was a growing ground swell of support for him. Further, he simply had always believed that he could win an elective position if he made the decision to seek it, whatever the office. He was confident in himself and in his community support.

From a strategic perspective, after analyzing various Higgs, Ford, and Hackett races, Herenton and his advisors had concluded that he could not count on even 5 percent of the white vote in a best-case scenario. The city was just too racially divided, not to mention the negative baggage many whites apparently perceived him to be carrying as a result of the Mahnaz Bahrmand affair and his alleged mismanagement as city school superintendent.[40] According to Herenton, there just was not enough time for him to adequately counter his tarnished image in a relatively small, but potentially supportive, segment of the white community.[41]

The key, then, was to generate a record turnout in the black community and minimize black votes for Hackett. Therefore, although Herenton vowed to speak across the entire city, it was quite clear that the overwhelming focus of his campaign would be on the African-American community. "I knew that in order for me to win this election, I had to motivate and inspire black people like they had never been inspired before. I also knew that I had to utilize our spiritual life as a rallying point. You have to draw upon the essence of a culture, a people, to get them to move during struggles and great transitions."[42]

Publicly, the issue of race would surface early and often. In a May

Wall Street Journal article, for instance, Herenton was quoted as saying
that "Memphis is still a city languishing in the mentality of the Old
South. It doesn't enjoy a good reputation as a color blind city."[43] He
would ceaselessly hammer home this theme throughout the campaign,
particularly as he exhorted black audiences to rise up and be heard on
election day. "You don't have the luxury to stay at home," he declared.[44]
He even chided them, stating that "[w]e ought to be embarrassed being
54.6 percent of this community and not be in control."[45]

It is essential, however, to remember that Herenton was not a black
separatist. He had long and enduring ties to the city's local branch of
the NAACP, including a strong personal friendship with Maxine Smith,
its tireless leader. Thus, despite a clear focus on arousing support in the
black community, he harbored a desire for better race relations as well.
If elected, he sincerely hoped he could elevate the city's black community while at the same time bringing the city together. For Herenton, despite the obvious obstacles, these were not seen as mutually exclusive
goals: "Above all, the African-American candidate must not apologize
for having as his or her primary objective to empower the Black community. And the White community has got to understand. The White community cannot look at us with fear, nor suspect, because everybody benefits if the Black condition is improved."[46]

It is also important to remember Herenton's well-established ties with
many of the city's business elites. His years of service on corporate
boards, including those of Holiday Inn and First Tennessee Bank, had
left him reasonably well connected in business circles. One of his primary goals was more and better jobs for the city's poor, and he believed
firmly that these local businesses could deliver them. Consequently,
despite occasional populist overtones,[47] Herenton remained a reliable
supporter of the economic establishment. Spurring economic development in the private sector would remain a high priority whether Hackett
or Herenton was elected. Herenton simply did not see helping business
and helping the poor as mutually conflicting goals; rather, they were
inseparable.[48]

Thus, despite talk of an impending racial and economic revolution in
Memphis were Herenton to be elected,[49] it should be remembered that,
at his core, Dr. Herenton was not only an advocate of improved race relations, but he was also a believer in a "supply-side" (or "trickle-down")
economics of sorts.[50] Rhetorical flurries and exaggerated community ex-

pectations aside, Herenton was very much a social, political, and economic "moderate."

What he would add to the administration of city policy would be a deep and sincere African-American consciousness. In that sense, things would change. In addition, he openly identified himself as a Democrat, being "more in tune with the Democrats' priorities."[51] Consequently, as somewhat more economically liberal than Mayor Hackett, Herenton would look more freely to the federal government for help and would demonstrate a greater faith in government to help in solving pressing city problems.

The Campaign Team

Herenton tapped attorney Charles Carpenter to be his campaign manager. Carpenter had not been part of the initial "Hawkins group" that had begun to explore the possibility of Herenton's candidacy, and he had never managed a political campaign. Nonetheless, Carpenter had attended the People's Convention and had persuaded Herenton that he was the candidate for the job. According to Herenton, this was going to be a nontraditional campaign in order to avoid the traditional results. Thus, he wanted a campaign manager who was not one of the old-line "pols" aligned with a particular Memphis faction. He believed that Carpenter was bright, honest, tough, and had an orderly lawyer's mind. Herenton had worked with him before, and Carpenter had urged Herenton to run for mayor on previous occasions.[52]

The remainder of the campaign organization was nearly in place by the end of June. Osbie Howard, an accountant and longtime Ford supporter, was selected to be the treasurer, assisted by accountant Frank Banks. Ron Redwing, an employee of the Catholic Diocese, was to handle media relations. Myrtis Rankin, a teacher and veteran of a number of Mississippi voter-registration drives, would head up voter registration. Real estate broker Eddie Walsh would direct the absentee ballot drive. Floyd Newsum, a career fire fighter, would be the volunteer coordinator. Herenton's personal pastor and a former city councilman, Reverend James Netters, was to be the official spiritual advisor, while twenty-six-year-old Reginald French, a former police officer, was in charge of getting out the vote on election day. Memphis State University's Allen Hammond and others would provide general campaign assistance.[53]

Felix Walker and Associates were retained as the primary professional campaign consultants. In addition, Creative Marketing Concepts of Germantown and Fresh Ideas of Memphis headed the list of advertising consultants.

As for the campaign's grassroots structure, government employee Henri Brooks, banker Jesse Turner Jr., bond broker Archie Willis, and educator Johnnie Turner were to coordinate the "wards and precincts" canvassing operation. Within each of the city's predominantly black precincts, individuals were assigned to oversee registration, absentee balloting, and getting out the vote on election day. In some instances, these precinct leaders actually went door-to-door in their designated neighborhoods.[54]

Conspicuously absent from the organizational chart was Harold Ford. From the outside, it looked as if the Congressman had decided to sit this one out. In reality, however, the campaign had asked him to remain on the sidelines, at least for now. According to Reverend Bill Adkins, "Willie Herenton had to be the focal point."[55] Former Ford associate Frank Banks notes that "Ford wasn't happy. He really didn't understand why they didn't want his help."[56]

Fund Raising

One of the first tasks the campaign organization faced was fund raising. It appeared obvious from early on that Herenton's campaign would be badly outspent. For example, in late February Mayor Hackett had filed his compulsory campaign financial statement, which indicated he had nearly a quarter of a million dollars already on hand, including carryover monies from his less than demanding 1987 race and a sizable amount raised at a 1990 appreciation dinner.[57]

Meanwhile, Herenton saw little point in asking either the white business elites or traditional black leaders for money, and he did not want to borrow money either. According to Herenton, "The black political establishment didn't support me because of jealousy. . . . I didn't go through their channels to start my campaign. I knew Hackett would get the white business money. And I didn't want to owe anybody anything."[58]

Shortly after the final unity conference, the *Commercial Appeal* estimated Herenton to have raised approximately fifty thousand dollars to that point, most of it raised at the Unity Summit meeting itself.[59] His July Fourth campaign kickoff dinner generated another ten thousand dollars from Teamsters Local No. 1196 and an additional fifty thousand dollars in pledges. These pledges included a ten-thousand-dollar contribution from the Federal Express Political Action Committee, which also gave the same amount to his opponent. In addition, Herenton attended a fund-raiser in Nashville, as well as traveling to Chicago for a fund-raiser organized by a group of Booker T. Washington High School alumni.

Locally, the Herenton campaign had been warned that high-profile fund-raising events in the white community were doomed to failure. For whatever reason, the campaign's two major attempts did indeed fall flat. When the campaign sent out two thousand invitations to members of the Memphis Bar Association, fewer than twenty attended a September 6 fund-raiser.[60] Thereafter, a similar session with local realtors was canceled entirely.[61]

Much of Herenton's funding ultimately came in the form of small individual contributions, a number of which came through the churches. Some of these smaller donations even came "in-kind." For example, someone would find soft drinks on sale and bring them to the campaign headquarters as a contribution. The volunteers, in fact, came to survive primarily on soft drinks and popcorn donated in this manner.

By September 23, as election day neared, campaign financial statements indicated that Hackett had raised some $675,000, nearly three times the $236,000 raised by Herenton. Besides the $10,000 from Teamsters' Local No. 1196, Herenton's largest single contributions had come from the Memphis Teachers' Association ($3,000), Mississippi Boulevard Christian Church ($3,300), the West Tennessee Annual Conference of the CME Church ($5,000), and a Washington-based Teamsters' union ($20,000). However, most of the money had been raised in relatively small amounts from some 1,500 separate individuals.[62]

After a final flurry of fund raising, Herenton closed the gap a bit. Including money raised after the election to help pay off campaign debts,[63] Herenton ended up having raised roughly one-half what the incumbent, Hackett, had succeeded in amassing. The final figures were approximately $743,000 for Hackett and $324,000 for Herenton.

Voter Registration

Along with fund raising, voter registration was a high priority for the Herenton campaign team. Herenton realized how important voter registration was to his chances for his success and voiced his concern: "We're going to reach into the bowels of the ghetto and find those people who have lost hope and given up."[64] Actually, the voter-registration drive was relatively simple. There were some limited efforts to register people door-to-door. In addition, a number of black churches also provided some assistance in this endeavor. However, the bulk of it was accomplished by organizing "teams" that were sent to grocery stores, laundromats, shopping malls, and housing projects.[65]

As indicated in chapter 5, more than fifty thousand African-American registrants had been added by the September 3 deadline. That exceeded an original goal of forty thousand. However, this only allowed the Herenton camp to maintain the same 51 to 49 percent advantage it had enjoyed in May. Nevertheless, it was a moral victory of sorts, given the increased difficulty involved in registering a generally lower-income population.

Herenton on the Stump

The campaign did indeed officially begin on the Fourth of July, beginning where it would end, at the Peabody Hotel. At a dinner for approximately one thousand Herenton supporters, Kenneth Whalum blasted Mayor Hackett for his lack of educational leadership; Congressman Ford claimed that the mayor had cost the city millions of dollars in federal aid by not working with the city's Congressional representatives; and Shep Wilbun urged supporters to make this their own "declaration of independence" night. Herenton then struck his own key themes as he spelled out his concerns for the underfunding of the city's public schools, for the city's racial division, and for continuingly depressing rates of poverty.[66]

As for disseminating his messages, there would be only limited money for radio and television ads. Nevertheless, as an alternative way of increasing visibility, the Herenton campaign did reserve the side panels on one hundred city buses at a cost of forty-one thousand dollars over the course of the three-month campaign. In addition, because Hackett ran such a low-visibility campaign in which he made very few quotable public statements, Herenton appeared to enjoy at least an equal share of the media's regular campaign coverage.[67]

The goal was to "dominate the media," and, in retrospect, Herenton believed that his campaign had been relatively successful at that. As for the coverage itself, he had no complaints, although he felt that Hackett was clearly the *Commercial Appeal*'s preferred candidate—contributing to Hackett's image of invincibility. In contrast, Herenton believed that the *Commercial Appeal* portrayed him as the black candidate least likely to be able to beat the incumbent mayor.[68]

In addition to relying on media presentations, Herenton spoke at numerous churches, civic-group meetings, open "town meetings," and small "meet-and-greet" occasions, besides touring the public-housing projects and canvassing black neighborhoods. Outside the black community, his appearances included speeches delivered before the Shelby County Republicans, the Kiwanis Club, B'nai B'rith, the Mid-South Jaycees, St. Mary's Episcopal School, Christian Brothers' University, the Memphis Ministers' Association, receptions at a handful of residences of white citizens, and a number of private meetings with various local business leaders.[69]

As the campaign progressed, although there really was no carefully orchestrated master plan as such,[70] Herenton utilized a very standard general strategy of attacking his opponent and his policies early, hoping that such attacks would cause Hackett to respond and possibly even to debate. The strategy was also an attempt to shake people's confidence in Hackett and get at least some to begin considering other options. Then, at a given point, the campaign would switch to the positive, focusing almost entirely on what Herenton could deliver as the alternative.

The case against Hackett had a number of dimensions. Most specifically, he was attacked for his alleged insensitivity to a variety of mounting human problems in the city, his inability to bring Memphis together racially, his campaign's alleged dirty tricks, and scandals in both the city's public housing authority and in its construction of the Pyramid Arena.

On August 1, Herenton called for an external audit of the city's financial dealings with the developers of the financially troubled Pyramid. Herenton accused Hackett of mismanaging the project and of lying to the public by suggesting that taxpayers would not ultimately be responsible for debts incurred by project developers. Or, as he simply could not resist saying, maybe Hackett just "doesn't understand the complex financial issues involved." To which Hackett responded that he "would not dignify his name-calling with a response."[71]

On August 3, at a meeting of the African-American People's Convention Organization, Herenton actually accused the Hackett administration of "meanness" in its policy priorities: "Any city that will place brick and mortar before its people is a mean city. Any city that won't educate its children is a mean city. Any city that keeps thousands of people in the housing projects and won't improve them is a mean city. So, I believe God has ordained his downtrodden to rise up and save this entire city."[72]

There was also the issue of the city's efforts to lure a National Football League team. Implied in some of Herenton's attacks was the notion that such a priority was just another example of the incumbent's concern for institutions rather than suffering people. Claiming "it would not be my highest priority," Herenton concluded that "Memphis's ability to secure professional sports franchises should be contingent on its success in dealing with the economic disparity problems among the citizens."[73] According to Eddie Walsh, Herenton's supporters had carefully analyzed this issue and come to the conclusion that it was of greatest concern to select middle- and upper-class east Memphis whites. Thus, there was no need to place high priority on riding this particular bandwagon.[74]

On August 23, Herenton referred to a host of city problems, ranging from the lack of adequate low-income housing to underfunding of the public schools, from crime to the lack of jobs; Herenton asserted that the incumbent mayor "would rather dodge tough issues than face them."[75] He also returned to one of his primary themes, which was that Memphis must begin to resolve its problems with race relations if it hoped to become as successful as a city like Atlanta.

Another potential issue was the recent departure of Holiday Inn's corporate headquarters. The move provided Herenton with an opportunity to challenge Hackett in his strong suit, his ability to lure and retain corporations. The problem here, however, was the fact that Herenton sat on the board of directors of Holiday Inn. Any attempts to capitalize on this particular issue were likely to backfire.

As September dawned, unable to prod the incumbent mayor into face-to-face issue debates or even into a public response to any of his remarks, Herenton stepped up his attacks. In a dizzying flurry of speeches to church congregations and town meetings, he hammered away at the decay in the city's downtown and in its neighborhoods and used the scourge of homelessness as a counter to Hackett's "sharing and caring city" themes. When speaking of Hackett in the context of such problems, he came to refer to him not by name, but as "the incumbent."[76]

Further, Herenton compared himself to Moses, ready to fight "mod-

ern day Pharaohs" and "evil in the land."[77] Not only was he critical of
Hackett's policy priorities, but he also criticized alleged dirty tricks in
the incumbent's campaign. Through his campaign manager, Charles Carpenter, for instance, he accused Hackett supporters of playing a dirty
trick when Mahnaz Bahrmand suddenly turned up as a fellow resident
in Herenton's apartment complex, even possessing the parking place
next to his. In addition, the media apparently had been tipped off when
Bahrmand moved in.[78] Further, another aide suggested that Herenton's
apartment had been bugged and that he was being surreptitiously watched
and followed.[79]

Meanwhile, there was some surprise in the Herenton camp that Hackett
had not gone on the attack himself, or at least attacked Herenton indirectly through others. They had been prepared for criticisms both of
Dr. Herenton's record while he was superintendent of schools and of
Herenton's alleged involvement in the Mahnaz Bahrmand affair. As a
matter of fact, they were actually hoping for some of these attacks as
they might well have proven useful in solidifying and galvanizing support in the black community.[80]

Far from being merely a negative campaign, however, Herenton emphasized the positive effects that this election would bring. Herenton argued that his election would evoke "pride and hope in the black people
of this city and Memphis [would] take a quantum leap forward" if he
were elected. In addition, he reassured whites that they would be treated
"justly" under a Herenton administration, and he challenged whites to
"help transform Memphis . . . to the renaissance of the South."[81]

As for specific issue positions, Herenton promised an economic development strategy that would produce more higher-paying manufacturing and white-collar positions, beyond the low-wage service jobs that
would likely accompany the incumbent's emphasis on making Memphis
a distribution center and tourist attraction. He also pledged increased
educational leadership and more school funding; a fairer shake for blacks
seeking city employment and contracts without resorting to affirmative-
action quotas; more police foot patrols, particularly in the highest crime
areas; more emphasis on drug education and treatment; and a revamp-
ing of the scandal-ridden public housing system.[82] He argued that all of
these goals could be achieved without having to raise local taxes to any
significant extent, in part by reducing waste, but also by diverting monies from ventures like the Pyramid and the new downtown trolley line,

and by finding a way to tax those crossing state lines to work in or visit Memphis.[83]

As he crisscrossed the city in the last two weeks of September, he began to tie up loose ends. For example, besides tougher law enforcement, he promised citizen review committees to help avoid abuse of police power.[84] He came out in favor of tax reform, preferring an income tax to the more regressive combination of property and sales taxes currently in place.[85] He defended his record as school superintendent, particularly the success of the optional schools program, while reminding voters of how other large cities had courted his services. And, at the Jewish Temple Israel, in a much more conciliatory tone, he even conceded that the incumbent mayor had done "a fairly good job."[86]

At the same time, three simple and very positive thirty-second television ads began to air, with the landmark Hernando De Soto Bridge in the background and an orchestral string arrangement on the soundtrack. Herenton spoke in general terms of his constructive vision for the city, emphasizing better race relations and affordable housing for all. "What Memphis needs today is leadership, not politics. . . . People working together can do anything. . . . Together, we can move Memphis forward."

The Rotary Club Debate

On Tuesday, October 1, with the election only two days away, the candidates finally met face-to-face at the Peabody Hotel. The televised event was sponsored by the local Rotary Club. Hackett and Herenton, both Rotary Club members, sat next to each other during the luncheon, smiling often as they chatted amicably. Each candidate also had a visible group of supporters sitting at adjacent tables. At Herenton's table were Carpenter, Reverend Adkins, NAACP lawyer Richard Fields, and Dr. Harry Moore, director of the local chapter of the National Conference of Christians and Jews and one of Herenton's few publicly declared white supporters.

In a rather uneventful forty-five-minute exercise, the candidates made speeches and then answered questions. Beyond reiterating his basic campaign themes in his opening remarks, Herenton had an opportunity to address a handful of key controversies in the question-and-answer segment. The first question dealt with OCI's negative external evaluation of the city schools under Herenton's leadership, which Herenton argued was methodologically invalid as he defended his tenure as superinten-dent. Later, he dispelled the notion that he would completely abandon Hackett initiatives like the drive for an NFL franchise, high-profile cul-tural exhibits, and downtown redevelopment.

Overall, Herenton felt that the Rotary Club "debate" really helped his campaign. In his view, it sharpened the contrast between the two can-didates, and he believed he noticed some of Hackett's white business leaders hanging their heads as the forum proceeded. It also helped ener-gize his supporters, lifting their confidence and enthusiasm.[87]

The Final Push

Although the Herenton campaign, like the Hackett campaign, did not conduct its own polls, independent polling had consistently shown Herenton trailing Mayor Hackett by at least 11 percentage points.[88] Yet, as Congressman Harold Ford asserted, "Anytime an incumbent gets less than 50 percent [in the polls], he's in trouble."[89]

Yet, a slighted Ford remained on the sidelines. As a matter of fact, he had even publicly mentioned the possibility of not putting out his "Ford ballot" this time. Herenton's campaign manager, Charles Carpen-ter, responded, "We don't need Ford's ballot and we don't need Ford."[90]

With the rift appearing to grow at a very inopportune time, Frank Banks arranged for Ford to call radio station WDIA while Herenton was being interviewed. In the subsequent public conversation, the two men made it clear that they had every intention of working together. Ford stated, "We're together in this pursuit," while Herenton added that "[w]e're going down the stretch hand in hand," and he personally called the Congressman after the show and requested his assistance.[91]

Finally, as September wound down and election day neared, the Con-gressman became a more visible presence on the campaign trail. For ex-ample, Ford and Herenton appeared together at dawn on September 27, shaking hands with arriving city sanitation workers. They then proceeded to a fund-raising breakfast, shook hands at a picnic in the Orange Mound neighborhood, attended a backyard political forum in south Memphis, and, with some seventy-five supporters, made a high-profile five-mile walk down Elvis Presley Boulevard in Whitehaven.

Ford also took the offensive, attacking Hackett for being two-faced in his currying of the black vote. As an example, he cited what he alleged were dual sets of campaign literature. The version circulated in the black community emphasized a number of Hackett's high-profile black appointments, while the white version stressed what Ford claimed was a veiled racist theme that had appeared in a number of his media ads. In a message that obviously could be read at least two different ways, voters were warned that they stood to "lose their voice" if they did not vote.[92] This turned out to be one of the only opportunities Herenton's supporters had to strike a defensive posture against an alleged Hackett attack on Dr. Herenton. They hoped it would be enough to help rally those last wavering voters.

Meanwhile, organizational endorsements began to trickle in. Besides Teamsters' Local No. 1196 and the 4,000-member Memphis Education Association, the campaign picked up the 1,000-member furniture workers' IUEE Local No. 282, the *Tri-State Defender*'s editorial endorsement, and the support of the (black) Memphis Baptist Ministerial Alliance, with its 260 members representing more than 300 churches.[93]

At the same time, open dissent within the black community was strongly frowned upon. For example, as indicated previously, a number of black groups threatened a citywide boycott of all McDonald's restaurants when black franchise owner George Jones publicly endorsed Dick Hackett.[94] Former Councilwoman Minerva Johnican, Reverend James Smith, and State Representative Alvin King, among a small group of others, were also severely chastised for making similar endorsements of the incumbent.[95] In addition, caller attacks on the incumbent mayor became so severe that black radio station WLOK canceled the popular Bill Adkins call-in show.[96]

Public support for Herenton from the Memphis white community was nearly nonexistent, however. Although there were a few whites at the campaign kickoff dinner, there were only five in a crowd of hundreds at the official opening of Herenton's campaign headquarters on a sunny Saturday afternoon. As of September 15, not one prominent white or white institution had gone on record in support of his candidacy.[97] Then, the day before the election, a handful of whites, mostly members of the local Peace and Justice Center, publicly endorsed Dr. Herenton.

On Tuesday morning, October 1, in a visit coordinated by Reverend Samuel Kyles, the Reverend Jesse Jackson stopped briefly in Memphis on his way to another engagement in Arkansas. He joined Herenton at a campaign breakfast in Whitehaven, after which the two men toured the

Fig. 23. W. W. Herenton, Reverend Jesse Jackson, Maxine Smith, and Others, at the Site of Martin Luther King Jr.'s Assassination. Jackson arrived late in the campaign to help rally support. Courtesy of Eddie Walsh.

Dixie Homes public housing project. Jackson then returned the next day and spent most of it on the stump with Herenton.[98]

That evening, election eve, Herenton and Jackson were joined by Martin Luther King III, who had been unable to make a September 7 fund-raiser at the Peabody. These events culminated with a huge final two-hour rally at the Bountiful Blessings Cathedral. The press estimated that there were some four thousand people in attendance, and seventeen thousand dollars was raised. Jesse Jackson reminded the frenzied crowd that "[t]his is a religious pilgrimage, not a political campaign."[99]

Such gatherings underscored the role the black churches played in Herenton's campaign. Besides providing money, forums, and registration help, a number of black churches also provided their buses for the "get out the vote" effort on election day.[100] Given the historic prominence of the church in the African-American community, Herenton was convinced that the campaign required the help of the black clergy. This was a "holistic" campaign approach, according to Herenton, and the black churches were an important part of the whole picture. Some ministers did not support him; but, as Herenton saw it, most recognized that he had the support of their congregations. In the end, Herenton viewed the churches as influential and very helpful overall, although some of his aides believed that many of the churches were not as helpful as they might have been.[101]

The efforts of ministers and many others would be necessary in order to turn out a sufficiently large African-American vote. At the first of his town meetings on September 11, Herenton warned a gathering of approximately two hundred supporters at the Princeton Avenue Baptist Church that they simply could not afford to stay home from the polls this time. The same message was driven home again and again on election day itself.

Herenton received the official endorsement of Congressman Ford, as he appeared as the mayoral candidate of choice on the well-known "Ford ballot." In addition, Herenton's name topped the normal array of election day "ballots" in the black community (e.g., the "Black Unity Ballot" of the Black Unity Coalition and the "John Ford" ballot).[102] The Ford endorsement also translated into a considerable amount of election-day assistance on the part of Ford and his experienced vote-canvassing operation. Ford himself took 150 volunteers and worked door-to-door in District 7 until after 7:00 P.M.[103]

Campaign aide Jim Wilkens was running the computer and watching turnout as election day unfolded. That allowed the campaign to target specific areas, where turnout appeared low, especially after 4:30 P.M. Supporters even went out with a band into the Thirty-Ninth ward. But generally, from early on, they had clear indications of a very large turnout.

Herenton and Reverend Adkins had been driving around the city, attempting to round up additional votes, when they noticed two street people holding Herenton signs at the corner of Third and McLemore. Upon approaching them, one stated, "Doc, I'm a crackhead, but I'm going to keep my head straight today so we can win this thing" as he reached into his soiled pocket and pulled out a brand new voter-registration card. Choked with emotion, Herenton turned to Adkins and said, "We're going to win. . . ."[104]

It was more of the same at the polls. Veteran poll coordinator Vera Lewis noted that she had never seen this many people with physical handicaps turning out to vote. "There were many in wheelchairs, some on canes and crutches, and I personally punched the choices for two blind people."[105]

As early as June 20, Eddie Walsh was projecting a 54 percent black turnout, with Herenton arguing that it would need to be even a little higher than that.[106] As things ultimately developed, both Walsh and Herenton were essentially correct.[107] Walsh also noted that, despite its tremendous success, this was one of the only black citywide campaigns in his recollection in which the candidate did not have to pay for church assistance, spots on endorsement ballots, or for most poll workers. The campaign had taken on such a momentum of its own that virtually everyone simply volunteered their services.[108]

In an election that ultimately turned out as close as this one was, every single vote was critical. Consequently, marshaling absentee voters would be even more important than normal. It is a slow and laborious process to locate each prospective absentee voter and then get that person to vote. Each vote gained can take a considerable amount of time.

The rules were clear and limiting. One was eligible to cast an absentee ballot if election day fell on a religious holiday, or if the person would be on jury duty, out of town, was more than sixty-five years of age, or in poor health. If qualifying under one or more of these provisions, the votes had to be cast in person at the downtown election commission sometime during the three weeks preceding election day. Election commission hours were 8:00 A.M. to 4:30 P.M., Monday through Friday, and 8 A.M. to 8 P.M. on September 24, 25, and 26, just prior to the October 3 election. Or a voter could mail in the ballot if required to be out of town on election day itself.

To gain absentee votes, Eddie Walsh preprinted the ballot request forms. Then, he and fifteen others helped applicants with the necessary documentation, targeting students going away to college as well as individuals in the military. Churches were asked to help identify the "sick and shut in" (e.g., those in nursing homes and senior-citizen centers). On one occasion, Herenton was persuaded to visit the disabled at the King's Daughters and Sons Home, which turned out to be a very moving experience for Herenton and generated a number of votes.

• • •

In the end, as the next chapter will portray rather graphically, every single vote did indeed turn out to be critical. Had any one of the above pieces been missing, Dr. Herenton would have been defeated. It took a record effort to win, and that is exactly what occurred in the Memphis black community.

Although never mentioned directly, and seldom referred to even indirectly, race had rather quickly become the issue. In the absence of any glaring policy disagreements or any strong personal attacks, the two mayoral campaigns sped along in an obviously parallel manner like two adjacent trains in the night. Herenton campaigned largely in the African-American community, Hackett in the white community. In the end, the only real question was which of these parallel endeavors would succeed in registering and turning out a larger share of its racial constituency.

Herenton admits to having been second-guessed at virtually every strategic turn by a variety of his supporters. And, although they had done no systematic citywide polling at any point in the campaign, he claims he could simply "feel the people." He was getting such positive feedback as he walked the African-American neighborhoods that he was just convinced he was on the right track.[109]

In 1969, Harry Holloway had noted the "inadvisability of [blacks] waging high pressure campaigns. Their campaign had included highly publicized rallies featuring such prominent visitors as Reverend Martin Luther King Jr. and Mahalia Jackson. For the future, Negro leadership concluded, such tactics would not be prudent, for they so aroused whites as to increase their vote beyond any gains in the Negro vote."[110]

The Herenton campaign was about to test the wisdom of those warnings in a different time and in a different setting.

8 The Election

As the sun rose in the Memphis sky on Thursday, October 3, it was the beginning of what was to become a historic day. W. W. Herenton was about to become the city's first African-American mayor, and only the third African American to win a citywide race in the city's history. Significant racial changes also would occur on the city council and the school board. More than one hundred consecutive years of white conservative rule was about to come to an end.

The weather was sunny and warm, ideal for a large voter turnout. And, indeed, voting was heavy in the morning and remained that way throughout the day. According to Reverend John Kerrick of St. Patrick's Church, an inner-city polling place, "You can feel the excitement in the air. There's always hype, but this time there's a sense of something really happening."[1] At Whitehaven High, in the middle of a black residential area, election workers were so busy that they did not have time to eat their sandwiches. Meanwhile, a hundred white citizens were waiting to vote when the polling place opened at St. Louis Church in an affluent east Memphis precinct.[2]

As the polls closed at 7:00 P.M., early returns suggested that the election would be very close and that Herenton had a chance to win. Then, as the final precinct ballots were counted, they showed Herenton with a slight lead. The absentee ballots, however, had yet to be counted, and both the Hackett and Herenton camps realized that these would include the votes of far more white than black voters. The only question was how

Fig. 24. Mayor-Elect W. W. Herenton and Campaign Assistant Eddie Walsh. Courtesy of Eddie Walsh.

many more. It was not until 2:00 A.M. that an anxious city had its answer. When all the nearly 248,000 ballots had been counted, Herenton was declared the winner by 172 votes (142 by final recount).

We will now proceed to dissect Herenton's victory in the mayor's race, as well as remarkable results in at-large races for city council, city court, and the school board. Analysis from earlier chapters will help explain why black candidates were as successful as they turned out to be in the 1991 municipal election. There were similarities and differences in the results for mayor as opposed to the other citywide races. The comparison not only sheds additional light on the mayoral race and the city's racial politics in general, but it also provides a welcome corrective to analyses that focus almost exclusively on mayoral elections.

The Mayoral Results

The final audited voting returns indicated that W. W. Herenton had received 122,596 votes (49.44 percent), while incumbent Richard C. Hackett received 122,454 votes (49.38 percent). A minor white candidate, Robert "Prince Mongo" Hodges, received just under 3,000 votes (1.18 percent). Herenton had prevailed over Hackett by a mere 142 votes—slightly more than one-half vote per precinct.[3]

Not only was the 1991 mayoral election the closest in the city's history, but it was also the most racially polarized. Our estimates indicate that 96 percent of the white voters cast their ballots for Hackett, while 99 percent of the black voters cast theirs for Herenton. Conversely, 1 percent of the blacks cast their votes for Hackett, while 3 percent of the whites opted for Herenton (the other 1 percent voted for Hodges).[4]

The "Mongo" Factor

Prince Mongo Hodges, a cult-like figure who sometimes dressed in a loincloth and purported to hail from the planet of Zambodia, appears to have been particularly popular among younger voters. A number of Hackett supporters expressed anger with him following the election, seeming to believe that Mongo had prevented their candidate from winning. As campaign manager Bill Boyd stated rather sarcastically, "Hurray for Mongo, joking and having fun."[5]

If Mongo had not run and his supporters had voted like other whites and blacks, we estimate that Hackett would have won the election with 50.14 of the vote. Nevertheless, many of Mongo's supporters appear to have been casting an anti–establishment vote and may well have chosen not to participate without him as an option. Most likely, then, Prince Mongo's candidacy did not alter the final mayoral results.

Mongo's candidacy did, however, become intertwined with the federal court decision to eliminate the runoff in mayoral elections. Without a runoff, Herenton won the 1991 election with a plurality of 49.44 percent of the votes cast. With the majority system that existed prior to the court decision, there would have had to have been a second election between Herenton and Hackett. Given the closeness of the first vote, it is unclear who would have won a runoff election.

One scenario would have led to Herenton's victory in such a runoff. According to this scenario, most of Prince Mongo's voters would have stayed home rather than turning out to vote for Dick Hackett. Meanwhile, tasting victory, blacks would have turned out in the same high percentages as they had in the general election. In addition, Herenton would have been a more credible candidate among monied interests and would have found it easier to raise campaign funds this time. He also would have been viewed as more viable among white voters and would have received more votes from white moderates.

A much different scenario might have led to a Hackett victory. The incumbent mayor had approximately $350,000 remaining in his campaign fund, while Herenton had used all the funds that he had raised. Further, Hackett would have gained an estimated sixty voters in a white area precluded from voting the first time due to confusion about whether these residents lived within the city limits. In addition, Hackett might well have turned out more conservative whites, who now perceived a realistic threat that a black man might occupy the mayor's office. We did interview one white couple the day after the election who said, "[I]f we only had known the election was going to be so close, we would have voted." Another white said to us, "I only voted for Herenton because I felt sorry for him that he was going to lose so badly."

At the very least, our two scenarios demonstrate that this was a hotly contested election in which any small change could well have affected the final results. Rather than focusing on such hypothetical minutia, however, we will attempt to explain the actual results by turning to the larger context within which this closely contested election occurred.

City Council Elections

We will first examine the other citywide races since they were a part of the same maelstrom that affected the mayoral election. Our analysis shows that many of the at-large races diverged in significant ways from the mayoral results. It is important to account for those differences in order to understand both the mayoral results and the existing state of interracial electoral politics in Memphis.

For reasons outlined in chapter 5, the Memphis City Council has contained a combination of seven district and six at-large representatives since the electoral reforms of 1966. In the 1991 elections for those at-large council positions, there was a significant amount of racial crossover voting. Unlike the mayoral race, white crossover was important for a number of black candidates, while black crossover was also quite important for a number of whites. Table 3 describes the crossover vote.

Table 3

Racial Crossover Voting for At-Large Candidates, 1991

Office	Candidate	White Crossover	Black Crossover	Percent Vote
Mayor	Herenton	3		49
	Hackett		1	49
Council 3	Whalum	13		48
	Edmunds		7	42
Council 5	Lowery	19		55
	Alissandratos		3	45
Council 4	Sonnenburg		53	74
	Taylor	11		26
Council 2	Leffler		24	49.8
	Barksdale		29	29
Council 1	Vander Schaff		15	49
	Howell	14		39
Board of Education 2	Lewis	40		61
	Blackburn		8	24
Board of Education 1	Todd		4	29
	Rhodes		8	24
City Court 1	Hunt	30		64
	Robinson		1	36
City Court 2	Kyle		38	49.5
	Rooks	5		26

The city's black majority was reflected in the district results, with African Americans winning four of those seven district seats. The major change in the city council, however, would be in the six at-large positions. Only one black had ever been victorious in one of these citywide elections, and all six of those seats were held by whites at the time of the 1991 election. With blacks winning two of the at-large positions in 1991, the city council's racial balance changed from ten whites and three blacks to a much narrower seven-to-six white majority.

The black victors were Kenneth Whalum, who gave up a safe district seat to run for an at-large post, and Myron Lowery, formerly a television reporter and a candidate for at-large posts in 1983 and in 1987. The white victors were all incumbents: Pat Vander Schaaf, Florence Leffler, Barbara Sonnenburg, and Tom Marshall. Leffler and Marshall had strong white opponents, Sonnenburg had only token opposition, and Vander Schaaf had two black opponents.

In position 3, black candidate Kenneth Whalum won 48 percent of the vote compared to 42 percent for his white opponent, incumbent Oscar Edmonds. A third black candidate, Charlotte Harper, received the remaining votes.

Edmonds had been in politics for thirty years, including service in both the state and county legislatures. He had held a position on the city council since 1975 and had become the leader of the Hackett voting bloc in that body. In his private life he was the owner of a construction supply company and a referee in the National Football League. He was also an unabashed Democrat.

The winning candidate, Kenneth Whalum, was a city council member and a minister at Olivet Baptist Church. He had decided to run for the at-large post instead of defending the safe district seat he had held for one term. Arguing that more blacks were needed on the city council in order for blacks to obtain their fair share of city resources, he believed that he "was one of the few blacks with the name recognition and willingness" to run for the citywide post.[6] A very contentious council member, he was outspoken in his opposition to Hackett and exuded a deep dislike for Edmonds, calling him "the single worst councilman" and a "flunky for Hackett."[7] Moreover, the two members had argued vehemently at many council meetings.[8]

A Whalum victory had not been expected, particularly given his lack of popularity in the white community. He was openly anti-Hackett and pro-black on many public policy issues, made little attempt to campaign among whites, and did not have any identifiable white campaign supporters. In addition, he had a black female opponent who had the potential of gaining votes among whites and blacks, especially from those in the education profession, since she was a public school teacher. Nonetheless, Whalum was elected with the help of a 13 percent white crossover vote. He appears to have benefited from, among other things, his name recognition as well as from questions raised about his opponent's voting record on behalf of developers.

In position 5, Myron Lowery was another black victor in an at-large council race, defeating A. D. "Andy" Alissandratos by a 55 percent to 45 percent margin. Lowery had formerly been a weekend news anchor for a local television station, and he left after charging racial discrimination when he was not made a weekday anchor. He had served on Congressman Harold Ford's staff and worked for Federal Express as a communications specialist. He had run unsuccessfully for at-large positions on two previous occasions. In 1983, he was overwhelmed by white Republican Bill Gibbons, while in 1987 he lost a closely contested race to Florence Leffler. Lowery was interested in "people" issues, strongly supporting increased funding for education and changes in city housing policies.

His opponent was longtime incumbent Andy Alissandratos. First elected to the council in 1971, Alissandratos was seen as its fiscal expert and was a staunch opponent of tax increases for any purpose, including education. He was a strong Hackett supporter and had supported costly endeavors such as the various downtown redevelopment projects. Lowery accused him of ignoring neighborhood and people needs in order to fund large ventures like the Pyramid.[9]

Lowery's victory is easier to explain than Whalum's. He had name recognition because of his work as a TV personality and his previous political races. Moreover, he had credibility as a knowledgeable observer of public policy from his years as a TV anchor. He was also familiar with running a citywide campaign. He was articulate and found it easy to communicate in mixed-race audiences. Beyond that, his views and rhetoric were racially neutral and thus appeared to register more positively with white voters. He received a 19 percent white crossover vote. Lowery's victory was partially attributable to Alissandratos's longevity on the city council. Alissandratos no longer appeared to be the dynamic guardian of the city treasury, but rather an aged conservative reflexively defending the status quo.

In position 4, white candidate Barbara Sonnenburg's comfortable victory (74 percent to 26 percent) over her black opponent, Danny Taylor, is also understandable. Taylor was a little-known car salesman with no political experience. Sonnenburg, on the other hand, had served two terms on the school board and three on the city council. She was part of a council voting bloc that had regularly opposed Mayor Hackett, and she was visibly involved in neighborhood issues. It was not unusual to see her lobbying for neighborhood interests at the meetings of the Board of

Adjustment, at hearings on roadways, or at most committee meetings of the city council. She received a 53 percent crossover from black voters.

In position 2, Florence Leffler's 49.8 percent to 29 percent victory over Gene Barksdale also was quite predictable. A one-term incumbent on the city council, Leffler had been a popular principal at Central High School and was a supporter of the arts. Although a fiscal conservative, she had joined in a number of voting alliances with blacks on the city council. Nevertheless, she was best known for her vehement opposition to additional school funding, arguing that the system was overly bureaucratic and additional funds would not find their way into the classroom. She had a black challenger, political novice Jimmie Berry, and a well-known white opponent, Gene Barksdale.

Barksdale was a former sheriff best known for having chained several prisoners to the gates of the federal prison to protest a court order preventing the transfer of sentenced local prisoners into the state correctional system. Further, Barksdale had garnered a substantial number of black crossover votes in his races for the sheriff's office, although he lost races for that position in 1986 and in 1990. In the end, he and Leffler managed a combined 53 percent crossover from black voters.

In position 1, Pat Vander Schaaf's 49 percent to 39 percent victory over a black opponent, Rai Howell, was more of a surprise. Vander Schaaf had been on the city council since 1975, chairing that body in 1979. Since then, she had run a weak fourth for city mayor in 1982. She suffered from a series of ailments, including a stroke in 1982 as well as back and neck injuries from a fall in 1988. Because of her health problems, she had missed 35 of 178 city council meetings, the worst record on the council. In addition, there were two pending lawsuits that challenged whether she was even a city resident. She was a fiscal conservative, suburban oriented, a strong supporter of Hackett, and a proponent of the big-ticket items such as the Pyramid. Her opponent argued that "she has not been a friend to education and she has failed to help the inner city."[10]

Vander Schaaf claimed that 1991 would be her last campaign and responded to attacks by saying, "I'm sick and tired of people snapping at my heels. I haven't been sitting around gathering dust for 16 years. I still have services to perform."[11] She was a seasoned politician with a number of citywide races under her belt. In addition, she had developed a broad base of support since she had worked on issues such as state child abuse and rape laws, was responsible for a city ordinance requiring the ticketing of those parking in handicapped spaces, and had also worked on an ordinance requiring smoke detectors in apartment buildings. Her opponent was Rai Howell, a newcomer to politics. She was a public-relations executive and an articulate candidate who was not well known by the population at large. Another black candidate, Kenneth Karney, took votes away from Howell.

Vander Schaaf won because there were two black candidates and because of the federal court decision that had outlawed runoff elections. She managed only 49 percent of the vote, compared to 51 percent for her two black opponents. Nonetheless, there was racial crossover voting in both directions. For instance, 14 percent of the whites crossed over for Howell, while 15 percent of the blacks crossed over for Vander Schaaf.

One of the more interesting races was for council position 6, with white incumbent Tom Marshall defeating white challenger Buckner "Buck" Welford by a 40 percent to 34 percent margin. Marshall, an architect by training and occupation, was city council chairperson at the time of the election. He was articulate, photogenic, and a political moderate on the city council. The major blot on his record was his opposition to a landmarks commission decision involving a building in which his firm had a vested interest.

Besides two relatively unknown black challengers—seamstress Cheryl Gatson and businessman Clifford Lewis—his major opponent was Buck Welford, a lawyer who ran a well-organized and well-financed campaign, although he did not have prior electoral experience. He was a Republican and the son of a prominent Memphian, United States Sixth Circuit Judge Harry Welford. He had maneuvered his candidacy to find a race in which he would not have a strong black opponent. He originally filed to oppose Vander Schaaf, who ended up with a strong black opponent in Rai Howell. Just before the deadline, Welford filed instead to oppose Marshall, who did not have well-recognized black opposition. Nonetheless, 46 percent of the black voters crossed over for Marshall, allowing him to win without a majority of the white vote.

School Board Elections

The Memphis city schools were governed by a single school board comprised of nine members. Although the precise size of the board had varied some over the years, all members had long been elected at-large, even after the electoral reforms of 1966. Following the racial unrest of 1968, however, the state legislature had intervened and altered that arrangement. Since 1970, there had been seven district seats and two members selected at-large.[12]

In 1991, blacks and whites split the two at-large elections for the school board. Sara Lewis was the black winner, while Bill Todd was the winning white candidate.

In position 2, Lewis defeated white incumbent James Blackburn, winning by a 61 percent to 39 percent margin. Lewis was a former administrator on the staff of the school board and was executive director of "Free the Children," a Shelby County antipoverty program that seemed to enjoy a positive image among whites. In the end, she garnered a white crossover vote of 40 percent.

White candidate Bill Todd prevailed in his school board race for position 1, but in a much more complex election. The sixty-year-old Todd was retired from the school system, where he had gained name recognition as the director of athletics. There were four black candidates, the best known being Dolores Elder Jones, who had been an administrator at the Memphis Housing Authority and an unsuccessful candidate for city council in 1987. Ultimately, Todd prevailed over white candidate Gail Rhodes by a 29 percent to 24 percent margin.

Rhodes was from the Midtown area, had been active in both her school and the city PTA and was viewed as progressive on educational reforms. She was known in Midtown and among PTA parents, but otherwise she had limited name recognition. Combined, she and Todd still managed 12 percent of the black vote.

City Court Elections

There were also two contested at-large races for positions on the city court. Blacks and whites split these two elections as well. Earnestine Hunt was the black winner, while Sara Kyle was the white electee.

In position 1, black incumbent Earnestine Hunt defeated white challenger Jim Robinson by a 64 percent to 36 percent margin. Robinson, a private attorney and formerly an assistant district attorney, had run for the position in the 1990 special election and had been easily defeated by the incumbent that year as well.

Hunt had previously worked in the public defender's office and in legal services and had been defeated for a county circuit court position in August of 1990. Three months later, she won a special election, defeating a relatively well-known white opponent, Sara Kyle. That 1990 victory made her only the second African American to win an at-large Memphis election. Her white crossover in 1990 was 5 percent in the general election and 14 percent in the runoff. It was 30 percent in 1991, the second-largest among the various black candidates that year.

Sara Kyle, after losing to Earnestine Hunt in November of 1990, was victorious in her 1991 city court race for position 2. She won by a 49 percent to 26 percent margin over a little-known black candidate who had never run for public office. There were also two other minor white candidates.

Kyle enjoyed considerable name recognition. She was the wife of a state senator, cousin of a U.S. Representative, and niece of a former governor of Tennessee. Further, she had gained name recognition from her 1990 city court race against Hunt. Whites cast most of their votes for Kyle, while 38 percent of blacks also crossed over to vote for her.

Analysis of the Citywide Elections

Historic changes took place in Memphis as a result of the 1991 election. An African American was elected mayor in a sharply contested race that ended more than a century of white conservative control of that office. In addition, blacks were elected to at-large positions on the city council, school board, and the city court.

We will now analyze this combination of races in an attempt to explain the results of this historic election. As the city's demographics evolved, there had become an increasing number of viable black candidacies, encouraging more blacks to seek elective office. Institutional changes both contributed to that demographic evolution and helped facilitate the translation of those numbers into electoral success. These trends, then, spurred by an effective Herenton campaign, culminated in record levels of black electoral participation in 1991. And this time, except at the mayoral level, the city's penchant for racially polarized voting moderated some and did not spell defeat for African-American candidates. Even the advantages of incumbency failed to stop the tide of racial change. Some would second-guess Mayor Hackett's campaign strategies; but, in the end, the undercurrents of change simply were not on his side.

Viability of Black Candidates

Our first proposition is that historical trends in Memphis politics pre-saged considerable black electoral success in 1991.

Electoral politics in the state of Mississippi suggest that victories in previous elections prompted additional black candidates to seek elective office. In large part, this trend occurred because, following successful campaigns, black voters believed that they had a realistic chance to elect fellow blacks to office and would turn out to support them. Their votes would finally count in a way they perceived as meaningful.[13]

In Memphis, we explored the possibility of such electoral momentum by considering the increasing number of viable African-American candidacies as the electoral environment changed to make victory more likely. In particular, we examined the number of viable black candidacies for at-large city council, city court, or school board positions. Viability is defined as a first- or second-place finish with at least 30 percent of the general election vote. Runoff elections were excluded to maintain comparability.

Table 4 shows that the number of black candidates finishing first or second went from two in 1975 to seven in both 1987 and 1991. The number of "viable" black candidates increased incrementally from zero in

Table 4

Viability of Black Candidates, 1971–1991

Year	Viable	Number	Average Viability	Average Vote
1991	5	7	71%	45%
1990 county	7	9	78%	35%
1987	2	7	29%	26%
1983	1	4	25%	28%
1979	0	1	0%	17%
1975	0	2	0%	19%
1971	0	0	0%	0%

1979, to one in 1983, two in 1987, and five in 1991. Thus, although 1987 and 1991 had the same number of black candidates, more of these candidates were viable in 1991.

We also compared the average vote of the black candidates over time. From a low of less than 20 percent in 1975 and 1979, the figures increased rather steadily to nearly half of the vote in 1991.

These data suggest that blacks made steady progress in running candidates who would then have a public reputation on which to run again. Beyond that, the increasing viability of the black candidates over time would seem to have given blacks more confidence that they could win elections. Thus, the number of viable black candidacies in 1991 can be traced to earlier efforts by black candidates at the mayoral and sub-mayoral levels.

As for winning elections, prior to 1990, Minerva Johnican was the only African American to have won a citywide Memphis election, winning an at-large city council post in 1983. Her victory, however, was due to a unique set of circumstances that created a temporary coalition between blacks and Republicans.

Earnestine Hunt's city court election in 1990, on the other hand, was a much better precursor of 1991. Without the special circumstances that surrounded the Johnican victory, Hunt captured most black votes, some white crossover votes, and other black candidates did not dilute her vote by appearing on the same ballot.

Still another precursor was the 1988 county assessor's race in which black candidate Michael Hooks won with a sizable number of white crossover votes. In addition, there were impressive black gains in the county races of 1990. For example, limiting analysis to city precincts only, there was a total of seven viable black candidates that year.[14] In addition, five of them won their countywide races, although none of them received a majority—even when looking only at city precincts. Each had at least two white opponents and was elected by a plurality, as there was no runoff provision in the county. White crossover voting was significant for two of the winners, however, helping elect Joe Brown as a criminal court judge and D'Army Bailey as a circuit court judge.

The 1990 county races were polarized in both the white and black communities, with 85 percent of the whites voting for white candidates and 89 percent of the blacks voting for black candidates. However, there was a substantial difference in bloc voting. Where 76 percent of blacks voted for the winning black candidate, only 52 percent of whites voted for the winning white candidate. Thus, both groups were polarized, but blacks made their votes count more by engaging in more bloc voting.

At the very least, 1990 demonstrated that an African American could win a citywide election. The key was there needed to be only one strong black candidate in a particular race. It also helped if there were at least two white opponents.

Electoral Context

Our second proposition is that institutional changes contributed to the evolution of a black majority and helped facilitate the translation of those numbers into electoral success.

One of the institutional changes was a successful stalling of the city's annexation policy. The annexation of Cordova, as described at length in chapter 5, made Herenton's margin of victory closer than it would have been without that annexation. If Memphis had not absorbed Cordova just prior to the 1991 election, Herenton would have won by 3,246 votes rather than by 142. Other citywide races were not effected.

Meanwhile, the residents of Hickory Hills, a white enclave in southeast Memphis, successfully stalled their proposed annexation in the courts. Using racial voting patterns from the rest of the city, it is possible to estimate the mayoral voting split had these voters been eligible to vote in the 1991 city election. Our estimates indicate that if Hickory Hills had been part of the city, Hackett would have received 10,868 more votes than Herenton. Thus, Hackett would have won the city's mayoral election by a 10,726-vote margin, although other citywide election winners likely would have remained the same.

The second institutional change that contributed to black electoral success was the repeal of Memphis's runoff provision. The federal judge hearing the Memphis voting-rights lawsuit issued an order in August of 1991. That order abolished the runoff for any election in which the entire city would be deciding the winner. Thus, candidates for city mayor, at-large city council seats, city court, and at-large school board positions no longer required a majority in order to win. This decision profoundly affected the 1991 elections.

The most dramatic impact of this ruling was upon the mayoral race. Once again, Herenton had received 49.44 percent of the votes, Hackett

49.38 percent, and Prince Mongo Hodges the remaining 1.18 percent. With a majority requirement, Hackett and Herenton would have met in a runoff, and Hackett could very well have retained his seat.

In addition, there were ten remaining citywide contests with at least two opponents. Four of the offices, yielding one white and three black winners, would not have required a runoff. Of the six races that would have required a second election, five of those 1991 victors were white and one was black. Three of the six contests would have had two white opponents in the runoff, while three would have been interracial.

The three interracial runoffs would have been for council position 1, where white candidate Vander Schaaf had won by plurality, council position 3, where black candidate Whalum had been comparably victorious, and city court position 2, where white candidate Kyle was victorious. Such runoffs probably would have precipitated more racially polarized voting patterns in both the white and black communities. Depending upon the turnout of blacks and whites, all three of the whites or all three of the blacks could have been elected. Ironically, there is at least the possibility that if Herenton had been elected in a runoff, then an additional black council member would have been elected, giving Herenton a black majority on the city council.

There is one other possibility. White crossover voting for black candidates might have been due to a feeling among these white voters that, without a runoff, they needed to vote for the black candidates who would be most apt to cooperate with the white community. With a runoff election, some white Memphians might have changed their voting patterns and voted for less viable whites in the general election.

A Black Crusade

Our third proposition is that the above trends, galvanized by an effective Herenton campaign, culminated in record levels of black electoral participation.

The stage had been set for a racial revolution in Memphis electoral politics. The viability of black candidacies was becoming increasingly apparent. Changes in annexation law had helped secure racial parity in the pool of eligible voters. Further, the elimination of the runoff meant that the door was clearly open, at least if the black community could unify around single black candidates and participate in record numbers.

W. W. Herenton emerged as the black "unity candidate" for mayor, and his candidacy succeeded in generating a quasi-religious fervor in the African-American community. Jesse Jackson noted: "This was a religious pilgrimage, not a political campaign." King's death was seen as the crucifixion and Herenton's election was the resurrection. "We were running a crusade. Crusades tend to beat campaigns."[15]

The participation level of black voters did indeed increase markedly in 1991. We will look at four measures of that participation: registration, turnout, fall-off, and absentee balloting.

Chapter 5 provided a discussion of registration and turnout. The data showed that black registration was at historically high levels in 1991, as it had been in 1983. It was approximately equal to the traditionally high registration rates in the white community. Black registration reached 87 percent of the eligible voters and was notably higher than in other comparable cities. Black turnout also reached a historically high level of just under 56 percent of the voting-age population. Thus, it too was higher than normal black turnout in other comparable cities and approximately the same as turnout in the Memphis white community. What made this turnout rate even more remarkable is the breadth and depth of black poverty discussed in chapter 3 above. The mobilization of such a relatively large proportion of the city's severely indigent population is particularly noteworthy.

Another important issue in considering black electoral participation is voting fall-off. Voting fall-off refers to the phenomenon whereby voters cast their votes in the highest profile races at the top of the ticket, but are increasingly likely not to vote in lower salience races further down the ballot. In a typical municipal election, the mayoral race not only engenders the greatest amount of interest from the media, but also attracts the largest number of votes.

In Memphis, focusing on the past three mayoral election years, the mayoral race did indeed lead the ballots in total votes for each of these elections. In 1983, average fall-off was 30 percent, dropping to 21 percent in 1987 and 17 percent in 1991.[16] A possible explanation for the decreasing fall-off is that Memphis elections are becoming more intense as more viable black candidates appear on the ballot, and both whites and blacks realize that black candidates have a chance of winning at-large elections, and, therefore, they realize how important voting for all offices is.

Because of the record levels of black turnout and the nature of the Herenton campaign crusade, we also calculated fall-off in the African-American community alone. Black fall-off was slightly higher in 1991. In 1983, it was 57 percent of the city's total fall-off, declining to 50 percent in 1987, and then increasing to 59 percent in 1991. It is quite possible that in 1991 there were a number of blacks who did not normally vote in elections and came to the polls for the sole purpose of voting for Dr. Herenton. As a result, the Herenton candidacy had slightly less impact in terms of its "coattail effects."[17]

We next examined the levels of black fall-off in the 1991 citywide elections in which black candidates were successful. The least black fall-off occurred in court position 1 (Hunt), council position 3 (Whalum), and school board position 2 (Lewis). Myron Lowery, in winning council position 5, experienced a much different pattern. His election was marked by a peculiarly high level of black fall-off. Those figures, consistent with racial reflexivity, suggest that the more accommodationist Lowery was left depending considerably more on white support than that of the other black winners.

Absentee ballots constitute a third issue in considering black electoral participation in the 1991 election. The highest drama of election night related to absentee ballots. In a typical Memphis election, the election commission counts absentee ballots prior to the precinct returns. O. C. Pleasant, chairperson of the Memphis Election Commission, said that the large number of 1991 absentee ballots had prevented an early count.[18] Ultimately, because of the lateness in counting these ballots, it was not until nearly 2:00 A.M. that the final election results were announced. The commission blamed the delay on a computer glitch that required the ballots to be entered a second time. The *Commercial Appeal* reported that the computer could not read the floppy disk upon which they were entered originally.[19]

Meanwhile, tensions mounted. All other ballots had been counted by 9:30 P.M., and the delay in counting the absentee votes was of concern to Herenton's supporters since these would be disproportionately white votes. Harold Ford then led a delegation of his supporters to the election commission where he engaged in a televised shouting episode, accusing black Election Commissioner O. C. Pleasant of being part of a plot to steal the election.[20] In a private meeting after the confrontation, Ford indicated he wanted to be present for the counting. Pleasant agreed, and Ford designated Frank Banks and Osbie Howard to oversee the counting. In addition, Circuit Court Judge James Swearengen and Chancellor Floyd Pete were at the election commission, and a legal brief had been prepared if the Herenton campaign decided it needed to secure the ballots.[21]

Although Herenton continues to believe that there was a "serious attempt to distort the results,"[22] in retrospect, it seems unlikely that a conspiracy was in the making. Commissioner Pleasant had previously been a Ford supporter; moreover, Hazel Strictland, a black election commission worker, supervised the counting in which four of the clerks recording information were black. In addition, the prospect of considerable governmental and media oversight after the fact would seem to have been a serious deterrent to any potential vote tampering.

Table 5 displays the data for absentee balloting.[23] It shows that the absentee ballots were more important in the 1991 elections than they had been in the previous two. In 1991, absentee ballots were 3.5 percent of the total ballots cast, while in 1983 and 1987 they averaged only 2 percent. The actual number was 8,224 in 1991, compared to 4,866 in 1983.

Table 5 also shows that blacks improved their percentage of these ballots. In 1983, their percentage was 24 percent of the total absentee ballots cast, 15 percent in 1987, and 32 percent in 1991. In addition, 1991 was even more impressive since blacks increased their actual number of absentee ballots. The Herenton campaign clearly improved its chances of winning through its successful facilitation of absentee balloting in the black community. Without that effort, Herenton would have lost the 1991 election, although other black winners would not have been affected.

Table 5

Absentee Ballots, 1983–1991

Year	Total Absentee Ballots	Absentee as Percent of Total Mayoral Vote	Absentee for Black Mayoral Candidates
1991	8,224	3.3%	32%
1987	3,249	1.9%	15%
1983	4,866	2.1%	24%

Racial Voting

Our fourth proposition is that, in light of the above developments, the city's penchant for racially polarized voting moderated somewhat for this election and did not work to the disadvantage of African-American candidates.

Polarization is a contextual factor that refers to the percentage of votes cast by all the voters of a racial group for the candidates of that race (e.g., black voters voting for black candidates). Chapter 5 demonstrated that polarization in mayoral elections had been equally high in the black and white communities from 1975 through 1991, and it often exceeded 90 percent. Yet, in 1991, polarization did not by itself produce victory for black candidates.

The 1991 mayoral election had polarization rates that approached 99 percent. It is worth noting, however, that polarization has not been as high for the other at-large offices. We computed polarization averages for all nonmayoral citywide races in 1983, 1987, and 1991 and found scores of 61 percent, 62 percent, and 65 percent, with white polarization exceeding black by an average of between 2 and 12 percent. Although polarization did vary considerably by individual office, no office showed the same high level of polarization as was found in the mayoral races.

Polarization is of less value to the success of a candidate of a racial group, however, if that group splits its vote among several of its own candidates for a particular position. Thus, we also examined racial bloc voting to see how blacks and whites held together in voting for a particular candidate.

Bloc voting is a contextual factor that refers to the percentage of citizens of one racial group who vote for the leading candidate of that racial group. Chapter 5 showed that racial bloc voting in mayoral elections varied somewhat from 1975 to 1991, although it often exceeded 90 percent. In 1991, bloc voting in the black community appeared to be essential to the election of W. W. Herenton.

Racial bloc voting has also been important in electing black and white candidates below the mayoral level; although, in general, it has not been nearly as pervasive in those elections. Looking at the averages for the 1983, 1987, and 1991 at-large races, the white means for bloc voting were 71, 74, and 68 percent respectively, while the black means were 73, 54, and 66 percent. Thus, there has been less bloc voting in the nonmayoral races, and it has not been as prevalent in the black community as in the white community.

The next measure of racial polarization to consider is the crossover voting pattern. In the 1991 at-large elections, some white incumbents proved to be at least relatively acceptable to the black community. Leffler in council position 2, Sonnenburg in council position 4, and Marshall in council position 6 garnered significant numbers of black votes. They had respective black crossovers of 24, 53, and 46 percent. Meanwhile, in court position 2, white candidate Kyle easily defeated black candidate Rooks, attracting a crossover vote of 38 percent.

Of the incumbent white victors, only Vander Schaaf in council position 1 did not win with a sizable number of black crossover votes. The splitting of the black vote by two candidates explained her victory. However, even as a Republican who had historically sided with other whites and Hackett on the city council, she still managed a black crossover of 15 percent.

Some black candidates also combined strong support in their own community with crossover votes to record solid victories in 1991. For example, Hunt and Lewis were the most successful black beneficiaries of white crossover voting. Hunt in city court position 1 had a high white crossover of 30 percent; while Lewis in school board position 2 had a white crossover of 40 percent. Even more essential to their elections, however, Lowery in council position 5 received a 19 percent white crossover vote, while Whalum in council position 3 received 13 percent.

The race-conscious strategies and race-based results found in the mayoral election were not nearly as apparent in other citywide contests featuring black and white candidates. In point of fact, those campaigns and results were noticeably more racially neutral, with record levels of racial crossover voting.

Such results give rise to the question of whether racial reflexivity had softened sufficiently to the point that Herenton could have won with a more deracialized strategy—at least as deracialized as Dick Hackett's. A deracialized strategy would obviously have been preferable as far as Herenton was concerned. Nonetheless, the Herenton camp concluded that recent events and Hackett's popularity minimized his chances of attracting much of a white crossover vote at the mayoral level.

The other side of that coin is that without Herenton's "unity crusade," there might not have been the record levels of black registration and turnout. The large turnout would not appear to have affected the easy elections of Sarah Lewis (school board) and Earnestine Hunt (city court).

However, a significantly lower black turnout might well have hurt both at-large council winners Kenneth Whalum and Myron Lowery, as well as W. W. Herenton himself—even had he somehow succeeded in attracting the degree of white crossover that Whalum and Lowery enjoyed.

White Liberals

> I wish some of my white friends would have publicly supported me, but
> that has not happened.

—Dr. Herenton, October 2, 1991

Related to the issue of race, our fifth proposition is that white liberals did not appear to have a significant impact on the 1991 Memphis elections.

As explained in chapter 1, there have only been a very limited number of white liberals exerting influence in Memphis politics. Although there has been some crossover voting, there has been no indication of a permanent white liberal voting bloc that would consistently support black mayoral candidates.

We do not have polling data to directly test the hypothesis that white liberals were more apt to vote for Herenton or any of the other black candidates. The lack of white crossover voting in the mayor's race suggests that there were probably not any identifiable white groups that voted for Herenton in large numbers. However, there was an identifiable white crossover in other at-large races that might be attributable to white liberals.

The Midtown area of Memphis has a reputation for being more liberal than the city as a whole. It includes professors from Rhodes College and the University of Memphis; government employees who work downtown; young people who inhabit the hundreds of apartments along the Poplar Corridor; gays who live throughout the area; aesthetes who love to work on beautiful old homes; environmentalists who support the recycling efforts of the city; and whites who feel comfortable living next to blacks and having their children attend integrated schools such as Peabody Elementary, Idlewild Elementary, Snowden Junior High, and Central High School. If there is a concentration of liberals in Memphis, it seems reasonably safe to assume that a disproportionate number of them would be found here.

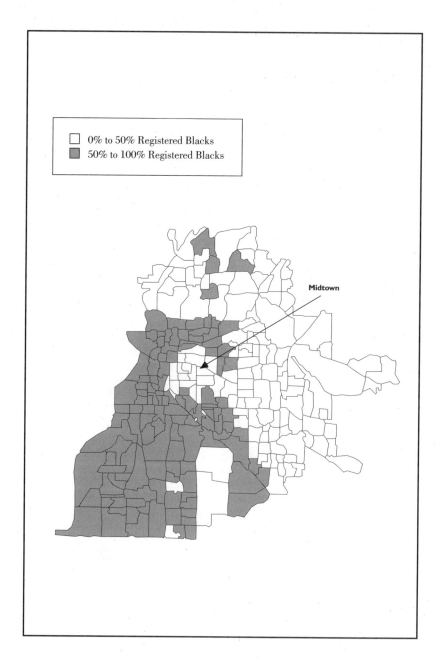

Fig. 25. The Midtown Precincts and Surrounding Voting Precincts in 1991.

It is difficult to precisely define Midtown, however, since its boundaries are reputational rather than legal. Thus, we used a two-part process to determine the precincts included in this area. We asked the Center for Neighborhoods, which works with neighborhood groups, for their definition of "Midtown." They chose the street boundaries of Jackson, Bellevue, Park, and Goodlett. Then, as Midtown is an area known to be racially integrated but with a white majority, we excluded precincts with black majorities from the rectangular definition provided by the Center for Neighborhoods.

Figure 25 shows Midtown as a white rectangle in the heart of Memphis. It is closer to downtown (just to its west) than to the more affluent east Memphis—located to the right of the map. Figure 25 also provides a racial context for understanding the election results. The Midtown area is an island of white voters surrounded largely by black voters. The darkened areas reflect precincts that had registration rates of at least 50 percent black. These figures reflect a highly segregated city. African Americans predominate in the areas surrounding the downtown. To the north and northwest, blacks are a majority in an area called north Memphis; to the south, they are a majority in south Memphis; and to the far south, they are a majority in an area ironically called Whitehaven. Besides Midtown, whites predominate in the more affluent areas to the east—referred to as east Memphis, to the north in a working class area called Frayser, and to the northeast in the more middle-class Raleigh area.

Figure 26 displays the Midtown precincts. These precincts reflect a diverse area that ranges from the large homes of Central Gardens to the more modest though architecturally unique houses of the Vollintine-Evergreen area. The Madison and Poplar Corridors contain many apartment buildings for young residents, while most other areas include many single-family homes and high levels of home ownership. Midtown includes Central Gardens, Hein Park, the Evergreen Historic District, Vollintine-Evergreen, Cooper-Young, and Annesdale Park.

We tested the hypothesis concerning white liberal crossover in the mayoral race. The crossover for Herenton in Midtown was 2 percent greater than for the city as a whole. Such a small difference led us to reject the hypothesis that there was any significant liberal Midtown crossover voting. Next, we thought that perhaps some sections of Midtown might be more apt to crossover for Herenton. Figure 26 also shows the areas in which the crossover was 5 percent or greater. We found four

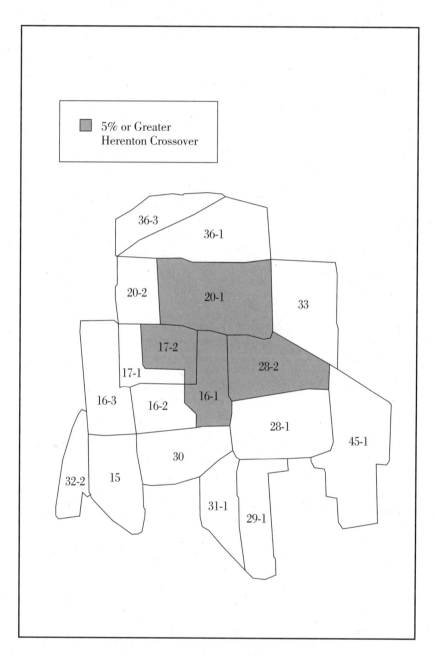

Fig. 26. The Midtown Precincts in 1991.

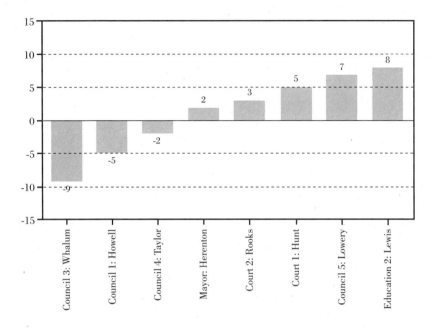

Fig. 27. White Crossover for At-Large and District Elections in Midtown, 1991.

areas with crossover that met this criterion. These areas roughly corresponded to the Evergreen Historic district, with upscale residents, and the Overton Square area, with a young residential base of unmarried people.

However, the numbers pale in comparison to crossover in other cities when we recognize that the highest mayoral crossover in any Memphis precinct was 7 percent. In Atlanta, for example, the white crossover for the city's first black mayor was 25 percent.[24] If Midtown is synonymous with white liberalism, the data suggest the lack of a clear white liberal vote for Herenton.

We next looked to see if there was more Midtown crossover in the other citywide races. The mean rate of crossover for both Midtown and the city as a whole was an identical 17 percent. Though there was substantial white crossover for a number of black candidates, Midtown did not show any unique inclination to cross the city's color barrier.

However, Figure 27 shows that white crossover did vary in Midtown, depending on the specific candidates. Viewed in conjunction with Table 3, we find Rooks (court position 2) and Taylor (council position 4) doing far better than they did citywide, while Hunt (court position 1), Lowery (council position 5), Lewis (school board position 2), Howell (council position 1), and Whalum (council position 3) did worse. It appears that the variation in Midtown crossover depended primarily on local factors. Whalum's opposition to the landmarks commission, which protects many of the older homes in this area, may have been one example.

It is also possible that the votes for black candidates might have emanated from whites other than those who are considered liberals. These voters may have been conservatives who believed their business interests would suffer unless they shared power with the black community. Further, the vote could have reflected parents who believed that incumbents on the school board were incapable of thoughtful policy decisions, and that the black judge on the city court had performed admirably during her short incumbency. The particular motivations of these voters may be too complex to call them white liberals.

Incumbency

Proposition number six is that the well-established advantages of incumbency failed to stop the 1991 tide of racial change in Memphis.

A truism of modern American politics is that incumbents enjoy a vast electoral advantage and are reelected in very high numbers. This appears to be true for the United States Congress, state governors, state legislatures, and even in local government.[25] Incumbents have the advantage of name recognition, the ability to raise funds as repayment for political favors, and the advantage of timing political events. They can, for example, announce public programs or appear at seemingly nonpolitical events as a way of keeping their names before the public. Incumbents also seem to engender public trust. In many cases the institution may be unpopular, but the representative from the institution may be able to gain the continuing support of the voters.[26] As a local example, historically the Memphis City Council has been unpopular, although incumbents on the council have usually been reelected.

We tested the incumbency explanation by examining the results of the 1991 election. In those races that had an incumbent on the ballot, 56 percent of those incumbents were reelected, while 44 percent were defeated. Although incumbents won slightly more than half of their races, they were not as successful as in previous city elections or as found in other large United States cities.[27] As a contrast, in 1987 all of the incumbents won reelection. In two elections prior to that, 70 percent (1983) and 86 percent (1979) of the incumbents were successful.

Consequently, the traditional incumbency advantages did not seem to have a decisive impact on the 1991 elections. The winners (Vander Schaaf, Leffler, Sonnenburg, Marshall, Hunt, and Sorak) had similar incumbency advantages as the losers (Hackett, Alissandratos, and Edmonds).

Focusing on Hackett, he had all the advantages noted above and enjoyed a relatively positive reputation after more than two terms in office. Alissandratos was a strong supporter of the Hackett program and enjoyed the reputation of being the preeminent financial expert on the city council. Edmonds was the leader of the Hackett faction on the city council, producing a policy record with which most citizens seemed to be pleased.

In addition, incumbency did not appear to be a consistently negative factor either, with one possible exception. Blackburn's loss in his attempt to retain his seat on the school board appeared to be the product of a negative retrospective vote. In evaluating his loss, Blackburn stated that "I know from the conversations I've had that there was a lot of unhappiness with the School Board. But there are a lot of tough decisions in the job and they're not pleasant for a lot of people."[28] The *Commercial Appeal* also concluded that his loss was due to unhappiness with the school board, since it was rare for school board incumbents to be defeated. In addition, white incumbents Mal Mauney and J. C. Williams had been defeated at the district level by white challengers Barbara Prescott and Chris Thomas.[29]

Overall, however, incumbency did not play a large role in the 1991 election since incumbents did not enjoy the vast advantage that would be expected. In addition, voters generally did not appear to be casting their vote in a negative, retrospective manner. Instead, it was an election caught in a political maelstrom, and even incumbents were swept out of the way in many cases.

Mayor Richard C. Hackett

Lastly, our seventh proposition is that, for all practical purposes, Mayor Hackett did not lose the 1991 mayoral election; he was defeated. In the end, given the electoral milieu, the tide of Memphis history was no longer on the side of the white conservative tradition.

Nevertheless, in any election determined by a margin of 142 votes out of 248,000 votes cast, there always will be second-guessing. Why did Hackett not spend more of his large campaign war chest? Were his campaign workers overconfident? Why did Hackett not pander to the city's racial divisions in order to spur a larger white turnout?

There are legitimate questions about Hackett's unwillingness to use all of his campaign funds. The expenditure issue is used by many political insiders to surmise that Hackett could have won the election by employing these funds effectively. For example, he could have used the money to make more phone calls and to target voters for increased turnout on the day of the election. That strategy may not have produced more voters, however. Buck Welford's at-large campaign for council position 6 shows that a well-financed campaign does not necessarily produce a victory and can produce a backlash against the candidate. Or, for another example, in the 1982 mayoral race, Mike Cody's enormous advantage in campaign expenditures did not produce a victory over Hackett.

There is also criticism of Hackett because his supporters did not show the intensity of earlier campaigns. However, chapter 6 demonstrates that Hackett understood the election would be close, and he showed incredible intensity throughout the campaign. The fact that his supporters assumed he would be victorious was not something Hackett could control. However, as the incumbent, Hackett used his position to raise funds and draw workers from the ranks of political appointees. These were both resources unavailable to Herenton.

Finally, a racially divisive strategy might have brought Hackett victory, but there is no certainty of that assessment either. In the process, Hackett might have lost some of his moderate white supporters. In general, he had to energize his white supporters in a way that did not create a reaction among blacks and moderate whites. He chose a stealth campaign, quietly meeting with voters in private backyard functions. In addition, as Hackett suggested, a racially divisive campaign might well have made the city ungovernable after the election, no matter which candidate won.

• • •

In summary, neither incumbency nor white liberals had much of an identifiable impact on the 1991 elections. The institutional context did play a role, however, because the elimination of the runoff left candidates less dependent upon the major demographic group in the community. In addition, changes in annexation laws were important because the addition of Hickory Hills would surely have produced a Hackett victory.

As for race specifically, it profoundly affected the 1991 mayor's election, virtually regardless of anything Mayor Hackett did or did not do. The same was true, but to a lesser extent, in the other at-large elections. Nevertheless, with impetus from a well-run Herenton campaign, black participation rates were at an all-time high, and that participation proved essential to black success in all but two of their citywide victories. In the end, the Herenton and black at-large victories of 1991 were part of a black electoral tide that had been pressing at the dam of white conservative control for more than a century, a dam that had finally begun to spring visible leaks in recent years and gave way in 1991.

Part III

Implications and Prospects for the Future

9 Conclusion: Racial Reflexivity in Memphis

Besides being one of the very closest and most racially polarized mayoral elections ever to occur in the United States, the election of Dr. W. W. Herenton in 1991 was a major event in Memphis political history. Looking at it in that historical context, we see key ways in which Memphis can be compared to other large southern cities. We also see ways in which this particular election varied from the first elections of African-American mayors in other large United States cities.

Racial Politics in Large Southern Cities

As in most all southern cities, the issue of race has played a prominent role in the evolution of Memphis politics. At the turn of the century, Memphis had its Jim Crow system of segregation, lynchings, and race riots. It also experienced a notable degree of violent and nonviolent resistance to such oppression, especially among poorer blacks more recently immigrating to the city. Nevertheless, conservative whites still dominated local politics from the late 1870s until 1991, although their ranks had begun to splinter some in the 1970s.

Earlier in the century, Bertram Doyle observed, "[T]he Negro masses look on the White man as chosen to rule and the ballot as a means to that end. . . . They accept their status as nonvoters and expect to be guided thereby."[1] Although Doyle may have been correct when analyzing much of the South in 1937, his conclusion did not apply even then to

Memphis. The city's history of discrimination and its service-based economy combined to spawn a large and exceptionally poor African-American lower class. This fact might lead one to expect relatively low levels of political participation. Yet, that has not been the case when looking at the overall history of electoral participation in the city's African-American community.

Memphis was one of the southern cities that allowed early black suffrage when it served the interests of white politicians. But, to a larger degree than almost anywhere else, African Americans were selectively marshaled to the polls in the first half of the twentieth century by the political machine of E. H. "Boss" Crump.[2] Despite their exceptionally low economic status as a community, blacks registered at surprisingly high rates, even by southern standards. They have voted at high rates as well, even after the demise of the Crump machine. As Harry Holloway put it, "[Memphis blacks] participated in elections more freely than any other southern Negroes."[3]

Despite such habits of political participation, blacks were unable to translate such efforts into electoral success. Whether intending to or not, the annexation of predominantly white suburbs, racially polarized voting, at-large elections, and a runoff provision combined to minimize the number of black elected officials.

Then, two important changes occurred. The state's annexation law was changed in 1974, slowing the rate of annexation and finally allowing blacks to reach numerical parity with whites. Then, in July of 1991, a federal judge struck the runoff provision in citywide elections. Consequently, a unified white majority could no longer automatically defeat any insurgent black candidacy. Nevertheless, in order to win citywide, blacks would normally need to unify behind single black candidates, and that had proven difficult, especially in recent years.

First Electing a Black Mayor

Among the largest fifty cities in the country that had a strong mayor system and a population that was even 40 percent black, only Memphis and St. Louis had failed to elect a black mayor by 1991.[4] In addition, many of these black mayors were first elected in cities with much smaller black populations than either St. Louis or Memphis. In racially mixed settings, the winning formula generally was predicated on an "accommodation" model of sorts. Whether intentionally or not, African-American candidates ran on platforms that were acceptable to a number of white liberals. Then, they subsequently won in coalition with those whites.[5] In more current parlance, blacks benefited from at least a partial "de-racialization" of local politics.[6]

W. W. Herenton's victory in Memphis, however, deviates significantly from the standard formula for electing an African-American mayor for the first time in a racially mixed city. Richard Hackett and the dominant white political culture ultimately were beaten by a combination of demographic and rule changes and a crusadelike Herenton effort that successfully tapped generations of African-American frustration.

Two realities are important to remember at the outset. First of all, Memphis has had an unusually small number of white liberals. Beyond that, its African-American community had often struggled to overcome its own internal divisions.

Whereas St. Louis had its "central corridor" of liberal whites,[7] a number of factors have contributed to the relative absence of such a group in Memphis throughout most of its history, a reality that has seriously restricted the opportunities for the kind of black-white liberal coalition found in other cities. The yellow fever epidemics of the 1870s led to the exodus of most of the more cosmopolitan white immigrants and the subsequent influx of much more parochial whites from surrounding rural areas. This demographic trend contributed to Memphis's having an exceptionally small number of white liberals from the beginning. Thereafter, the city remained reasonably insular, surviving largely as a commercial center built around the cotton trade and later as a magnet for companies seeking cheap, non-unionized local labor. Thus, at least until the quite recent developments discussed in chapter 1, there has been very minimal ethnic influx, no liberal foundations to speak of, and little liberal leadership forthcoming from the heads of local businesses, churches, or civic organizations.

Secondly, as has been even more of a problem in St. Louis and some other cities,[8] the Memphis black community has long contained its own significant social and economic differences, leading to various political fissures. In particular, there has been a sizable core of very poor people, and they often have been militant, rebellious, and difficult to incorporate into mainstream electoral politics. Most notably, since blacks began to contest citywide elections in the mid-1970s, it has not been uncommon for each of these contests to have more than one black candidate attempting to appeal to an often alienated majority of the city's black population.

Consequently, Herenton's campaign began with two "black unity" conventions. This process succeeded in delivering a single African-American candidate, but it also placed some distance between Herenton and a number of the city's liberal whites, a quite small group to begin with. Further, when compared to the standard formula discussed in the introduction, Herenton ended up with virtually no support among predominantly white groups, few white endorsements, and few white votes. Meanwhile, there was no strong second white candidate to split the white vote. The only mass-circulation newspaper in the city endorsed the white incumbent, besides having run a relatively recent series of highly critical articles on Herenton's private life as well as on his tenure as school superintendent. And, although race was a powerful undercurrent throughout, the two campaigns ran parallel to each other, with few attacks and few discussions about issues. Instead, both groups of supporters concentrated on registering and turning out their own racial constituencies. In the end, despite the immensity of the social and economic impediments discussed in chapter 3, black participation rates surged to remarkably high levels, and that turnout proved essential to Herenton's narrow win and also to success in all but two of blacks' citywide victories.

Dr. Herenton won thanks to an extraordinary level of black support and without having to appeal to the white community. Yet, if the city had been able to continue its annexations of predominantly white suburbs, our findings indicate that it is nearly certain Herenton would have been defeated. It is less clear what a runoff election would have meant; however, in an electorate this closely divided, a runoff might well have led to a reversal as well.

Memphis appeared to have reached that threshold of racial divisiveness, or "point of racial reflexivity," as we have chosen to call it, which all but precluded successful interracial accommodation. That political reality severely limited the chances of deracialized city politics, at least at the mayoral level.

Had Memphis history developed differently, allowing the city to retain a larger number of more liberal whites, this degree of racial reflexivity might not have evolved. White candidates would have had to have been more racially neutral in order to win, while black candidates could have withstood the defection of the most race-conscious blacks by regularly supplementing their vote totals with a reasonable number of white votes.

Nevertheless, there is some evidence that white liberals, or at least moderates, have been re-emerging as the city has diversified over the past quarter century. And, when looking at the level of crossover voting in a number of the 1990 and 1991 citywide races, it is clear that this diversification finally has begun to appear in the city's election returns. It is conceivable that a relatively successful Herenton stewardship could help cement and build upon that evolution.

W. W. Herenton and the Challenge of Racial Reflexivity

> The issue of Higgs' race may play a part in the [1976 mayoral] contest. But color is not likely to be the deciding factor. There are many fair-minded citizens, black and white, who have shown they are more concerned with the quality of candidates and issues than with the candidate's race. Whatever the outcome of the Higgs-Chandler battle, one thing is certain—we have turned a corner in Memphis politics.
>
> —Judge D'Army Bailey, October 13, 1976

Judge Bailey may have been a bit premature in those conclusions. Richard Murray and Arnold Vedlitz studied a variety of large southern cities and concluded in a 1978 journal article that Memphis voting was by far the most racially polarized. In particular, white support of black candidates was exceptionally low.[9] They noted that "Memphis . . . has been so highly polarized along racial lines in recent years that it has been most difficult for local blacks to align with any substantial element of the white population."[10]

Yet, following the 1991 city elections, Mayor Herenton seemed to have inherited at least a small window of opportunity in which to cultivate and expand what had the potential of becoming the first interracial governing coalition in Memphis in more than a century. To accomplish this, however, he would have to provide sufficient policy rewards to the black community, a core constituency that was likely to stay disproportionately very poor regardless of any actions he may take.[11] At the same time, he would have to reassure whites, especially the more mobile middle- and upper-class whites, that he was truly "the mayor of all the people."[12]

This promised to be a difficult task. Like most other black mayors first elected in racially mixed cities, Herenton took office amidst a majority white city council,[13] a predominantly white bureaucracy (especially significant in the always thorny matter of police conduct),[14] a relatively mobile white middle class watching every move, and a largely white mass media recording those moves.[15]

In addition, like his black mayoral counterparts, Herenton faced pressure to be even more moderate than his white predecessors in order to gain and hold the confidence of local corporate elites.[16] In his first post-election decision, for example, Herenton journeyed to Atlanta to learn from Maynard Jackson and Andrew Young.[17] He returned and appointed a transition team of virtually all corporate leaders. Yet, as the awareness of such constraints has grown in an increasing number of other cities, so has black voter unrest.[18]

Alternative Futures

Let us consider five possible scenarios. The first three would allow for a return of conservative white dominance in Memphis politics. One is a middle-ground arrangement. And the last would culminate in the kind of interracial governing coalition alluded to above.

In the first possibility, the "Reversal of 1991" scenario, the African-American community remains reasonably united, at least to the point that strong black candidates do not rise up to challenge incumbents such as Mayor Herenton. However, in races in which these single black candidates are pitted against strong single white opponents, anything short of another "crusadelike" effort could leave them on the short end of the narrow electoral margin this time. As it may well be difficult to replicate the historic participation levels of 1991, unless Herenton can find a fair number of white crossover votes, there could conceivably be a return of conservative white domination of Memphis politics.

The second alternative is the "Black Disunity" scenario. As much of the black community remains poor and grows frustrated with the compromises required of black elected officials in an interracial setting, the novelty of having a black mayor and more black councilpersons may begin to wear off. If the African-American community, rife with alienation and suspicion, returns to its internal divisiveness, this too could lead back to white conservative control. Even in a city where the majority of voters are black, multiple black candidates competing with single white opponents could well spell electoral success for the white challengers. In addition, such a return could be cemented by the next scenario.

A third possibility is the "Return of a White Majority" scenario. A short period of white governmental control could lead to a new round of annexations. And should the federal courts decide that such annexations are constitutionally acceptable even if they end up altering the racial balance in citywide elections, such population additions could tip the demographic scales sufficiently to allow a return of another extended period of white conservative rule. Or, if black elected officials are required by fiscal necessity to initiate annexations, such annexations would be likely to raise fewer constitutional problems but could well result in a similar long-term electoral shift.

The "Whites as Moderators" scenario is a fourth possibility. If the black population remains large enough to preclude much of a chance for white elected officials to regain governmental control in the foreseeable future, a factionalized black community could still allow white voters to play a moderating role. In New Orleans in 1986, for instance, Sidney Barthelemy, the more conservative of the two black candidates, garnered 86 percent of the white vote and only 28 percent of the black vote on his way to defeating the more racially conscious William Jefferson.[19] Similarly, in 1989, moderate black candidate Michael White won the mayor's office with only 30 percent of Cleveland's black vote.[20]

In the final scenario, "Interracial Coalition," Mayor Herenton and the city council are able to overcome racial reflexivity by successfully appeasing both the black and white communities without igniting racially reflexive backlash. However, not only does this require exceptionally astute political compromises, but also it is complicated by some rather fundamental disagreements between large segments of the black and white communities. Earl and Merle Black, for example, recently found clear ideological differences between southern blacks and whites.[21] Such disagreements over the appropriate level of governmental taxing and spending exist in Memphis as well.[22] Nonetheless, white and black Memphians still agree in their evaluations of most of the city's policy objectives and public services,[23] which encourages hope for the possibility of an interracial governing coalition.

At the very least, it may be possible to develop a working alliance between liberal and moderate blacks and whites, those not as prone to racially reflexive suspicion. In what Raphael Sonenshein refers to as a "unified model" of biracial coalition, participating blacks and whites must come to grips with their separate and shared interests as well as their mutual contributions.[24]

The seeds for such a development can be seen in the crossover voting especially apparent and critical in a number of the nonmayoral citywide races that occurred in 1990 and 1991. Should Mayor Herenton's leadership succeed in helping to cement that coalition, a progressive black-white governing majority might well be able to weather either internal divisions within the black community or further annexations, both of which could lead to a return of conservative white domination in the city of Memphis. Mayor Herenton sums up his hopes for the city in the following way:

> We have come a long way to the arrival of this new day. We must remember that our heritage is full of accounts of what can occur when we surrender to our all too human frailties of fear, prejudice and misunderstanding. But with the dawning of this new day, we have the opportunity to change the course of our civic history.
>
> As your new mayor, not for just a few, but for all Memphians, I envision a great and vital metropolis rushing excitedly towards the 21st century, a century which will feature a Memphis that proudly boasts equal opportunity and access, racial justice and peace, cultural unity and harmony—for all.[25]

Epilogue

The 1995 city elections served to validate and extend what had begun in the seminal election four years earlier. This time, incumbent Mayor W. W. Herenton easily won reelection, garnering nearly 75 percent of the vote, although he faced only token opposition and voter turnout was at a record low. Nevertheless, he managed a white crossover vote that approached 40 percent, nearly four times higher than any black mayoral candidate had ever attracted. In citywide elections for school board and city court, on the other hand, there was less evidence of racial crossover voting, as black candidates won every contested citywide post. And with at-large elections now eliminated for city council, African Americans won seven of those thirteen seats, although the new districts did not allow for much racial crossover, given the city's degree of residential segregation.

In the mayor's race, Dr. Herenton flexed his political muscles early. He began by lining up a local Who's Who of corporate backers and amassing a three-hundred-thousand-dollar war chest as early as April, well before any serious opposition had begun to develop.[1] Then, in July, as prospective opponents were just beginning to emerge, the *Commercial Appeal* ran a poll that showed the mayor's approval rating at more than 75 percent, with two-thirds of those polled supporting his reelection—including a majority of the white community.[2]

Given such an impressive approval rating, it was no surprise that only token opposition emerged. It was also no surprise that the incumbent mayor campaigned on his record, promising to maintain his fiscal management while continuing initiatives designed to spur job creation, increase downtown redevelopment, increase the construction of low-income housing, and improve race relations. With this message, Herenton crisscrossed the city, focusing on his crucial black base but also making many more overt appeals to prospective white supporters this time.

Suggesting a degree of racial reflexivity, however, opposition to Herenton gradually began to surface in the black community. In particular, this opposition began to appear after the mayor referred to Congressman Harold Ford as a "power-hungry maniac,"[3] made a highly visible appearance at the victory celebration of Jim Rout, the victorious white Republican candidate for county mayor, and then tacitly endorsed Republican gubernatorial candidate Don Sundquist by choosing not to make a formal endorsement of his Democratic opponent. Those incidents combined with what black leaders such as Vernon Ash, Teddy Withers, and William Larsha deemed to be an abandonment of his 1991 pledge to concentrate on problems in the African-American community led to a series of harsh rebukes, especially in the pages of the *Tri-State Defender*.[4]

Nevertheless, Herenton's campaign fund grew to more some five hundred thousand dollars, and his endorsements soared. He was formally endorsed by Republicans Sundquist and Rout, Bartlett Mayor Bobby Flaherty, the *Commercial Appeal*, the *Tri-State Defender*, the Shelby County Democrats, the police and firefighters' unions, AFSCME Local 1733, the AFL-CIO Labor Council, the electrical workers' union, the Building Trades Council, and the Memphis Educational Association. Jim Baker, a salesman and registered Republican, the most viable of the mayor's three announced opponents, failed to receive a single major endorsement.[5] Even the local Republican Party opted not to endorse a candidate, a symbolic victory for Herenton.

As election day neared, there was little indication of any major countertrends developing. A poll by the conservative *Memphis Business Journal* showed the mayor with a countywide approval rating of 65 percent, nearly identical to that of County Mayor Rout.[6] Then, two weeks before the election, in the only published election poll, Herenton led Baker 64 percent to 6 percent, with more than a quarter of the city's respondents opting not to indicate a preference.[7] Meanwhile, African Americans maintained a 51 percent majority of those registered, with whites at 41 percent and "others" at 8 percent.

When the returns were counted on October 5, the obvious was confirmed. Mayor Herenton had swept to reelection, defeating Baker by a margin of 74 percent to 24 percent. Homogeneous precinct analysis indicated that Herenton had held his black base, receiving more than 97 percent of the African-American vote. In addition, he had captured nearly 40 percent of the white vote, with support ranging from 15 percent in some blue-collar neighborhoods to more than 50 percent in some of the wealthier white areas.[8]

The submayoral races were conducted under very different circumstances than the 1991 elections. The 1991 elections had eleven at-large races excluding the mayor, although only ten were contested. White crossover ranged from 5 to 40 percent, while black crossover ranged from 1 percent to 53 percent (see Table 3). Four years later there would be only six at-large elections, and only 4 of them were contested.

The change was brought about by the voting rights lawsuit discussed in chapter 5 and it dramatically affected the city council. The 1991 city council had seven whites and six blacks. Two of the at-large positions were held by blacks and four by whites. In May of 1995, the city council passed a "super district" plan to replace the former at-large positions. Each super district would elect three council members. The eastern super district was primarily white, while the western super district was primarily black.

Ironically, if the at-large system had been in effect in 1995, blacks would have won all six of the seats rather than splitting the seats with white winners. Black turnout was estimated at about 55 percent, while white turnout was at about 45 percent. Further evidence is provided by the four contested at-large elections for judge, school board, and court clerk. All of the victors were African Americans.

Three of the black victors won by substantial margins. City court incumbent Walter Evans received 68 percent of the vote. He was opposed by a little-known white challenger who had the additional liability of a husband running for city council with strong opposition from Republicans and midtown residents.

Also in the city court elections, neophyte black candidate Jayne Chandler won a very narrow victory over white incumbent Nancy Sorak.

It was a campaign without any racial rancor. Sorak had been so popular that she had not drawn an opponent in 1991. She enjoyed widespread support in the black community and was endorsed by the *Tri-State Defender* in 1995. In fact, she received about 34 percent of the black vote, which in the end was not enough to overcome the relative size of the black turnout and a 23 percent white crossover to Chandler. Chandler had run an effective door-to-door campaign, but there was also suspicion that at least some of her white crossover votes resulted from a confusion of family names, since Chandler was the name of a former white mayor, Wyeth Chandler, who had subsequently become a local judge.

One of the most bitter at-large races was for a school board position. Black incumbent Sara Lewis was opposed by a well-financed white attorney, Mike Robb. Lewis had won easily in 1991 when she defeated an unpopular incumbent with 61 percent of the vote. However, her 1995 campaign became mired in controversy because of financial irregularities at the Free the Children program, which she directed. In addition, some white parents were concerned that she was not an enthusiastic supporter of the optional schools program. In the end, however, Lewis still won 64 percent of the vote, in large part because she maintained a solid black base of support. Her white crossover was only 15 percent, however, compared to 40 percent in 1991.

Finally, Thomas Long was elected as city court clerk by a 31 to 29 plurality over his white opponent, Joe Cooper. Long enjoyed the endorsements of both a former clerk and an incumbent court clerk and Congressman Harold Ford. His campaign was hampered, on the other hand, by charges that employees of the clerk's office were being pressured to campaign for Long. Probably because of the controversy and the Ford endorsement, Long had the lowest white crossover of any at-large black candidate, only 12 percent. His opponent, Joe Cooper, had the second-highest black crossover, some 31 percent. Cooper had served in an administrative capacity in the offices of prominent black political leaders, including Assessor Michael Hooks, Court Clerk John Ford, and Court Clerk Minerva Johnican. He also ran an energetic campaign, although it was set back by a reminder to voters that at one time he had been convicted of bank fraud.

Two of the at-large candidates did not draw opponents. Black incumbent Judge Earnestine Hunt-Evans was popular with both blacks and whites. White incumbent school board member Bill Todd, on the other hand, would surely have been defeated if he had drawn a viable black opponent.

Overall, then, the 1991 and 1995 submayoral elections witnessed a limited amount of selective crossover by both black and white voters, depending upon the record and campaign of the candidate. Nonetheless, the bulk of both the black and white communities continued to vote along racial lines. Thus, as in 1995, as long as the city retains its black majority, Memphis at-large races are likely to continue to be dominated by African-American candidates.

Mayor Herenton won reelection, as have virtually all the first blacks to be elected mayor in other large United States cities.[9] However, two things are worth noting. First of all, Herenton faced only token opposition. Second, the turnout rate was significantly lower than in any Memphis election since the mayor-council form was adopted in 1966. Only approximately 36 percent of eligible voters turned out in 1995, compared to 65 percent in 1991 and a previous low of 47 percent in 1987. Consequently, the degree of evolution in the city's interracial politics still has not really been tested. That test will occur when a prominent white conservative receives the endorsement of the local Republican Party in opposing Mayor Herenton—or another black candidate—in a hotly contested election likely to attract a much larger turnout. Meanwhile, a considerable amount of racial polarization continued to appear in the lower salience elections for school board and city court.

Internal divisions within the black community, combined with further annexations of predominantly white outlying areas, could still result in a return of conservative white domination in the city of Memphis. The challenge to Herenton will be to continue developing a progressive black-white governing majority, and the 1995 mayoral election results do suggest a significant first step in that direction.

Notes

Preface

1. For example, see Eugene Webb, Unobtrusive Measures (Chicago: Rand McNally, 1966).
2. Ecological regression analysis allows us to estimate the proportion of votes cast for candidates by black and white voters. In Memphis, the Shelby County Election Commission collects information on the race of registrants that makes it possible to draw these estimates. Homogeneous precinct analysis provided a check on the regressions by examining voting patterns of precincts that are 90 percent white and 90 percent black. These are not polling data, but aggregate data that provide the relationship between the racial composition of the precinct and the vote for a candidate. The data are not actual votes, but rather are estimates of voting patterns. Though these aggregate data require a caution because they do not represent individual votes, the reader will become aware that they do reflect voting patterns of individuals.

There are some anomalies in these very complex data sets. First, we compared census information, collected every ten years, to registration information collected more frequently. Interpolation procedures were used for the years between the censuses. Second, registration information includes blacks, whites, and others. An estimating technique based on the proportion of whites and blacks in a precinct allocated the "others" to black and white categories. Third, black and white registration information is available from 1951, though turnout information is only available from 1979. Lastly, estimated voting patterns for a future annexation area were based on voting patterns of a comparable newly annexed area.

Our study employs the double regression method that is suggested in the literature. Our form of ecological regression is based on Bernard

Groffman, Michael Migalski, and Nicholas Noviello, "The Totality of Circumstances Test in Section 2 of the 1982 Extension of the Voting Rights Act: A Social Science Perspective," Law & Policy 7 (Apr. 1985): 199–223.

Introduction

1. Roscoe Martin, foreword to V. O. Key, *Southern Politics in State and Nation* (New York: Knopf, 1949), xxxix.
2. For example, see Key, *Southern Politics,* chapter 1; Harry Holloway, *The Politics of the Southern Negro* (New York: Random House, 1969), chapter 1.
3. Key, *Southern Politics,* 5.
4. See David Matthews and James Prothro, *Negroes and the New Southern Politics* (New York: Harcourt, Brace, and World, 1966), 13–15; Key, *Southern Politics,* chapter 25.
5. For example, see ibid.; Blaine Brownell and David Goldfield, *The City in Southern History* (Port Washington, N.Y.: Kennikat, 1977); Robin Kelley, "We Are Not What We Seem," *Journal of American History* 80 (June 1993): 75–112; Michael Honey, *Southern Labor and Black Civil Rights* (Champaign: Univ. of Illinois Press, 1993); Jack Bass and Walter DeVries, *The Transformation of Southern Politics* (New York: Basic Books, 1976); Reese Cleghorn and Pat Watters, *Climbing Jacob's Ladder* (New York: Harcourt, Brace, and World, 1967); Benjamin Mays, *Born to Rebel* (New York: Scribner's, 1971).
6. Paul Lewinsohn, *Race, Class and Party: A History of Negro Suffrage and White Politics in the South* (New York: Russell and Russell, 1963).
7. Holloway, *The Politics of the Southern Negro,* 21–27; Mays, *Born to Rebel.*
8. Holloway, *The Politics of the Southern Negro,* 23.
9. For example, see Kelley, "We Are Not What We Seem"; Honey, *Southern Labor and Black Civil Rights*; Kenneth Goings, "Lynching, African-Americans and Memphis," unpublished paper.
10. Bass and DeVries, *The Transformation of Southern Politics,* 55. See also Key, *Southern Politics,* 651; Cleghorn and Watters, *Climbing Jacob's Ladder.*
11. Margaret Price, *The Negro Voter in the South* (Atlanta: Southern Regional Council, 1957), 72–81; Richard Murray and Arnold Vedlitz, "Race, SES and Voting Participation in Large Southern Cities," *Journal of Politics* 39 (Nov. 1977): 1064–72.
12. For example, see John Jacob, "Black America, 1993: An Overview," in National Urban League, *The State of Black America 1994* (New York: National Urban League, 1994), 3–4.
13. For example, see Matthews and Prothro, *Negroes and the New Southern Politics,* chapter 1; Marvin Olsen, "Social and Political Participation of

Blacks," *American Sociological Review* 35 (Aug. 1970): 682–95; Laura Stein and Carol Kohfeld, "St. Louis' Black-White Elections," *Urban Affairs Quarterly* 26 (Dec. 1991): 238–39; Price, *The Negro Voter in the South*, 30; James Jalenak, "Beale Street Politics" (Yale Univ. honors thesis, 1961), chapter 9.

14. For example, see Holloway, *The Politics of the Southern Negro*, chapter 1 and p. 329; Robert Lane, *Political Life* (Glencoe, Ill.: Free Press, 1959), 249.

15. See Charles V. Hamilton, "The Patron-Recipient Relationship and Minority Politics," *Political Science Quarterly* 94 (Summer 1979): 211–28.

16. For example, see Robert Alford and Eugene Lee, "Voting Turnout in American Cities," *American Political Science Review* 62 (Sept. 1968): 796–813. As for the impact of urban governmental form on political participation in general, see John Kessel, "Governmental Structures and Political Environment," *American Political Science Review* 57 (Sept. 1963): 615–20; Robert Duggar, "The Relation of Local Government Structure to Urban Renewal," *Law and Contemporary Problems* 26 (Jan. 1961): 49–69; Robert Salisbury, "St. Louis Politics," *Western Political Quarterly* 13 (June 1960): 498–507.

17. See Key, *Southern Politics*, 75, 649; Alexis de Tocqueville, *Democracy in America*, edited by Phillips Bradley (New York: Knopf, 1951); Louis Hartz, *The Liberal Tradition in American Politics* (New York: Harcourt, Brace, 1955); Ira Katznelson and Mark Kesselman, *The Politics of Power* (New York: Harper, Brace, and Jovanovich, 1987), 261.

18. For example, see Robert Dahl, *Democracy in America* (Chicago: Rand McNally, 1976), 359–62.

19. For example, see Jeffrey Henig, "Race and Voting," *Urban Affairs Quarterly* 28 (June 1993): 544–45; Richard Murray and Arnold Vedlitz, "Racial Voting Patterns in the South," *Annals of the American Academy of Political and Social Science* 439 (Sept. 1978): 29–39; David Goldfield, *Cotton Fields and Skyscrapers* (Baltimore: Johns Hopkins Univ. Press, 1982); Holloway, *The Politics of the Southern Negro*, 321; Brownell and Goldfield, *The City in Southern History*, 17. All of these sources seem to contradict earlier findings noted in Price, *The Negro Voter in the South*, 72–81.

20. Although ours is an original conception, this analysis draws heavily on the teachings of Charles V. Hamilton, as well as on those of William Nelson and Phillip Meranto, *Electing Black Mayors* (Columbus: Ohio State Univ. Press, 1977).

21. For example, see Peter Ross Range, "Capital of Black Is Bountiful," *New York Times Magazine*, Apr. 7, 1974; Steven V. Roberts, "He's One of Us," *New York Times Magazine*, Feb. 24, 1974; *New York Times*, June 24, 1991.

22. Robert Starks and Michael Preston, "Harold Washington and the Politics of Reform in Chicago: 1983–1987," in Rufus Browning, Dale Rogers Marshall, and David Tabb, eds., *Racial Politics in American Cities* (New York: Longman, 1990), 88–107.

23. See Mylon Winn, "The Election of Norm Rice as Mayor of Seattle," *PS: Political Science & Politics* 23 (June 1990): 159.

24. For the purposes of this book, a "liberal" as opposed to a "conservative" is one who tends to favor more governmental intervention in the private-enterprise economy, both in order to regulate business in a way that requires businesses to be more socially responsible and in order to redistribute resources from the "haves" to the "have-nots." There is also a social dimension to liberalism, which is more tolerant of multiculturalism.

25. *New York Times*/WBBM-TV poll, cited in the *New York Times*, Apr. 6, 1989.

26. See *New York Times*, June 13, 1989. A comparable pledge to avoid race baiting also was taken in Birmingham in 1983. See *Washington Post*, Oct. 13, 1983.

27. William Riordan, ed., *Plunkitt of Tammany Hall* (New York: Dutton, 1963), 45–49.

28. As an example of this literature, see Chandler Davidson, *Biracial Politics* (Baton Rouge: Louisiana State Univ. Press, 1972); Rufus Browning, Dale Rogers Marshall, and David Tabb, *Protest Is Not Enough* (Berkeley: Univ. of California Press, 1984); Georgia Parsons, "Racial Politics and Black Power in the Cities," in George Galster and Edward Hill, eds., *The Metropolis in Black and White* (New Brunswick, N.J.: Center for Urban Policy Research, 1992), 166–89.

For case studies, see J. Phillip Thompson, "David Dinkins' Victory in New York City: The Decline of the Democratic Party Organization and the Strengthening of Black Politics," *PS: Political Science and Politics* 23 (June 1990): 145–48; Saundra Ardrey and William Nelson, "The Maturation of Black Political Power: The Case of Cleveland," *PS: Political Science and Politics* 23 (June 1990): 148–54; Robert Starks and Michael Preston, "Harold Washington and the Politics of Reform in Chicago: 1983–1987," *Black Electoral Politics* 2 (1990): 88–107; Clarence Stone, "Race and Regime in Atlanta," *Black Electoral Politics* 2 (1990): 125–39; Huey Perry, "The Evolution and Impact of Biracial Coalitions and Black Mayors in Birmingham and New Orleans," *Black Electoral Politics* 2 (1990): 140–52; Avian Asher, Arthur Goldberg, John Mollenkopf, and Edward Rogowsky, *Changing New York City Politics* (New York: Routledge, 1991); Raphael Sonenshein, *Politics in Black and White* (Princeton, N.J.: Princeton Univ. Press, 1993); William Grimshaw, "Is Chicago Ready for

Reform?" in Melvin Holli and Paul Green, eds., *The Making of the Mayor, Chicago 1983* (Grand Rapids, Mich.: Eerdmans, 1984).

29. See Charles V. Hamilton, "De-Racialization: Examination of a Political Strategy," *First World* 11 (Mar./Apr. 1977): 3–5; Symposium, *Urban Affairs Quarterly* 26 (Dec. 1991): 181–227; Symposium, *PS: Political Science and Politics* 23 (June 1990): 160–90; Davidson, *Biracial Politics*; Robert Huckfeldt and C. W. Kohfeld, *Race and the Decline of Class in American Politics* (Champaign: Univ. of Illinois Press, 1989), 91; Nelson and Meranto, *Electing Black Mayors*, 329.

30. Robert Smith, "Recent Elections and Black Politics," *PS: Political Science and Politics* 23 (June 1990): 160.

31. *Commercial Appeal*, Oct. 10, 1991.

1. White Politics

1. Goldfield, *Cotton Fields and Skyscrapers*, 11. We use Goldfield's thematic construct to frame our historical review of the white political culture in Memphis.

2. For example, see Charles Crawford, *Yesterday's Memphis* (Miami: Seemann, 1976).

3. For example, see Denoral Davis, "Against the Odds" (Ph.D. diss., State Univ. of New York at Binghamton, 1987), 48.

4. See ibid.; Gerald Capers, *The Biography of a River Town* (New York: Vanguard Press, 1966), 47–48, 79.

5. See Crawford, *Yesterday's Memphis*; John Hope Franklin, *From Slavery to Freedom* (New York: Knopf, 1980).

6. Sandra Vaughn, "Memphis: Heart of the Mid-South," in Robert Bullard, ed., *In Search of the New South: The Black Urban Experience in the 1970s and 1980s* (Tuscaloosa: Univ. of Alabama Press, 1989), 99.

7. See Shields McIlwaine, *Memphis Down in Dixie* (New York: Dutton, 1948).

8. Crawford, *Yesterday's Memphis*; Brownell and Goldfield, *The City in Southern History*, 16.

9. Brownell and Goldfield, *The City in Southern History*, 16. See also Lawrence Larsen, *The Rise of the Urban South* (Lexington: Univ. Press of Kentucky, 1985), 40.

10. George Lee, *Beale Street* (New York: R. O. Ballou, 1934), 13. See Capers, *The Biography of a River Town*, 47–49; Crawford, *Yesterday's Memphis*; Franklin, *From Slavery to Freedom*; David Tucker, *Memphis Since Crump* (Knoxville: Univ. of Tennessee Press, 1980), chapter 1; Lee, *Beale Street*, 15–16. For the prominence of Beale Street, see Lewinsohn, *Race, Class and Party*, 139.

11. For example, see Clayton Robinson, "Impact of the City on Rural Immigration to Memphis: 1880–1940" (Ph.D. diss., Univ. of Minnesota, 1967); Roger Biles, *Memphis in the Great Depression* (Knoxville: Univ. of Tennessee Press, 1986).

12. Goldfield, *Cotton Fields and Skyscrapers*, 64. This was a period in which southern urbanism lagged behind northern urbanism more than at any time in history.

13. Denoral Davis, "Against the Odds," 48.

14. Kathleen Berkeley, *"Like a Plague of Locusts": Immigration and Social Change in Memphis, Tennessee* (Los Angeles: UCLA Press, 1980), 4.

15. Robinson, "Impact of the City on Rural Immigration to Memphis," 5. The Irish later played a role as government officials and had substantial representation in the fire and police departments.

16. Ibid.

17. John Ellis, "Disease and the Destiny of a City: The 1878 Yellow Fever Epidemic in Memphis," *The West Tennessee Historical Papers* 28 (1974): 76.

18. Ibid., 82.

19. Ibid., 82, 87.

20. For example, see Ellis, "Disease and the Destiny of a City," 75–89. And for a more general account of rural influence on urban politics in the South, see Goldfield, *Cotton Fields and Skyscrapers*; Earl Black and Merle Black, *Politics and Society in the South* (Cambridge, Mass.: Harvard Univ. Press, 1987).

21. Goldfield, *Cotton Fields and Skyscrapers*, 94.

22. Biles, *Memphis in the Great Depression*, 6. Also see Rayford Logan, *The Betrayal of the Negro* (London: Collier and Macmillan, 1965), 300.

23. John Harkins, *Metropolis of the American Nile* (Oxford, Miss.: The Guild Bindery Press, 1982), 104. See also William Miller, *Mr. Crump of Memphis* (Baton Rouge: Louisiana State Univ. Press, 1964), 8.

24. Gerald Capers, *The Biography of a River Town* (New York: Vanguard Press, 1966), 216.

25. For example, see the *Commercial Appeal*, Feb. 17, 1991; Memphis and Shelby County Planning Commission, *Annexation: A Must for a Growing Memphis* (Sept. 1967).

26. Yung Wei and H. R. Mahood, "Racial Attitudes and the Wallace Vote," *Polity* 3 (Summer 1971): 532–49.

27. Goldfield, *Cotton Fields and Skyscrapers*, 8.

28. A "spot market" is a market in which a commodity is sold for immediate delivery. For example, see Franklin Edwards and Cindy Ma, *Futures and Options* (New York: McGraw-Hill, 1992), 78.

29. Harkins, *Metropolis of the American Nile*, 95–96.

30. Robert Sigafoos, *Cotton Row to Beale Street* (Memphis: Memphis State Univ. Press, 1979), 75.
31. Biles, *Memphis in the Great Depression,* 19.
32. Sigafoos, *Cotton Row to Beale Street,* 85.
33. Goldfield, *Cotton Fields and Skyscrapers,* 160.
34. Sigafoos, *Cotton Row to Beale Street,* 86.
35. Gerald Capers, "Memphis: Satrapy of a Benevolent Despot," in Robert Allen, *Our Fair City* (New York: Vanguard, 1947), 226.
36. Daniel Elazar, *American Federalism* (New York: Crowell, 1972), 106–7.
37. See Jack Holmes, "The Underlying Causes of the Memphis Riot of 1866," *Tennessee Historical Quarterly* 17 (1958): 292–96; Altina Walker, "Class and Race in the Memphis Riot of 1866," *Journal of Social History* 18 (Winter 1984): 233–46; James Gilbert Ryan, "The Memphis Riots of 1866," *Journal of Negro History* 62 (1977): 243–57; James Hathaway, "A Social History of the Negro in Memphis" (Ph.D. diss., Yale Univ., 1934), 77–80; A. A. Taylor, *The Negro in Tennessee, 1865–1880* (New York: Associated Publishers, Inc., 1941), 86; *Tri-State Defender,* July 6, 1991.
38. See Holloway, *The Politics of the Southern Negro,* 281, 286–87; Tucker, *Memphis Since Crump,* 118–21, 133–36.
39. For examples, see Honey, *Southern Labor and Black Civil Rights,* 61–63; *Memphis World,* June 29 and July 9, 1948; *Press-Scimitar,* Oct. 18–21, 1971; Oct. 28, 1971; Dec. 6, 1971; Dec. 10, 1971; Oct. 1, 1973; Oct. 9, 1973; Apr. 8, 1975; *Commercial Appeal,* Aug. 6, 1916; Jan. 12–15, 1983; Jan. 25, 1983; Feb. 23, 1983; Nov. 10, 1984; Tony Jones, "How Police Board Evolved," *Tri-State Defender,* Nov. 12–16, 1994.
40. For example, see Sandra Vaughn, "Memphis: Heart of the Mid-South," 105.
41. Capers, "Memphis: Satrapy of a Benevolent Despot," 216. See also Elazar, *American Federalism,* 106–7; Logan, *The Betrayal of the Negro,* 300. For a more general discussion of the racial divide in southern politics, see Joel Williamson, The Crucible of Race (New York: Oxford, 1984); Paul Lewinsohn, *Race, Class and Party: A History of Negro Suffrage and White Politics in the South* (New York: Russell and Russell, 1963); V. O. Key, *Southern Politics in State and Nation* (New York: Knopf, 1949), chapters 1, 24, 25, and 30; Holloway, *The Politics of the Southern Negro,* 26; Brownell and Goldfield, *The City in Southern History,* 17; James Geschwender, "Social Structure and the Negro Revolt," *Social Forces* 43 (1964–65): 248–56.
42. William Miller, *Memphis During the Progressive Era* (Memphis: Memphis State Univ. Press, 1957), 23.
43. John Terreo, "Reporting by Memphis Newspapers Prior to the 1866 Race Riot and During the 1968 Sanitation Strike: A Historical Study" (master's thesis, Memphis State Univ., 1987), 47–48.

44. Gloria Brown Melton, "Blacks in Memphis, Tennessee, 1920–1955" (Ph.D. diss., Washington State Univ., 1982), 49.

45. Biles, *Memphis in the Great Depression*, 14.

46. See T. O. Fuller, *The Inter-Racial Blue Book* (Memphis: Inter-Racial League, 1925).

47. Holloway, *The Politics of the Southern Negro*, 297.

48. Ibid., 27–28.

49. Lester Lamon, *Black Tennesseans, 1900–1930* (Knoxville: Univ. of Tennessee Press, 1977), 223.

50. Jalenak, "Beale Street Politics," 92.

51. Laura Stein and Arnold Fleischman, "Newspaper and Business Endorsements in Municipal Elections," *Journal of Urban Affairs* 9 (Fall 1987): 325–36.

52. *Commercial Appeal*, Oct. 6, 1993.

53. See Kenneth Neill, "Mr. Crump: The Making of a Boss," *Memphis Magazine* (Oct. 1972): 28–37.

54. See Capers, "Memphis: Satrapy of a Benevolent Despot," 221; Holloway, *The Politics of the Southern Negro*, 278.

55. For example, see Jalenak, "Beale Street Politics," chapter 2; David Tucker, *Lieutenant Lee of Beale Street* (Nashville: Vanderbilt Univ. Press, 1971), 18–19; Walter Adkins, "Beale Street Goes to the Polls" (Ph.D. diss., Ohio State Univ., 1935), 22–25. It should also be noted that the poll tax was virtually the only legal impediment to voting imposed by the state of Tennessee. A "white primary" later was allowed by local option, but the Memphis area turned it down.

56. See Miller, Mr. Crump of Memphis; Key, Southern Politics, chapter 4; Capers, "Memphis: Satrapy of a Benevolent Despot," 216–34; Waldo Zimmerman, "Mr. Crump's Legacy," *Memphis Magazine* (Oct. 1984): 14–18, 87–89.

57. Capers, "Memphis: Satrapy of a Benevolent Despot," 226, 230; Roger Biles, "Ed Crump Versus the Unions," *Labor History* 25 (Fall 1984): 533–52; Honey, *Southern Labor and Black Civil Rights*.

58. For example, see Honey, *Southern Labor and Black Civil Rights*; Annette Church and Roberta Church, *The Robert R. Churches* (Ann Arbor: Univ. of Michigan Press, 1974), 189; Zimmerman, "Mr. Crump's Legacy," 87.

59. In both 1950 and 1951, Memphis was named the "cleanest" city in America. On seventeen other occasions, it was also named the "quietest." See Capers, "Memphis: Satrapy of a Benevolent Despot," 222.

60. Ibid.

61. Robinson, "Impact of the City on Rural Immigrants to Memphis," 31.

62. Biles, *Memphis in the Great Depression*, 29.

63. Capers, "Memphis: Satrapy of a Benevolent Despot," 225.

64. Biles, *Memphis in the Great Depression*, 30.

65. Capers, "Memphis: Satrapy of a Benevolent Despot," 218.

66. Ibid., 254–55.

67. See *Press-Scimitar*, Dec. 6, 1940.

68. Harkins, *Metropolis of the American Nile*, 142.

69. Ibid., 146.

70. Tucker, *Memphis Since Crump*, 160.

71. See Joan Beifuss, *At the River I Stand* (Memphis: B & W Books, 1985), 165. Beifuss does an excellent job of chronicling the events related to the strike and the assassination.

72. Jackson Baker, "Profile of Henry Loeb," *Memphis Magazine* (Jan. 1980), 26.

73. Harkins, *Metropolis of the American Nile*, 143.

74. Interview with a Loeb staff member.

75. Cornell Christian, "Blood and Strife Bought Dignity for City Workers," *Commercial Appeal*, Feb. 28, 1993.

76. Baker, "Henry Loeb," 28.

77. Thomas Cowan, *Values and Policy in Shelby County, Tennessee* (Memphis: Christian Brothers College Study, 1979), 18.

78. John Daniel, "Memphis 1975: The Campaign Strategy of a Black Political Candidate" (honors thesis, Southwestern at Memphis College, 1976), 7.

79. Harkins, *Metropolis of the American Nile*, 143.

80. Baker, "Henry Loeb," 29.

81. Ibid., 31.

82. Ibid., 27.

83. Harkins, *Metropolis of the American Nile*, 149.

84. Beifuss, *At the River I Stand*, 165.

85. Ibid., 163.

86. Interview with a Loeb staff member.

87. Baker, "Henry Loeb," 25.

88. Jalenak, "Beale Street Politics," 66–69.

89. Baker, "Henry Loeb," 29–30.

90. Ibid., 30. This controversy is further documented by William Wright, *Memphis Politics: An Example of Racial Bloc Voting* (New York: McGraw-Hill, 1962).

91. Baker, "Henry Loeb," 28.

92. Interview with a Loeb staff member.

93. William Street, "Black Vote Figures Heavily in Races," *Commercial Appeal*, Sept. 21, 1971.

94. Ed Weathers, "Wyeth Chandler: The Man in City Hall," *Memphis Magazine* (July 1981): 60.

95. Interview with a Chandler staff member.
96. Weathers, "Wyeth Chandler," 61.
97. Ibid., 62.
98. Interview with a Chandler staff member.
99. This race has been very effectively chronicled by Daniel, "Memphis 1975."
100. Ibid., 24.
101. Ibid., 45–46.
102. Ibid.
103. One author of this book sponsored such a get-together, since he had known Higgs professionally through an internship program. He invited residents of the neighborhood and college professors.
104. Daniel, "Memphis 1975," 32–33.
105. Ibid., 38–48.
106. Ibid.
107. Ibid., 49.
108. Harkins, *Metropolis of the American Nile*, 170.
109. *Commercial Appeal*, Sept. 19, 1987.
110. For a general discussion of early white leadership in the struggle for black civil rights in the South, see John Egerton, *Speak Now Against the Day* (New York: Knopf, 1994). Or, for a local example, see David Waters, "Lynching Drove Rabbi to Lead Local Klan Attack," *Commercial Appeal*, Mar. 26, 1995.
111. For example, see Tucker, *Memphis Since Crump*, chapters 7 and 8.
112. Ibid., 163.
113. For example, see Neal Pierce, "Sparking an Economic Comeback in Memphis," *National Journal*, Apr. 11, 1987, 889.

    As of the 1990 census, the city of Memphis contained approximately six hundred thousand residents. Shelby County encompassed those six hundred thousand and roughly another two hundred thousand in both incorporated and unincorporated outlying areas. Shelby County adopted a strong mayor-council system in 1974, and it gradually assumed administrative responsibility for such countywide services as health care, property assessment, and land-use planning. The city provided its citizens with all other services (including schools), while the county provided basic services for those living outside the city limits. Bill Morris was Shelby County mayor from 1978 to 1994.
114. Michael Kirby, *Memphis Poll 1993*, City of Memphis, Finance Division, 1993.
115. For example, of the seventy-seven largest cities in the United States, Memphis ranks seventy-fifth in the percentage of residents speaking a native language other than English, and seventy-sixth in the percentage of its people born in a foreign country. See the Department of Commerce, *City*

and County Data Book 1994 (Washington, D.C., Government Printing Office, 1994), xxix.

116. Nicholas Lemann, *The Promised Land* (New York: Alfred Knopf, Inc., 1991), chapter 1.

117. Selma Lewis, "Social Religion and the Memphis Sanitation Strike" (Ph.D. diss., Memphis State Univ., 1976), 154.

118. The reference is to community organizer Saul Alinsky. For more detail, see Saul Alinsky, *Rules for Radicals* (New York: Random House, 1971).

119. Terreo, "Reporting by Memphis Newspapers," 58.

120. Sigafoos, Cotton Row to Beale Street, 337.

121. *Commercial Appeal*, Oct. 1, 1993.

122. For more discussion of whether the "New South" is more myth or reality, see Bullard, *In Search of the New South*; Chet Fuller, "I Hear Them Call It the New South," *Black Enterprise* 12 (Nov. 1981): 41–43.

2. The Hackett Years

1. Ed Weathers, "A Tale of Two Mayors," *Memphis Magazine* (May 1984): 92.

2. Charles Bernsen, "Different Paths Converge in Race for City Mayor," *Commercial Appeal*, Sept. 2, 1991.

3. Marc Perrusquia, "Hackett: Mayor's Priority Is Economic Development," *Commercial Appeal*, Jan. 14, 1990.

4. Ibid.

5. Jim Balentine, "Mayor Hopefuls Vow 'Clean' Race," *Press-Scimitar*, Oct. 13, 1982.

6. Richard C. Hackett, personal interview, Dec. 1, 1992; Weathers, "A Tale of Two Mayors," 97.

7. *Commercial Appeal*, Jan. 22, 1990.

8. Weathers, "A Tale of Two Mayors," 93.

9. Ibid.; Kay Pittman Black, "Dick Hackett: Peanut Butter Sandwiches and a Sense of Thrift," *Press-Scimitar*, Nov. 6, 1982.

10. Kay Pittman Black, "Hackett Refuses to Echo Blasts," *Press-Scimitar*, Nov. 23, 1982.

11. Balentine, "Mayor Hopefuls Vow 'Clean' Race."

12. Jim Balentine, "13 Qualify for Mayor's Race," *Press-Scimitar*, Oct. 12, 1982.

13. Pollster John Bakke, cited in Kay Pittman Black, "Politics Watchers Say Class, Race Will Pick Mayor," *Press-Scimitar*, Nov. 13, 1982.

14. Ford Worthly, "Booming American Cities," *Fortune*, Aug. 17, 1987, 30–36.

15. John Branston, "The Hackett Style," *Commercial Appeal*, Jan. 26, 1986.

16. Kay Pittman Black, "New Mayor Won't Have Bodyguards," *Press-Scimitar*, Dec. 10, 1982.

17. Kay Pittman Black, "Hackett: Hard Worker with the Common Touch," *Press-Scimitar*, Dec. 21, 1982.
18. Weathers, "A Tale of Two Mayors," 78.
19. Charles Bernsen, "Different Paths Converge in Race for City Mayor," *Commercial Appeal*, Sept. 2, 1991.
20. Branston, "The Hackett Style."
21. Weathers, "A Tale of Two Mayors," 79.
22. Black, "Hackett: Hard Worker with the Common Touch."
23. *Commercial Appeal*, Nov. 5, 1992; Bernsen, "Different Paths Converge in Race for City Mayor."
24. Broughton quoted in Bernsen, "Different Paths Converge in Race for City Mayor."
25. Ibid.
26. Weathers, "A Tale of Two Mayors," 93; Clark Porteous, "He Delves Into Complaints First-Hand," *Press-Scimitar*, Dec. 12, 1973.
27. Perrusquia, "Hackett: Mayor's Priority Is Economic Development."
28. Richard C. Hackett, personal interview, Dec. 1, 1992.
29. Jerry Huston and Jimmie Covington, "Hackett's Tax Agenda and Tenure Are Fodder for Critics," *Commercial Appeal*, Sept. 29, 1991.
30. Richard C. Hackett, speech to Rotary Club, WMC TV-5, Oct. 1, 1991.
31. Debt service, for instance, only increased from 15 to 18 percent of total budget. General obligation debt actually declined in current dollars from 434.5 million in 1983 to 403.3 million in 1990. And the debt to value of property ratio declined from 16 percent to 11 percent during that time. For example, see Huston and Covington, "Hackett's Tax Agenda and Tenure Are Fodder for Critics."
32. Richard C. Hackett, personal interview, Dec. 1, 1992.
33. Richard C. Hackett, Speech to the Rotary Club.
34. Charles Bernsen, "Hackett and Herenton Back City Tax Reform," *Commercial Appeal*, Sept. 25, 1991.
35. Deborah Lohse, "100 Metro Area Tax Bills," *Money*, Jan. 1993, 99–101. These figures also mean that housing is cheaper to purchase in Memphis, in addition to the city having a lower tax burden for appraised value.
36. Anna Byrd Davis, "Which Tax Delivers the Most Burdens the Least?" *Commercial Appeal*, Feb. 15, 1993.
37. However, the fact that Tennessee in general is a low property tax state can be seen in the fact that both Nashville and Knoxville ranked lower than Memphis.
38. Charles Bernsen, "Herenton Inherits City of Promise, Problems," *Commercial Appeal*, Dec. 29, 1991.
39. International Paper eventually settled in east Memphis, brought many of its employees from New York, and many of those employees chose to live

in areas outside the city. This move indicates the problems of trying to stimulate job growth in the city, as the areas outside the city may end up drawing away much of the economic development.

40. Working with those in the private and public sector, he was able to get the state of Tennessee to pledge twenty-five million dollars for research facilities and chairs of excellence in pediatric research shared by the university and St. Jude. Mission for Memphis, a group of business leaders, was able to raise nineteen million dollars from private donors. And the city also provided St. Jude with an adjacent building, previously used by Memphis Light Gas and Water.

41. *Commercial Appeal*, Mar. 29, 1991.

42. Weathers, "A Tale of Two Mayors," 97.

43. Kay Pittman Black, "Hackett Woos Support from Voters He 'Lost,'" *Press-Scimitar*, Jan. 21, 1983.

44. Allan Brettman, "Ramses Showing Wide Reach," *Commercial Appeal*, May 13, 1987.

45. Thomas Jordan, "Partners," *Commercial Appeal*, Mar. 29, 1987. Shortly after Hackett's defeat, the city's NFL bid failed, as Charlotte and Jacksonville were selected instead.

46. The bureau was not able to provide information on the number of visitors coming from outside the city.

47. Jerry Huston, "Memphis Targets '93 for Tourism Delights," *Commercial Appeal*, Feb. 21, 1993.

48. Thomas Jordan and Charles Bernsen, "Mayor Veers Moderately from Conservative Image," *Commercial Appeal*, Oct. 2, 1983.

49. John Beifuss, "Downtown Dreams Find Concrete Footing," *Commercial Appeal*, May 30, 1993.

50. Charles Bernsen, "Catalogue of Events in the Development of the Pyramid," *Commercial Appeal*, Sept. 10–15, 1989.

51. Charles Bernsen, "Pyramid Plans Mesh with Shlenker," *Commercial Appeal*, Sept. 15, 1989.

52. Gary Moore, ". . . and the Mall Came Tumbling Down," *Memphis Flyer*, June 24, 1992.

53. John Fisher, "HUD Letter to MHA Chairman," *Commercial Appeal*, Aug. 3, 1991.

54. Marc Perrusquia and Jerry Markon, "Mayor Says MHA Officials Must Go," *Commercial Appeal*, Jan. 22, 1992.

55. "Wade Resigns, Agrees to Fee to 'Consult,'" *Commercial Appeal*, Sept. 18, 1984.

56. See *Tri-State Defender*, Mar. 16, 1991.

57. Paula Wade, "HUD Tells Memphis to Spend Surplus," *Commercial Appeal*, Sept. 1, 1989.

58. City of Memphis, *CHAS: Five Year Comprehensive Housing Affordability Strategy*, City of Memphis, Division of Housing and Community Development, Oct. 1991, 9, 11, 24, 27, 28, and 32.

59. Enterprise Foundation, *Memphis, Tenn: An Assessment Report on Housing Needs, Programs and Public/Private Partnership Opportunities* (Columbia, Md.: Enterprise Foundation, 1992), 13, 15, 17.

60. Charles Bernsen, "Mayor Touts 5-Year Plan to Renovate, Add Housing," *Commercial Appeal*, Sept. 15, 1994.

61. Michael Kirby, "Implementation and the Code Enforcement Process," unpublished paper presented at the annual meeting of the Urban Affairs Association, Vancouver, Apr. 1991.

62. Dave Hirschman, "Cooper Project Lives Again," *Commercial Appeal*, Oct. 25, 1990.

63. Richard C. Hackett, speech to Rotary Club, WMC TV-5, Oct. 1, 1991.

64. Guy Reel, "Others Hold the Reins, but School Funding Is Big Mayoral Issue," *Commercial Appeal*, Sept. 22, 1991.

65. Ibid.

66. Bernsen, "Mayor Touts 5-Year Plan."

3. Black Politics

1. For out-migration, see Vaughn, "Memphis: Heart of the Mid-South," 102; Jimmie Covington, "Jobs in '80s Revamped Population of County: Young Blacks Left and Whites Arrived," *Commercial Appeal*, May 26, 1992.

2. For example, see Vaughn, "Memphis: Heart of the Mid-South," 99–115; Ira Berlin, *Slaves Without Masters* (New York: Pantheon, 1974).

3. Holloway, *The Politics of the Southern Negro*, 272; Jalenak, "Beale Street Politics," chapters 7 and 9. For a more general discussion of antebellum southern cities as incubators for black leaders, see Berlin, *Slaves Without Masters*; Daniel Thompson, *Negro Leadership Class* (Englewood Cliffs, N.J.: Prentice-Hall, 1963).

4. Holloway, *The Politics of the Southern Negro*, 302.

5. See F. Ray Marshall and Arvil Van Adams, "Negro Employment in Memphis," *Industrial Relations* 9 (May 1970): 308–23; Katherine McFate, ed., *The Metropolitan Area Fact Book* (Washington, D.C.: Joint Center for Political Studies, 1989); Davis, "Against the Odds"; Vaughn, "Memphis: Heart of the Mid-South"; Melton, "Blacks in Memphis, Tennessee"; Jalenak, "Beale Street Politics," 163–66; Goldfield, *Cotton Fields and Skyscrapers*. As for black community fissures and mass suspicion of black leaders, see Charles Williams Jr., "Two Black Communities in Memphis, Tennessee: A Study in Urban Socio-Political Structure" (Ph.D. diss., Univ. of Illinois, 1982).

6. George Lee letter appearing in the *Baltimore Afro-American,* June 8, 1929. Also see his comments in *The Messenger* (July 1925): 252–53.

7. *Commercial Appeal,* July 18, 1993. See also Cindy Wolff, "Distribution Jobs Are a Boon to Area; Experts Also Want Manufacturing," *Commercial Appeal,* July 3, 1994.

8. For example, see Lewinsohn, *Race, Class and Party,* 139; Davis, "Against the Odds," 211.

9. See Lee, *Beale Street,* 13.

10. W. E. B. DuBois, *The Souls of Black Folks* (Chicago: McClung, 1903).

11. See Melton, "Blacks in Memphis, Tennessee," 32.

12. *Press-Scimitar,* Apr. 19, 1952. See also Church and Church, *The Robert R. Churches.*

13. See Vaughn, "Memphis: Heart of the Mid-South," 100; Lewinsohn, *Race, Class and Party,* 139.

14. See Vaughn, "Memphis: Heart of the Mid-South," 113–15.

15. Davis, "Against the Odds," 223. Also, see Kenneth Wald, "The Electoral Base of Political Machines," *Urban Affairs Quarterly* 16 (Sept. 1980): 6.

16. See William Cohen, "Negro Involuntary Servitude in the South, 1865–1940," *Journal of Southern History* 42 (Feb. 1976): 39.

17. Davis, "Against the Odds," 50–55.

18. Ibid., 292–96. See also Jalenak, "Beale Street Politics," 32, 163–66.

19. See Vaughn, "Memphis: Heart of the Mid-South," 112.

20. Goldfield, *Cotton Fields and Skyscrapers,* 166.

21. Ibid., 191.

22. Ibid., 166.

23. U. S. Department of Commerce, Bureau of the Census, *Census of the Population, 1990* (Washington, D.C.: Government Printing Office, 1991).

24. Booker T. Washington, *Up from Slavery* (Garden City, N.Y.: Doubleday, 1963).

25. Lamon, *Black Tennesseans.*

26. *Chicago Defender,* Apr. 24, 1915.

27. *Commercial Appeal,* Aug. 14, 1916.

28. Ibid., Oct. 22, 1916. And similarly, see *Chicago Defender,* May 28, 1918.

29. *Commercial Appeal,* Dec. 4, 1916.

30. See John Dollard, *Caste and Class in a Southern Town* (New Haven: Yale Univ. Press, 1938), 290.

31. Howard Rabinowitz, *Race Relations in the South, 1865–1890* (New York: Oxford Univ. Press, 1978), 336. Specifically, see *Commercial Appeal,* Nov. 11, 1916; Oct. 29, 1916; Aug. 6, 1916; *Chicago Defender,* Mar. 2, 1918. See also Melton, "Blacks in Memphis, Tennessee," 202.

32. Holloway, *The Politics of the Southern Negro,* 287.

33. For example, see Melton, "Blacks in Memphis, Tennessee," 363–64; Vaughn, "Memphis: Heart of the Mid-South," 107; Holloway, *The Politics of the Southern Negro*, 287. As for the 1968 sanitation strike, see Beifuss, *At the River I Stand*; Tucker, *Memphis Since Crump*, chapters 3 and 9; Robert Bailey, "The 1968 Memphis Sanitation Strike" (master's thesis, Memphis State Univ., 1974).

34. For example, see Honey, *Southern Labor and Black Civil Rights*; *Memphis World*, Aug. 8 and Aug. 25, 1944; *Chicago Defender*, Sept. 22, 1917; May 1, 1920; Tucker, *Memphis Since Crump*, chapter 3.

35. *Memphis World*, Aug. 8 and 25, 1944.

36. See Beifuss, *At the River I Stand*; Bailey, "The 1968 Memphis Sanitation Strike"; Tucker, *Memphis Since Crump*, chapter 9.

37. Tucker, *Memphis Since Crump*, 161.

38. See Melton, "Blacks in Memphis, Tennessee," 14.

39. See Price, *The Negro Voter in the South*, 68.

40. For example, see Melton, "Blacks in Memphis, Tennessee," 363–64; Vaughn, "Memphis: Heart of the Mid-South," 107.

41. See Melton, "Blacks in Memphis, Tennessee," 253.

42. Tucker, *Memphis Since Crump*, 142.

43. *Commercial Appeal*, Sept. 20, 1982.

44. Attorney John Ryder, former Republican county chairman, quoted in Jackson Baker, "Election Aftermath as Simple as Black and White?" *Memphis Flyer*, Aug. 13–19, 1992.

45. For example, see Adkins, "Beale Street Goes to the Polls," 6. Also note, however, that Tennessee had one of the smallest African-American populations in the South, e.g., see V. O. Key, *Southern Politics in State and Nation*, 10. For context of historical black voting patterns, see Jalenak, "Beale Street Politics," 175; William Brink and Louis Harris, *Black and White* (New York: Simon and Schuster, 1966), 74; Holloway, *The Politics of the Southern Negro*, 346.

46. For example, see Tucker, *Lieutenant Lee of Beale Street*, chapter 1; Taylor, *The Negro in Tennessee*, 155, 233, and 249.

47. For example, see Nate Hobbs, "Can Shelby GOP Attract Blacks to the Party?" *Commercial Appeal*, Feb. 27, 1994.

48. See Lynette Wrenn, "Commission Government in the Gilded Age," *Tennessee Historical Quarterly* 47 (Winter 1988): 216–26.

49. Joseph Cartwright, *The Triumph of Jim Crow* (Knoxville: Univ. of Tennessee Press, 1976), 137–39.

50. The Tennessee Supreme Court upheld the constitutionality of the poll tax in *Biggs* v. *Beeler* 180 Tenn 198.

51. For example, Robert Church Jr. was chosen as a delegate to the Republi-

can National Convention in 1896 and to each of the conventions from 1912 through 1940. His daughter, Roberta, was elected to the executive committee of the Tennessee Republican Party in 1952. Her father had been the only black on that committee earlier in the century. See *The Colored American*, Mar. 24, 1900; *Press-Scimitar*, Aug. 20, 1952.

52. For example, see *Commercial Appeal*, Oct. 21, 1916. See also Church and Church, *The Robert R. Churches*; Roger Biles, "Robert R. Church, Jr., of Memphis," *Tennessee Historical Quarterly* 42 (Winter 1983): 362–83.

53. See Melton, "Blacks in Memphis, Tennessee," 41–42; Lamon, *Black Tennesseans*; Biles, "Robert R. Church, Jr., of Memphis."

54. Holloway, *The Politics of the Southern Negro*, 272 and 346. See also Jalenak, "Beale Street Politics," chapters 7 and 9.

55. Jalenak, "Beale Street Politics," 114.

56. *Memphis World*, Aug. 3, 1960.

57. For example, see Linda Williams, "White-Black Perceptions of the Electability of Black Candidates," *National Political Science Review* 2 (1990): 45–64.

58. Brink and Harris, *Black and White*, 74.

59. For example, see Vaughn, "Memphis: Heart of the Mid-South," 100.

60. W. C. Handy, ed., *A Treasure of Blues* (New York: C. Boni, 1949), 18.

61. For example, see Jalenak, "Beale Street Politics," chapter 2; Jonathan Daniels, "He Suits Memphis," *Saturday Evening Post*, June 10, 1939; Randolph Meade Walker, "The Role of the Black Clergy in Memphis During the Crump Era," *West Tennessee Historical Papers* 33 (Oct. 1979): 33.

62. Lewinsohn, *Race, Class and Party*, 162. See also Holloway, *The Politics of the Southern Negro*, 280; Price, *The Negro Voter in the South*, 31; Gunnar Myrdal, *The American Dilemma* (New York: Harper and Brothers, 1949), 486; Jalenak, "Beale Street Politics," chapter 2.

63. Lewinsohn, *Race, Class and Party*, 120, 138, and 162.

64. For example, see Biles, "Robert R. Church, Jr., of Memphis," 362–82; Adkins, "Beale Street Goes to the Polls," 59; Lewinsohn, *Race, Class and Party*, 139–41; Tucker, *Memphis Since Crump*, 18–19 and 133; Vaughn, "Memphis: Heart of the Mid-South," 116.

65. For example, see Tucker, *Memphis Since Crump*, chapter 1; Williams, "Two Black Communities in Memphis, Tennessee," 40–42.

66. Early levels of black voter registration cannot be determined precisely, however, because there were no systematically collected records prior to 1951 when Tennessee first adopted a permanent voter registration law. Yet, it is clear when examining the first official records available that the Crump machine, at least in its late stages, had not been registering the large majority of black voters. Only 20 percent were registered in 1951,

and that was after the first of a number of large registration drives. For example, see Wright, *Memphis Politics*, 27. As for declining rewards, see Ralph Bunche, *The Political Status of the Negro in the Age of FDR* (Chicago: Univ. of Chicago Press, 1973), 493–502.

67. Holloway, *The Politics of the Southern Negro*, 291. See also Tucker, *Memphis Since Crump.*

68. For example, see Melton, "Blacks in Memphis, Tennessee," 330–32.

69. See Matthews and Prothro, *Negroes and the New Southern Politics*, 148–62.

70. See Bass and DeVries, *The Transformation of Southern Politics*; Holloway, *The Politics of the Southern Negro*, 327 and 335–36; Key, *Southern Politics in State and Nation*, 648.

71. See David Tucker, *Black Pastors and Leaders, 1819–1972* (Memphis: Memphis State Univ. Press, 1975); Walker, "The Role of the Black Clergy in Memphis," 38–43; Rabinowitz, *Race Relations in the Urban South*, chapter 2.

72. See Tucker, *Black Pastors and Leaders*; Walker, "The Role of the Black Clergy in Memphis," 29–47; Lewinsohn, *Race, Class and Party*, 140–41; Jalenak, "Beale Street Politics." For a more general discussion of the role of the black church in southern politics, see Charles V. Hamilton, *The Black Preacher in American Politics* (New York: Morrow, 1972); Franklin Frazier, *The Negro Church in America* (New York: Schocken Books, 1964); St. Clair Drake and Horace Cayton, *Black Metropolis* (New York: Harper and Row, 1945); Holloway, *The Politics of the Southern Negro*, 22–23; Price, *The Negro Voter in the South*, 68–69; Key, *Southern Politics*, 654.

73. See Wright, *Memphis Politics*, 8.

74. *Memphis World*, Nov. 11, 1955, article described in Melton, "Blacks in Memphis, Tennessee," 346–47.

75. See Jalenak, "Beale Street Politics," 82; Vaughn, "Memphis: Heart of the Mid-South," 117; Holloway, *The Politics of the Southern Negro*, 291.

76. "Single-shot voting" is a strategy whereby voters cast fewer than their allocated number of votes in order to increase the likelihood of electing a preferred candidate or candidates. For example, if a voter may vote for as many as five people to fill five vacancies in a multimember district, the voter might cast a vote for only the most preferred candidate so that votes for the others do not decrease the most preferred candidate's chances of election. Examples of the white reaction to this practice can be seen in the *Commercial Appeal*, Sept. 17 and 18, 1958.

77. For example, see *Memphis World*, July 4, 1959.

78. Jalenak, "Beale Street Politics," 66 and 69; *Commercial Appeal*, June 17, 1959.

79. *Commercial Appeal*, Aug. 2, 1959.
80. Wright, *Memphis Politics*, 31.
81. *Press-Scimitar*, Oct. 18, 1963. See also Oct. 12, 1963, 12; Oct. 16, 1963; Nov. 4, 1963.
82. See Holloway, *The Politics of the Southern Negro*, 286.
83. *Commercial Appeal*, Feb. 6, 1966.
84. For example, see Holloway, *The Politics of the Southern Negro*, 298–99.
85. Ibid., 293.
86. See Tucker, *Memphis Since Crump*, 141.
87. For detailed analysis, see *Press-Scimitar*, Feb. 12, 1976.
88. For example, see *Commercial Appeal*, Sept. 20, 1982; Williams, "Two Black Communities in Memphis, Tennessee," 103–6; Jalenak, "Beale Street Politics," 120–21.
89. For good general reference on blacks in Memphis and in Tennessee, see Taylor, *The Negro in Tennessee*.
90. *Press-Scimitar*, Feb. 12, 1976. See also the *Commercial Appeal*, Sept. 22, 1976; Oct. 11, 1976.
91. There was a runoff election in both 1975 and 1979.
92. Williams, "Two Black Communities in Memphis, Tennessee," 101–2.
93. For example, see Kay Pittman Black, "Whites Financing Higgs, Ford Says," *Press-Scimitar*, Aug. 10, 1983.
94. See Terry Keeter, "John Ford Endorses Gibbons in Mayor Race," *Commercial Appeal*, Sept. 9, 1987.
95. *Commercial Appeal*, Oct. 25, 1987.
96. Ibid.

4. Dr. W. W. Herenton

1. Much of this and subsequent discussions of Herenton's background have been drawn from the following four accounts: Vernon E. Ash, *Dr. W. W. Herenton* (Memphis: Withers Photographe, 1992); Larry Conley, "Profile: Willie Herenton," *Memphis Magazine* (Dec. 1980): 33–40; Cornell Christian and Michael Kelley, "Fight for Equity Keeps Herenton in the Ring," *Commercial Appeal*, Sept. 2, 1991; Larry Conley, "Willie Herenton Speaks Out," *Memphis Magazine* (Nov. 1989): 38–49.
2. Christian and Kelley, "Fight for Equity Keeps Herenton in the Ring."
3. Herenton quoted in Vernon Ash, "Herenton Poses Plan for Black Summit," *Tri-State Defender*, Mar. 16–20, 1991.
4. Herenton quoted in Leanne Kleinmann, "Pluck, Luck or Politics?" *Memphis Magazine* (Feb. 1992): 42.
5. Herenton, quoted in Conley, "Profile: Willie Herenton," 40.

6. Ash, *Dr. W. W. Herenton*, 14.

7. Ibid.

8. Conley, "Profile: Willie Herenton," 37; Ash, *Dr. W. W. Herenton*, 26.

9. Christian and Kelley, "Fight for Equity Keeps Herenton in the Ring."

10. Herenton quoted in ibid.

11. Ibid.

12. Kleinmann, "Pluck, Luck or Politics," 28.

13. Herenton quoted in Conley, "Profile: Willie Herenton," 38.

14. Christian and Kelley, "Fight for Equity Keeps Herenton in the Ring."

15. Conley, "Willie Herenton Speaks Out," 42.

16. *Press-Scimitar*, Dec. 6, 1978.

17. See Williams, "Two Black Communities in Memphis, Tennessee," 69–70.

18. Brown quoted in Kleinmann, "Pluck, Luck or Politics," 28.

19. Herenton quoted in Conley, "Profile: Willie Herenton," 37.

20. Blackburn quoted in Kleinmann, "Pluck, Luck or Politics," 29.

21. Sonnenburg quoted in ibid., 29.

22. Mauney quoted in Conley, "Profile: Willie Herenton," 38.

23. Herenton quoted in Ash, "Herenton Poses Plan for Black Summit."

24. For example, see George Noblit and Thomas Collins, "School Flight and School Policy: Desegregation and Resegregation in the Memphis City Schools," *Urban Review* 10 (Fall 1978): 203–12.

25. For example, the city's top administrators remained approximately half white and half black throughout his tenure as superintendent. See Jimmie Covington, "Herenton's Fast Start in Schools Was Stalled by Turmoil," *Commercial Appeal*, Sept. 29, 1991.

26. Herenton quoted in Conley, "Profile: Willie Herenton," 36.

27. Herenton quoted in ibid., 35.

28. These programs grew to the point that they existed in twenty-six separate schools by the time Herenton retired as superintendent in June of 1991.

29. Herenton quoted in Conley, "Profile: Willie Herenton," 34.

30. John Branston, "Herenton Says Working Style Won't Change," *Commercial Appeal*, Sept. 27, 1989.

31. See Edward W. Hill and Heidi Marie Rock, "Race and Inner-City Education," in George Galster and Edward Hills, eds., *The Metropolis in Black and White* (New Brunswick, N.J.: Center for Urban Policy Research, 1992), 124. New York's dropout rate is estimated to be 40 percent, with Chicago, Cleveland, Detroit, and Milwaukee having rates between 40 and 50 percent.

32. The ACT test is a basic college-entrance exam, designed to predict a student's likelihood of academic success in college. The range of test scores is between 1 and 36.

33. *Commercial Appeal*, Sept. 29, 1991.
34. Conley, "Willie Herenton Speaks Out," 42. The discrepancies between SAT and ACT averages apparently have to do with the different populations that took these two exams.
35. Conley, "Willie Herenton Speaks Out," 42.
36. Covington, "Herenton's Fast Start in Schools Was Stalled by Turmoil."
37. Herenton quoted in Conley, "Profile: Willie Herenton," 33.
38. *Commercial Appeal*, Sept. 29, 1991.
39. The Memphis school budget is semi-autonomous. Each year, the superintendent proposes an operating budget to the board, which then reviews it and, in turn, passes along its final proposed budget to the city council for approval. As a modified special district, the Memphis city schools do not have their own taxing authority, although the city council designates a fixed percentage of the city property tax to go to school funding. The city and county governments also allocate additional funds to the schools, although these funds make up only a small proportion of the school system's overall revenues. Thereafter, however, expenditure decisions are left largely to the schools, with minimal governmental interference.
40. Trends in "current dollars" are deceiving, as they do not consider the impact of economic inflation. For example, after a period of 20 percent inflation, a dollar is actually worth only eighty cents in real buying power. Thus, given the unusually high inflation rates during the late 1970s, it is clear that the "real" increase in the city schools' budget was a good deal less than the "current" dollar figure suggests.
41. The lack of air-conditioning in the city schools has been significantly improved since the mid-1980s. In-wall air-conditioning units have been added to the large majority of city classrooms. According to an internal document of the Memphis City Schools, as of the beginning of the 1994 school year, 101 (67 percent) of the schools were fully air-conditioned, seventeen (11 percent) were partially air-conditioned, four (3 percent) were beginning this renovation, and twenty-nine (19 percent) were not air-conditioned at all—some of these latter schools were slated for closing in the foreseeable future.
42. *Commercial Appeal*, Sept. 29, 1991.
43. For example, see Curtis Johnson, "The Truth on Herenton as School Supt." *Tri-State Defender*, Sept. 14–18, 1991.
44. Conley, "Profile: Willie Herenton," 36.
45. Branston, "Herenton Says Working Style Won't Change."
46. *Commercial Appeal*, July 11, 1989.
47. *Commercial Appeal*, July 6, 1989.
48. Final report, quoted in *Commercial Appeal*, Sept. 27, 1989.

49. Organization Consultants, Inc., *Memphis City Schools: A Study of Personnel Policies, Practices, and Procedures*, Sept. 1989. See also *Commercial Appeal*, Sept. 27, 1989.

50. Conley, "Willie Herenton Speaks Out," 45.

51. Ibid., 45.

52. *Commercial Appeal*, July 6, 1989; Sept. 21, 1989.

53. *Commercial Appeal*, July 6, 1989.

54. Conley, "Willie Herenton Speaks Out," 40–41.

55. Ibid., 48.

56. Ibid., 40.

57. Christian and Kelley, "Fight for Equity Keeps Herenton in the Ring."

58. Ibid.

59. *Commercial Appeal*, Sept. 21, 1989.

60. Conley, "Willie Herenton Speaks Out," 40.

61. Ibid., 42.

62. Ibid., 41.

63. Ibid., 48–49.

64. Christian and Kelley, "Fight for Equity Keeps Herenton in the Ring."

65. *Commercial Appeal*, Sept. 21, 1989.

66. Kleinmann, "Pluck, Luck or Politics," 29.

67. Ibid.

68. Terry quoted in ibid., 29.

69. Herenton quoted in ibid.

70. Herenton quoted in Conley, "Profile: Willie Herenton," 40.

71. Smith quoted in Kleinmann, "Pluck, Luck or Politics," 40.

72. Ash, *Dr. W. W. Herenton*, 6.

73. Herenton quoted in Ash, "Herenton Poses Plan for Black Summit."

74. Herenton quoted in Kleinmann, "Pluck, Luck or Politics," 42.

75. Ibid.

5. The Electoral Context

1. Up to 1991, Memphis had a runoff provision in its election law. If one candidate received a majority in the first contest, the "general election," then there was no need for a second "runoff" election. If there was only a plurality winner in the general election, however, then the top two candidates would face each other in the runoff. The figures explicitly identify which elections were runoffs. All other elections are general elections.

2. The 1975 election is well chronicled by Daniel, "Memphis 1975."

3. As a hypothetical example of polarization, black voters cast their vote as follows: black candidate A receives 60 percent of the black vote, black

candidate B receives 30 percent of the black vote, and white candidate C receives 10 percent of the black vote. The black polarization score would be 90 percent.

4. Congressman Harold Ford's general mode of endorsement is described in chapter 3 above.

5. For example, see Murray and Vedlitz, "Racial Voting Patterns in the South," 29–48. They studied the racial voting patterns of Atlanta, Houston, Dallas, New Orleans, and Memphis from 1960 to 1977.

6. As a hypothetical example, black voters cast their vote as follows: black candidate A receives 60 percent of the black vote, black candidate B receives 30 percent of the vote, and white candidate C receives 10 percent of the vote. The black bloc-voting score would be 60 percent.

7. These data reflect percentages of the total vote and not the percentage of white voters.

8. Except for the 1982 general election, there were slight differences between our regression analyses and our homogeneous precinct analyses. These ranged from 2 to 5 percent. We used the regressions and assumed that the homogeneous precincts had random errors. Even if the homogenous precinct analyses were utilized, however, that would not have changed our findings.

9. The census indicated that Memphis had approximately 1 percent "others," who were primarily categorized as Asians. These are not the same "others" reflected in the registration statistics, since some citizens do not want to specify their race. The election commission classifies these latter registrants as "others."

10. The available census categories in earlier years did not precisely match the voting population.

11. John Harkins, *Metropolis of the Nile*, 162.

12. For example, see ibid.

13. For example, see *Commercial Appeal*, Oct. 6, 1992.

14. Election commissioner quoted in ibid.

15. These cities were Nashville, Charlotte, San Antonio, Atlanta, Columbus, Indianapolis, Birmingham, Kansas City, New Orleans, Milwaukee, Detroit, Cincinnati, Baltimore, Chicago, Minneapolis, St. Louis, and Boston. Collecting these data was arduous, and there were several other cities that were not able to provide information. This data-collection effort provided additional respect for the Shelby County Election Commission, which does such a fine job collecting and disseminating registration and voting information to the public.

16. Both registration and turnout were computed by using voting age population.

17. These data total 100 percent of registrants. For example, if 80 percent of the registrants are white, then 20 percent of the registrants are black. The Memphis and Shelby County Election Commission records reflect a small number of "others," most of whom are either black or white. The "others" were assigned to black and white using the estimation procedure described in the preface.

18. Wright, *Memphis Politics*, 4–5.

19. Jalenak, "Beale Street Politics," 27.

20. Ibid., 23.

21. Thomas Ripey, "Changes in the Formal Structure of Municipal Government and Their Effect on Selected Aspects of the Legislative Process" (Ph.D. diss., Univ. of Kentucky, 1973), 96.

22. Wright, *Memphis Politics*, 2.

23. *Tri-State Defender*, June 8, 1983.

24. For example, if 60 percent of voting-age blacks are registered, then 40 percent are not registered.

25. M. Margaret Conway, *Political Participation in the United States* (Washington, D.C.: CQ Press, 1991), 28.

26. Frank R. Parker, *Black Votes Count* (Chapel Hill: Univ. of North Carolina Press, 1990), 164.

27. Ibid., 138–39.

28. Conway, *Political Participation in the United States*, 23–25.

29. *Commercial Appeal*, Feb. 10, 1991.

30. Jalenak, "Beale Street Politics," 31.

31. These data total 100 percent of turnout. For example, if 80 percent of the turnout is white voters, then 20 percent of the turnout is black voters.

32. The 1990 race was the only one without a mayoral contest, since it involved only a judicial office and county races.

33. For example, if 60 percent of voting-age blacks turn out, then 40 percent do not.

34. See Memphis and Shelby County Planning Commission, *Annexation: A Must for a Growing Memphis*; *Commercial Appeal*, Feb. 17, 1991.

35. Ibid.

36. For a fuller discussion of the fiscal implications, see Jimmie Covington, "Memphis Has 'Sprung Some Big Leaks,'" *Commercial Appeal*, July 31, 1994.

37. Tucker, *Memphis Since Crump*, 172.

38. *Press-Scimitar*, Aug. 31, 1982.

39. *Commercial Appeal*, Feb. 6, 1986.

40. Kirby, *Memphis Poll 1993* and *Memphis Poll 1994*, 1993–94.

41. See Chapter 113, Tennessee Public Acts of 1955, Sec. 6-308, et. seq.

42. When asked to interpret the act, the Tennessee Supreme Court handed

down two important rulings. First, it decided that the test of reasonable-
ness would be that the "overall well being" of both areas would have to improve. *Tennessee* v. *Pigeon Forge,* Tenn. 599 SW 2nd 545 (1980s). Second,
the court recognized the city's burden of proof and the fact that the "fairly
debatable" precedent had been supplanted. However, they also noted that
cities have a right to "orderly growth and development," especially to avoid
being hemmed in by unsafe, unsanitary, and substandard rural housing.
Pirtle v. *Jackson,* Tenn. 560 SW 2nd 400 (1977).

43. Memphis and Shelby County Office of Planning and Development, *Southeast Memphis Annexation Area,* Nov. 1987.

44. Norwood quoted in Calvin Burns, "Justice Dept. Lawsuit Stuns City," *Tri-
State Defender,* Feb. 23–27, 1991.

45. Nationwide, 70 percent of all candidates leading in the general election are
subsequently successful in a runoff. The comparable figure for African-
American candidates is only 50 percent. Thus, blacks seem to be disadvantaged by a runoff system, in that more would have been elected without it. See
Charles Bullock and Loch Johnson, *Runoff Elections in the United States*
(Chapel Hill: Univ. of North Carolina Press, 1992), 114. Bullock and Johnson
warn, however, that many of these white majorities might also prove capable
of adapting to a plurality system if it was required to defeat black candidates.

46. See *Commercial Appeal,* June 17, 1959.

47. *Commercial Appeal,* Apr. 15, 1966.

48. For example, see *Commercial Appeal,* May 13, 1966.

49. *Press-Scimitar,* May 17, 1966.

50. *Commercial Appeal,* Feb. 18, 1966.

51. The three dissenters were Jesse Turner, Vasco Smith, and Russell Sugarmon.

52. For example, see Tucker, *Memphis Since Crump,* 152–61.

53. This change was upheld by the United States Supreme Court in *Thornburg*
v. *Gingles* 478 U.S. 30 (1986).

54. See Figures 12, 13, and 14 for an empirical demonstration of this claim.

55. *United States* v. *City of Memphis,* Western District of Tennessee, Case
number 91–2139. For the significance of form on electoral participation
and results, see John Kessel, "Governmental Structure and Political Environment," *American Political Science Review* 61 (Sept. 1963): 615–20;
Robert Salisbury, "St. Louis Politics," *Western Political Quarterly* 13 (June
1960): 498–507; Robert Duggar, "The Relation of Local Government
Structure to Urban Renewal," *Law and Contemporary Problems* 26 (Jan.
1961): 49–69; Donald Rosenthal and Robert Crain, "Structure and Values
in Local Political Systems," *Journal of Politics* 28 (Feb. 1966): 169–96;
Charles Adrian and Oliver Williams, *Four Cities* (Philadelphia: Univ. of
Pennsylvania Press, 1961).

56. For example, see Ford Nelson, "Councilmen Hang Tough on Voting Suit," *Tri-State Defender*, Sept. 5, 1992.
57. For example, see ibid.

6. The Hackett Campaign

1. Branston, "The Hackett Style."
2. Ibid.
3. Ibid.
4. Dr. John Bakke, personal interview, Aug. 26, 1994.
5. Michael Kelley, "Unofficial Results: 172-Vote Win over Hackett," *Commercial Appeal*, Oct. 4, 1991.
6. To our knowledge, John Bakke's polls were the only systematic citywide polls conducted during the course of the campaign. Immediately after Labor Day, the Bakke polls showed Hackett leading Herenton citywide by a margin of 43 percent to 26 percent, with 20 percent undecided. That lead narrowed in a poll conducted roughly two weeks prior to the election, with Hackett now ahead 39 percent to 27 percent and 24 percent undecided. Then, the weekend before the election, his polling showed Hackett leading 38 percent to 27 percent with 22 percent undecided. As for the undecideds, twice as many blacks as whites fell into this category across all three polls.

    In terms of race, the second poll had shown Hackett support slipping in the black community (dropping from 12 percent to 10 percent). The final one showed it slipping to the point (10 percent to 5 percent) that Herenton now appeared to have at least a chance to win should the disproportionate number of black undecided voters support him at comparable rates.
7. Richard C. Hackett, personal interview, Dec. 1, 1992.
8. Ibid.
9. WMC TV-5, newscast, Oct. 2, 1991.
10. Richard C. Hackett, personal interview, Dec. 1, 1992.
11. John Bakke, "Legislative Report," Memphis Library Channel, Oct. 4, 1991.
12. Jerry Huston and Charles Bernsen, "Hackett, Herenton Adopt Classic Campaign Strategy," *Commercial Appeal*, Sept. 10, 1991.
13. Richard C. Hackett, personal interview, Dec. 1, 1992.
14. WMC TV-5, newscast, Sept. 9, 1991; Sept. 11, 1991; Sept. 18, 1991.
15. See *Commercial Appeal*, Sept. 22, 1991.
16. WMC TV-5, newscast, Aug. 29, 1991.
17. WMC TV-5, newscast, Sept. 9, 1991.
18. Jerry Markon, "Hackett Backs SCI, but Won't Appear," *Commercial Appeal*, Sept. 13, 1991.

19. *Commercial Appeal*, Sept. 11, 1991.
20. *Commercial Appeal*, Sept. 12, 1991.
21. *Commercial Appeal*, Sept. 18, 1991.
22. Huston and Bernsen, "Hackett, Herenton Adopt Classic Campaign Strategy."
23. Ibid.
24. *Commercial Appeal*, Sept. 13, 1991; Sept. 28, 1991; Oct. 1, 1991; Oct. 2, 1991.
25. Cornell Christian, "Mayoral Race Hits Stretch," *Commercial Appeal*, Oct. 1, 1991.
26. Jerry Huston and Jerry Markon, "Mayoral Candidates Address Racial Issues," *Commercial Appeal*, Sept. 27, 1991.
27. *Commercial Appeal*, Oct. 2, 1991.
28. Richard C. Hackett, personal interview, Dec. 1, 1992.
29. "Hackett Wins Endorsement of Fire Union," *Commercial Appeal*, Aug. 17, 1983; *Charter and Related Laws, City of Memphis* (Tallahassee, Fla.: Municipal Code Corporation, 1967), p. HRA-27.
30. Terry Keeter, "Gibbons Cites Employee Pressure," *Commercial Appeal*, Sept. 5, 1987.
31. Terry Keeter, "Event Raises $300,000 for Hackett," *Commercial Appeal*, Jan. 10, 1991.
32. Marc Perrusquia, "Richard Hackett," *Commercial Appeal*, Jan. 14, 1990.
33. Michael Kelley, "Election Fund-Raising Will Show in Ad Blitz," *Commercial Appeal*, Sept. 16, 1991.
34. *Polk's Memphis City Directory* (Memphis: R. L. Polk and Company, 1990). This directory yielded 82 percent of the occupations.
35. These are estimates gained by examining individual items presented in the financial disclosure forms and assigning them to categories. The expenditures were from 1990 and 1991.
36. These are estimates obtained by categorizing the specific expenditures listed by the candidates in their election commission filings before and after the election.
37. Charles Bernsen, "Record Spent by Herenton and Hackett; Equal Costs," *Commercial Appeal*, Nov. 22, 1991.
38. Ibid.
39. Ibid.
40. Ibid.; Richard C. Hackett, personal interview, Dec. 1, 1992.
41. Hackett contributor John Shea quoted in the *Memphis Flyer*, Aug. 29, 1993.
42. Jackson Baker, "Cash Register," *Memphis Flyer*, Aug. 29, 1993.
43. Charles Bernsen, "Hackett Faces Off with Herenton in Voter Registration," *Commercial Appeal*, June 28, 1991.
44. Charles Bernsen, "Largest City Voter Sign-Up Has 32,000 Last-Day Forms," *Commercial Appeal*, Sept. 4, 1991.

45. Interviews with Hackett campaign workers.

46. Richard C. Hackett, personal interview, Dec. 1, 1992.

47. Richard C. Hackett, Rotary Club debate, WMC TV-5, Oct. 1, 1991.

48. Richard C. Hackett, personal interview, Dec. 1, 1992.

49. Kelley, "Herenton's 'Crusade': Late Kick Wins Race," *Commercial Appeal*, Oct. 6, 1991.

50. Ibid.

51. Huston and Markon, "Mayoral Candidates Address Racial Issues."

52. Jerry Huston and Jimmie Covington, "Hackett's Tax Agenda and Tenure Are Fodder for Critics," *Commercial Appeal*, Sept. 29, 1991.

53. Louis Graham, "Hackett Rides Time-Tested Path," *Commercial Appeal*, Feb. 27, 1983.

54. Cornell Christian, "Herenton Says City Race Relations Will Be Major Issue of Campaign," *Commercial Appeal*, Aug. 24, 1991.

55. Charles Bernsen, "Herenton, Hackett Give Early Signals on Strategy," *Commercial Appeal*, Aug. 4, 1991.

56. Christian, "Mayoral Race Hits Stretch."

57. Charles Bernsen, "Herenton, Hackett Vie for Racial Crossover," *Commercial Appeal*, Sept. 15, 1991; "Bishop Ford Says COGIC Is Neutral in Mayoral Race," *Tri-State Defender*, Sept. 21–25, 1991.

58. Charles Bernsen, "Hackett and Herenton Seek Broader Support," *Commercial Appeal*, Sept. 19, 1991.

59. "Possible City-Wide Boycott of McDonald's Restaurant," *Tri-State Defender*, Aug. 17–21, 1991.

60. Calvin Burns, "Ministers Say Hackett Is Their Man," *Tri-State Defender*, Aug. 17–21, 1991; Bernsen, "Herenton, Hackett Vie for Racial Crossover."

61. William Larsha, "Hackett Is Hacking It," *Tri-State Defender*, May 18–22, 1991.

62. Arelya Mitchell, "Here Am I, O Hackett, Send Me," *Tri-State Defender*, Aug. 17–21, 1991.

63. Calvin Burns, "WLOK's Owner Admits Mayor's Call Preceded Adkin's Cancellation," *Tri-State Defender*, Sept. 28–Oct. 2, 1991.

64. Walker and Associates, *Headliners* 6 (Dec. 1985).

65. Richard C. Hackett, personal interview, Dec. 1, 1992.

66. Ibid.

67. William Larsha, "Shelby County Democrats Refuse to Endorse Herenton," *Tri-State Defender*, Aug. 31–Sept. 4, 1991.

68. Kelley, "Herenton's 'Crusade': Late Kick Wins Race."

69. "For Mayor: Hackett Can Succeed—That's the Key," *Commercial Appeal*, Sept. 29, 1991.

7. The Herenton Campaign

1. Ford and Herenton quoted in Ash, *Dr. W. W. Herenton,* 36.
2. Ford quoted in *Tri-State Defender,* Mar. 9, 1991, 12.
3. As examples of black reservations, see the letter by O. Z. Evers in the *Tri-State Defender,* Feb. 16–20, 1991; William Larsha, "A Way to Really Defeat Hackett," *Tri-State Defender,* Mar. 2–6, 1991.
4. See Vernon Ash, "Wilbun Releases Plan for Summit to Include All Black Citizens," *Tri-State Defender,* Feb. 16–20.
5. The formal pact read, "We the undersigned, by our signature, agree to formulate, organize and convene an African-American Convention/People's Summit for the sole purpose of selecting a consensus African-American candidate for Mayor of Memphis. We further agree, by our signature, to bind ourselves to the results of the African-American Convention/People's Summit."
6. *Commercial Appeal,* Mar. 2, 1991.
7. *Commercial Appeal,* Feb. 27, 1991.
8. Besides these names, the *Tri-State Defender* also listed the following individuals as prospective nominees: D'Army Bailey, Roscoe Dixon, Willie Jacox, Minerva Johnican, George Jones, Rufus Jones, J. O. Patterson Jr., Jim Perkins, Isaac Richmond, Gary Rowe, and Teddy Withers. See *Tri-State Defender,* Apr. 20–24, 1991.
9. W. W. Herenton, personal interview, July 6, 1992.
10. From the proposal for an open summit, presented by Councilman Wilbun at a press conference on Feb. 7. See reprint in the *Tri-State Defender,* Feb. 16, 1991.
11. Although the final rules did not limit participation to African Americans alone, it did apportion ward and precinct delegates according to "turnout by African Americans during the most recent election for President of the United States . . . " For a full description of convention rules, see *Tri-State Defender,* Apr. 6–10, 1991.

    This question was also raised vis-à-vis Harold Ford's "Black Summit (Issue) Workshops." And, although no whites chose to attend, Ford claimed that the meetings had been open to any Memphian, even though others claimed to have tape recordings that showed the contrary. See *Tri-State Defender,* Apr. 27–May 1, 1991; June 8–12, 1991.
12. For example, see Arelya Mitchell, "Vander Schaaf Opposes People's Convention at Coliseum," *Tri-State Defender,* Apr. 20–24, 1991.
13. Ibid. For a fuller discussion of the controversy surrounding the debated decision as to whether to restrict the convention to African Americans, see *Tri-State Defender,* Mar. 9–13, 1991; May 18–22, 1991.

14. There was considerable variation in attendance estimates. The official count was approximately five thousand. The *Tri-State Defender* reported it at nearly forty-five hundred. The *Commercial Appeal* reported it as closer to eighteen hundred. For a discussion of possible reasons for these discrepancies, see Arelya Mitchell, "Close to 5,000 Attend Convention," *Tri-State Defender*, May 3–7, 1991.

15. Eddie Walsh, personal interview, June 5, 1992.

16. For a concise summary of the proposed People's Platform, see *Tri-State Defender*, Apr. 27–May 1, 1991. For the full text, see *Tri-State Defender*, May 18–22, 1991.

17. For a fuller articulation of these initial appeals, see the full text of his June 1 speech to the People's Delegates Convention, reprinted in the *Tri-State Defender*, June 22–26, 1991.

18. Letter published in the *Tri-State Defender*, May 3–7, 1991. See also his editorial in the *Tri-State Defender*, May 11–15, 1991.

19. See William Larsha, "Peoples' Convention Is Not Divisive," *Tri-State Defender*, Apr. 6–10, 1991; Arelya Mitchell, "Vander Schaaf Opposes People's Convention at Coliseum."

20. Charles Bernsen, "Herenton Outwits Pundits to Become Black Choice," *Commercial Appeal*, June 17, 1991.

21. *Wall Street Journal*, May 31, 1991.

22. From W. W. Herenton, personal interview, July 6, 1992. See also Vernon Ash, "Herenton Poses Plan for Black Summit," *Tri-State Defender*, Mar. 16–20, 1991.

23. Nelson quoted in *Commercial Appeal*, Mar. 2, 1991.

24. See Vernon Ash, "Leadership Summit Canceled," *Tri-State Defender*, June 8–12, 1991.

25. See ibid.

26. Herenton quoted in the *Commercial Appeal*, May 25, 1991.

27. See editorial in *Tri-State Defender*, May 18–22, 1991.

28. Bernsen, "Herenton Outwits Pundits"; Ash, "Leadership Summit Canceled"; Calvin Burns, "Analyst Predicts Herenton Victory Possible," *Tri-State Defender*, June 1–5, 1991.

29. W. W. Herenton, personal interview, July 6, 1992.

30. Ibid.

31. *Commercial Appeal*, June 16, 1991; June 17, 1991.

32. Withers quoted in Ash, "Leadership Summit Canceled."

33. *Tri-State Defender*, June 22–26; *Commercial Appeal*, June 17, 1991.

34. For highlights of the five-hundred-page report of the Summit Task Force Coordinators, see *Tri-State Defender*, June 22–26, 1991.

35. W. W. Herenton, personal interview, July 6, 1992.
36. Herenton and Wilbun signed in advance, while Muhammad signed on the day of the convention. According to Wilbun, Higgs agreed to sign if he participated, but ultimately chose to forgo participation.
37. Arelya J. Mitchell, "No Other Blacks Should Run for City Mayor," *Tri-State Defender*, June 22–26, 1991.
38. *Tri-State Defender*, June 22–26, 1991.
39. For the text of his withdrawal statement, see *Tri-State Defender*, June 22–26, 1991.
40. For example, see Jackson Baker, "Against All Odds," *Memphis Flyer*, Aug. 15–21, 1991.
41. W. W. Herenton, personal interview, July 6, 1992.
42. Herenton quoted in Kleinmann, "Pluck, Luck or Politics," 41.
43. Herenton quoted in *Wall Street Journal*, May 31, 1991.
44. Herenton quoted in *Commercial Appeal*, Sept. 12, 1991.
45. Herenton quoted in Ford Nelson, "Herenton to Hackett: You Can Run, but You Can't Hide," *Tri-State Defender*, Aug. 31–Sept. 4, 1991.
46. Herenton quoted in the *Tri-State Defender*, Mar. 23–27, 1991.
47. For example, see Nelson, "Herenton to Hackett: You Can Run, but You Can't Hide."
48. For example, one of the first things Herenton did following his election was to visit Maynard Jackson and Andrew Young in Atlanta. He sought advice about how best to begin replicating Atlanta's economic successes. Upon his return, one of his first official acts was to appoint a transition team that comprised virtually all corporate elites.
49. For example, see Mitchell, "No Other Blacks Should Run for City Mayor"; Jackson Baker, "People's Choice," *Memphis Flyer*, June 22–26, 1991, 7; Arelya Mitchell, "Herenton Is the People's Choice," *Tri-State Defender*, May 3–7, 1991.
50. For detailed accounts of this basic economic philosophy, see Jude Wanninski, *The Way the World Works* (New York: Basic, 1978); George Gilder, *Wealth and Poverty* (New York: Basic, 1981); Irving Kristol, *Two Cheers for Capitalism* (New York: Basic, 1978); Milton Friedman, *Capitalism and Freedom* (Chicago: Univ. of Chicago, 1962); Arthur Laffer and James Seymour, *The Economics of the Tax Revolt* (New York: Harcourt, Brace, and Jovanovich, 1979).
51. Herenton quoted in Jerry Huston, "Candidates Shun Partisan Labels," *Commercial Appeal*, Sept. 21, 1991.
52. W. W. Herenton, personal interview, July 6, 1992.
53. Other campaign committee chairpersons included Rick Hall (T-shirts and

caps), Anthony Pittman (youth committee), Latricia Ingram (phone bank), and George Burnett (signs). Hattie Jackson was the office manager and Patricia Powers the assistant office manager. For brief biographies of a number of these advisors, see *Commercial Appeal*, Sept. 24, 1991.

54. Eddie Walsh, personal interview, June 18, 1993.
55. Adkins quoted in *Commercial Appeal*, Jan. 1, 1992.
56. Banks quoted in *Commercial Appeal*, Jan. 1, 1992.
57. *Commercial Appeal*, July 14, 1991.
58. Herenton quoted in *Commercial Appeal*, Jan. 1, 1992.
59. *Commercial Appeal*, June 17, 1991. See also *Tri-State Defender*, June 22–26, 1991.
60. *Commercial Appeal*, Jan. 1, 1992.
61. *Commercial Appeal*, Sept. 15, 1991.
62. *Commercial Appeal*, Sept. 16, 1991.
63. For a listing of major post-election contributors to Herenton, see *Commercial Appeal*, Dec. 5, 1992.
64. Herenton, quoted in *Commercial Appeal*, May 25, 1991.
65. For example, see listing of that day's registration sites in *Tri-State Defender*, Sept. 7–11, 1991.
66. *Commercial Appeal*, July 5, 1991.
67. Although formal content analysis was not employed, this conclusion was reached after reviewing the recorded coverage of both the *Commercial Appeal* and WMC-TV.
68. W. W. Herenton, personal interview, July 6, 1992.
69. For example, see his speaking schedule for Sept. 26, reported in the *Commercial Appeal*, Sept. 27, 1991.
70. Eddie Walsh, personal interview, June 5, 1992.
71. *Commercial Appeal*, Aug. 2, 1991; *Tri-State Defender*, Aug. 3–7, 1991; Aug. 10–14, 1991.
72. Herenton quoted in *Tri-State Defender*, Aug. 10–14, 1991.
73. Herenton quoted in *Commercial Appeal*, Sept. 12, 1991.
74. Eddie Walsh, personal interview, June 5, 1992.
75. Herenton quoted in *Commercial Appeal*, Aug. 24, 1991.
76. *Commercial Appeal*, Sept. 22, 1991.
77. *Commercial Appeal*, Aug. 4, 1991.
78. Charles Carpenter in an interview on the Bill Adkins WLOK radio show, Aug. 19, 1991. As it turned out, Herenton already had a house under construction, and he moved out shortly thereafter. See Charles Bernsen, "When Teacher Moves In, Herenton Moves Out; His Aide Claims Setup," *Commercial Appeal*, Aug. 25, 1991; Calvin Jones, "Bahrmand Denies Po-

litical Harassment," *Tri-State Defender*, Aug. 31–Sept. 4, 1991.

79. *Tri-State Defender*, Aug. 10–14, 1991.

80. Eddie Walsh, personal interview, June 5, 1992.

81. Herenton quoted in *Commercial Appeal*, Aug. 4, 1991.

82. For more on alleged mismanagement in the city's public housing authority, and a possible cover-up by the *Commercial Appeal*, see *Tri-State Defender*, Sept. 14–18, 1991; Sept. 21–25, 1991.

83. *Commercial Appeal*, Aug. 25, 1991. These principles were formally presented as a platform on Sept. 6, 1991. See *Commercial Appeal*, Sept. 7, 1991.

84. *Commercial Appeal*, Sept. 25, 1991.

85. Charles Bernsen, "Hackett and Herenton Back City Tax Reform," *Commercial Appeal*, Sept. 25, 1991.

86. *Commercial Appeal*, Sept. 29, 1991.

87. W. W. Herenton, personal interview, July 6, 1992.

88. As indicated in the previous chapter, John Bakke conducted the only systematic polling during the campaign. Immediately after Labor Day, the Bakke poll showed Hackett leading Herenton citywide by a margin of 43 percent to 26 percent, with 20 percent undecided. That lead narrowed in a poll conducted roughly two weeks prior to the election, with Hackett now ahead 39 percent to 27 percent, with 24 percent undecided. Then, the weekend before the election, his polling data showed Hackett leading 38 percent to 27 percent, with 22 percent undecided.

89. Ford quoted in *Commercial Appeal*, Jan. 1, 1992.

90. Carpenter quoted in ibid.

91. Ibid.

92. See Vernon Ash, "Hackett Sends Black/White Voters Different Literature," *Tri-State Defender*, Oct. 5–9, 1991.

93. For further discussion of the ministerial endorsement, see Calvin Burns, "Ministerial Group Endorses Herenton Unanimously," *Tri-State Defender*, Aug. 24–28, 1991.

94. *Tri-State Defender*, Aug. 17–21, 1991.

95. See Arelya Mitchell, "Here Am I, O Hackett, Send Me"; see also a number of other articles and letters to the editor published in that issue.

96. See *Tri-State Defender*, Sept. 7–11, 1991; Sept. 28–Oct. 2, 1991.

97. *Commercial Appeal*, Sept. 15, 1991.

98. See Calvin Burns, "Herenton Gains Jackson Support," *Tri-State Defender*, Oct. 5–9, 1991.

99. Jackson quoted in *Commercial Appeal*, Jan. 1, 1992.

100. For examples, see *Tri-State Defender*, July 20–24, 1991; July 27–31, 1991.

101. W. W. Herenton, personal interview, July 6, 1992; Eddie Walsh, personal interview, June 18, 1993. And, for examples, see "Prayer Rallies to Be Held for Herenton," *Tri-State Defender*, Sept. 28–Oct. 2, 1991.

102. For a discussion of traditional black political groups and their "ballots," see William Larsha, "New Role for Black Political Groups," *Tri-State Defender*, Aug. 17–21, 1991.

103. *Commercial Appeal*, Oct. 4, 1991.

104. *Commercial Appeal*, Jan. 1, 1992.

105. See Jo Evelyn Grayson, "Man in Wheelchair Walks Mile to Vote for Herenton; Profiles in Voting Courage," *Tri-State Defender*, Oct. 12–16, 1991.

106. These predictions were made at the previously discussed June 20 meeting in Herenton's school board office.

107. As discussed in the next chapter, the actual black turnout was estimated to be 56 percent.

108. Eddie Walsh, personal interview, June 5, 1992. It should be noted, however, that the June 1 and Sept. 24 campaign finance reports indicate that the campaign ultimately paid $5,000 to Charles Carpenter, $2,750 to Patricia Powers, $2,750 to various campaign workers, $1,400 to poll workers, $1,250 to Fred Williams, $1,000 to TJuania Wood, $860 to Osbie Howard, and $650 to J. P. Netters.

109. W. W. Herenton, personal interview, July 6, 1992.

110. Holloway, *The Politics of the Southern Negro*, 284.

8. The Election

1. William Thomas, "Voters Start Early, Crowd Lines at Polls," *Commercial Appeal*, Oct. 4, 1991.

2. Ibid.

3. The final audit by Watkins, Watkins, and Keegan showed 609 "overvotes," meaning instances in which more votes were cast than the number of people who signed in at the polls. According to their report, "[T]he differences are unreconciled and the causes undetermined." The Hackett camp seriously weighed a legal challenge based on these discrepancies, but in the end decided that "a challenge . . . would not be appropriate given the nature of the irregularities which have occurred, the limitations of the state law and the information available to us under state law and election commission procedures." Robert "Prince Mongo" Hodges had not received enough of the total vote to pose a challenge under existing election law.

   For discussion of this matter, see Terry Keeter, "Election Gets Official Seal," *Commercial Appeal*, Oct. 15, 1991; Charles Bernsen, "Advisers

Concluded Challenge too Difficult," ibid.; John Branston, "The Election After Math," *Memphis Flyer*, Oct. 17–23, 1991.

4. The reader will note that these are estimates that might vary slightly from the actual vote. However, even if there is some variance, it does not change our conclusion that there was very little crossover by blacks or whites. See the preface for an explanation of our empirical methods.

5. John Beifuss, "Emotions Slide between Cheers, Tears for Hackett," *Commercial Appeal*, Oct. 4, 1991.

6. *Commercial Appeal*, Oct. 2, 1991.

7. *Commercial Appeal*, Aug. 2, 1991.

8. Charles Bernsen, "Filings Pull Surprises in Council Races, Not Mayor," *Commercial Appeal*, Aug. 5, 1991.

9. Jerry Markon, "Contrasts Mark Race in Position 5," *Commercial Appeal*, Sept. 19, 1991.

10. Jerry Markon, "Mrs. Vander Schaaf, Challengers Differ on Importance of Tourism," *Commercial Appeal*, Aug. 28, 1991.

11. Ibid.

12. For example, see Tucker, *Memphis Since Crump*, 152–61.

13. Parker, *Black Votes Count*, chapter 7.

14. A caution is in order since one of the candidates was included as viable since she won, even though she did not meet the 35 percent threshold.

15. Michael Kelley, "Herenton's 'Crusade': Late Kick Wins Race." See also Vernon Ash, "Herenton's Victory 'Inspired by God,'" *Tri-State Defender*, Oct. 12–16, 1991.

16. Memphis "fall-off" was calculated by comparing the number of mayoral votes to the number cast for each of the other offices. For the interracial analysis, we used a proportional method for each precinct by multiplying black registrants times the difference and then summing these to get city-wide numbers. The results were also cross-checked against racially homogeneous precincts.

17. A "coattail effect" occurs when voters come out primarily to vote for a person at the top of the ticket, but while they are there they also vote for and help elect others further down the ballot who are seen as aligned with the person at the top of the ticket. Therefore, those elected with this help are said to have ridden to election on the top candidate's "coattails."

18. Calvin Burns, "Pleasant Says Herenton Got Close to 10% of White Vote," *Tri-State Defender*, Oct. 12–16, 1991.

19. Terry Keeter, "Absentee Votes Settled, but Raw Feelings Remain," *Commercial Appeal*, Oct. 5, 1991.

20. Burns, "Pleasant Says Herenton Got Close to 10% of White Vote."

21. Keeter, "Absentee Votes Settled, but Raw Feelings Remain."

22. W. W. Herenton, personal interview, July 6, 1992.
23. These are the final audited results, which differ from earlier published results.
24. Clarence Stone, *Regime Politics: Governing Atlanta, 1946–1988* (Lawrence: Univ. Press of Kansas, 1989), 79–80. See also Stone, "Race and Regime in Atlanta," 125–39; Perry, "The Evolution and Impact of Biracial Coalitions and Black Mayors in Birmingham and New Orleans," 140–52; Thompson, "David Dinkins' Victory in New York City," 145–48; Ardrey and Nelson, "The Maturation of Black Political Power: The Case of Cleveland," 148–54; Starks and Preston, "Harold Washington and the Politics of Reform in Chicago," 88–107; Stein and Kohfeld, "St. Louis' Black-White Elections," 240.
25. For example, see Marcus Pohlmann, "The Electoral Impact of Partisanship and Incumbency Reconsidered: An Extension to Low Salience Elections," *Urban Affairs Quarterly* 13 (June 1978): 495–503.
26. See Paul Abramson, John Aldrich, and David Rhode, *Change and Continuity in the 1980 Election* (Washington, D.C.: Congressional Quarterly Press, 1982), chapter 7.
27. For example, see Pohlmann, "The Electoral Impact of Partisanship and Incumbency Reconsidered."
28. Blackburn quoted in Guy Reel, "Old Guard of Schools Takes Losses," *Commercial Appeal*, Oct. 5, 1991.
29. Ibid.

9. Conclusion: Racial Reflexivity in Memphis

1. Bertram Doyle, *The Etiquette of Race Relations* (Chicago: Univ. of Chicago Press, 1937), 139–40.
2. For a discussion of the relative uniqueness of this political alliance, see Wald, "The Electoral Base of Political Machines."
3. Holloway, *The Politics of the Southern Negro*, 280. See also Myrdal, *The American Dilemma*, 486; Price, *The Negro Voter in the South*, 31.
4. Of the nation's twenty-five largest cities with populations that were at least 30 percent black, Memphis was the very last to elect an African-American mayor. See Vaughn, "Memphis: Heart of the Mid-South," 118; *Commercial Appeal*, Oct. 25, 1987.
5. As examples of this literature, see Davidson, *Biracial Politics*; Leonard Cole, "Electing Blacks to Municipal Office: Structural and Social Determinants," *Urban Affairs Quarterly* 10 (Sept. 1974): 17–39; Thomas Pettigrew, "When a Black Candidate Runs for Mayor: Race and Voting Behavior," in Harlan Hahn, ed., *People and Politics in Urban Society* (Beverly Hills, Calif.: Sage, 1971), 99–105; Browning, Marshall, and Tabb,

Protest Is Not Enough; Parsons, "Racial Politics and Black Power in the Cities."

For case studies, see Bruce Ransom, "Black Independent Electoral Politics in Philadelphia: The Election of Mayor W. Wilson Goode," in Michael Preston, Lenneal Henderson, and Paul Puryear, eds., *The New Black Politics: The Search for Political Power* (New York: Longman, 1987), 256–89; Thompson, "David Dinkins' Victory in New York City," 145–48; Ardrey and Nelson, "The Maturation of Black Political Power: The Case of Cleveland," 148–54; Starks and Preston, "Harold Washington and the Politics of Reform in Chicago," 88–107; Stone, "Race and Regime in Atlanta," 125–39; Perry, "The Evolution and Impact of Biracial Coalitions and Black Mayors in Birmingham and New Orleans," 140–52; Asher, Goldberg, Mollenkopf, and Rogowsky, *Changing New York City Politics*; Sonenshein, *Politics in Black and White*; Grimshaw, "Is Chicago Ready for Reform."

6. See Hamilton, "De-Racialization: Examination of a Political Strategy," 3–5; Symposium, *Urban Affairs Quarterly* 26 (Dec. 1991): 181–227; Symposium, *PS: Political Science and Politics* 23 (June 1990):160–90; Davidson, *Biracial Politics*; Huckfeldt and Kohfeld, *Race and the Decline of Class in American Politics*, 91; Nelson and Meranto, *Electing Black Mayors*, 329.

7. See Stein and Kohfeld, "St. Louis' Black-White Elections," 227–48.

8. Ibid.; Sonenshein, *Politics in Black and White*, 11–13.

9. Murray and Vedlitz, "Racial Voting Patterns in the South," 29–40.

10. Ibid., 39.

11. For a discussion of the severe economic problems faced by virtually all southern cities, see Bullard, *In Search of the New South*; David Perry and Alfred Watkins, eds., *The Rise of the Sunbelt Cities* (Beverly Hills, Calif.: Sage, 1977); John Kasarda, "Caught in the Web of Change," *Society* 21 (Nov./Dec. 1983): 41–47; William Julius Wilson, *The Truly Disadvantaged* (Chicago: Univ. of Chicago Press, 1987), 180–81.

12. For example, see Nelson and Meranto, *Electing Black Mayors*, 329.

13. See *Christian Science Monitor*, Jan. 8, 1985. In terms of the more general issue of predominantly white city councils, see Albert Karnig, "Black Representation on City Councils," *Urban Affairs Quarterly* 12 (Dec. 1976): 223–43; Thomas Dye, *Politics in States and Communities* (Englewood Cliffs, N.J.: Prentice-Hall, 1985), 304–5. And for the reasons these councils remain disproportionately white, e.g., nonpartisan and at-large elections, see Thomas Dye and Theodore Robinson, "Reformism and Black Representation on City Councils," unpublished paper cited in Dye, *Politics in States and Communities*, 305; Richard Engstrom and Michael McDonald, "The Election of Blacks to City Councils," *American Political Science Review* 75 (June 1981): 344–54.

14. For examples, see *New York Times*, Apr. 5, 1991; Mar. 22, 1982; *Washington Post*, Apr. 9, 1983; Stone, *Regime Politics: Governing Atlanta, 1946–1988*, 156–58; William Nelson, "Black Mayors as Urban Managers," *Annals of the American Academy of Political and Social Sciences* 439 (Sept. 1978): 62; Roger M. Williams, "America's Black Mayors: Are They Saving the Cities?," *Saturday Review/World*, May 4, 1974, 10–13 and 66; Starks and Preston, "Harold Washington and the Politics of Reform in Chicago"; Jeffrey Hadden, Louis Masotti, and Victor Thiessen, "The Making of the Negro Mayors, 1967," *Trans-action* 5 (Jan./Feb. 1968):21–30.

As for the police, there is a clearly identifiable difference in the ways Memphis whites and blacks view their performance. For example, see Kirby, *The Memphis Poll 1994*, 16.

15. For example, see Nelson, "Black Mayors as Urban Managers," 64; for a particular example of this struggle (Mayor Richard Arrington and the *Birmingham News*), see *New York Times*, Nov. 9, 1981.

16. For example, see Raphael Sonenshein, "Biracial Coalition Politics in Los Angeles," *PS: Political Science and Politics* 19 (Summer 1986): 586; for some of the dilemmas faced by New York City Mayor David Dinkins in this regard, see *New York Times*, Mar. 8, 1991; Nelson, "Black Mayoral Leadership," 191; Stone, *Regime Politics: Governing Atlanta, 1946–1988*; Range, "Capital of Black Is Bountiful"; Roberts, "He's One of Us"; Peter Eisinger, *The Politics of Displacement* (Madison Wisc.: Institute for Research on Poverty, 1980); Peter Binzen, "Business Community Sees Reason for Hope," *Philadelphia Inquirer*, Jan. 8, 1984; Hadden, Masotti, and Thiessen, "Making of the Negro Mayors"; Paul Friesema, "Black Control of Central Cities: The Hollow Prize," *Journal of the American Institute of Planning* 35 (Mar. 1969): pp. 75–83.

17. For discussion of the Atlanta experience in this regard, see *New York Times*, Oct. 29, 1981; Mack Jones, "Black Political Empowerment in Atlanta," *Annals of the American Academy of Political and Social Sciences* 439 (Sept. 1978): 111–12; M. Dale Henson and James King, "The Atlanta Public-Private Romance," in R. Scott Foster and Renee Berger, eds., *Public-Private Partnership in America* (Lexington, Mass.: Lexington Books, 1982), 293–337; "The Capitalist Gospel According to Reverend Young," *Atlanta Constitution*, Sept. 22, 1983; *Atlanta Constitution*, July 24, 1983; Susan Clarke, "More Autonomous Policy Orientations," in Clarence Stone and Heywood Sanders, eds., *The Politics of Urban Development* (Lawrence: Univ. Press of Kansas, 1987); Adolph Reed, "A Critique of Neo-Progressivism in Theorizing about Local Policy Development," in Stone and Sanders, *The Politics of Urban Development*; Stone, *Regime Politics: Governing Atlanta, 1946–1988*, especially chapters 6–7.

18. For example, see Bryan Jackson, "Black Political Power in the City of the Angels," in Lucius Barker, ed., *Black Electoral Politics* (New Brunswick, N.J.: Transaction, 1990), 169–75; Charles Bernsen, "Detroit," *Commercial Appeal*, Jan. 31, 1991; *New York Times*, Apr. 3, 1989; Aug. 28, 1989; Feb. 28, 1991.

19. For example, see *New York Times*, Mar. 1, 1986.

20. For example, see Dana Milbank, "Cleveland's Mayor Shuns Black Themes to Court White Votes," *Wall Street Journal*, Oct. 11, 1991.

21. Black and Black, *Politics and Society in the South*, chapters 9–10.

22. Kirby, *The Memphis Poll 1994*, 25.

23. Ibid.

24. Sonenshein, *Politics in Black and White*, chapter 16.

25. Herenton quoted in Ash, *Dr. W. W. Herenton*, 3.

Epilogue

1. Supporters included the likes of Fred Smith, Pitt Hyde, Ron Terry, Joe Orgill, Ira Lipman, and Thomas Farnsworth. For a more complete list of such early contributors, see the *Commercial Appeal*, Apr, 9, 1995; Apr. 23, 1995.

2. *Commercial Appeal*, July 16, 1995.

3. *Commercial Appeal*, July 29, 1994; Aug. 2, 1994.

4. For example, see *Tri-State Defender*, Sept. 10–14, 1994; Jan. 7–11, 1995; Apr. 1–5, 1995; June 17–21, 1995; July 29–Aug. 2, 1995; *Commercial Appeal*, Sept. 21, 1994.

5. Besides Herenton and Baker, the other two announced candidates for mayor were "Prince Mongo" Hodges and a convicted pornographer, Ernie Lunati, who ran on a platform that stressed the need to "cane" convicted felons.

6. *Memphis Business Journal*, Sept. 25–29, 1995.

7. *Commercial Appeal*, Sept. 24, 1995.

8. *Commercial Appeal*, Oct. 6, 1995; Oct. 7, 1995.

9. See Michael Preston, "Big-City Black Mayors," in Lucius Barker, ed., *Black Electoral Politics* (New Brunswick: Transaction, 1990), 134–35.

Bibliography

Abramson, Paul, John Aldrich, and David Rhode. *Change and Continuity in the 1980 Election.* Washington, D.C.: Congressional Quarterly Press, 1982.

Adkins, Walter. "Beale Street Goes to the Polls." Ph.D. diss., Ohio State Univ., 1935.

Adrian, Charles, and Oliver Williams. *Four Cities.* Philadelphia: Univ. of Pennsylvania Press, 1961.

Alford, Robert, and Eugene Lee. "Voting Turnout in American Cities." *American Political Science Review* 62 (Sept. 1968).

Alinsky, Saul. *Rules for Radicals.* New York: Random House, 1971.

Ash, Vernon E. *Dr. W. W. Herenton.* Memphis: Withers Photographe, 1992.

Ardrey, Saundra, and William Nelson. "The Maturation of Black Political Power: The Case of Cleveland." *PS: Political Science & Politics* 23 (June 1990).

Asher, Avian, Arthur Goldberg, John Mollenkopf, and Edward Rogowsky. *Changing New York City Politics.* New York: Routledge, 1991.

Bailey, Robert. "The 1968 Memphis Sanitation Strike." Master's thesis, Memphis State Univ., 1974.

Baker, Jackson. "Against All Odds." *Memphis Flyer,* Aug. 15–21, 1991.

———. "Cash Register." *Memphis Flyer,* Sept. 18–22, 1991.

———. "People's Choice." *Memphis Flyer,* June 20–26, 1991.

———. "Profile of Henry Loeb." *Memphis Magazine,* Jan. 1980.

Bass, Jack, and Walter DeVries. *The Transformation of Southern Politics.* New York: Basic Books, 1976.

Beifuss, Joan. *At the River I Stand.* Memphis: B & W Books. 1985.

Berkeley, Kathleen. *Like a Plague of Locusts.: Immigration and Social Change in Memphis, Tennessee.* Los Angeles: UCLA Press, 1980.

Berlin, Ira. *Slaves Without Masters.* New York: Pantheon Books, 1974.

Biles, Roger. "Ed Crump Versus the Unions." *Labor History* 25 (Fall 1984).

———. *Memphis in the Great Depression.* Knoxville: Univ. of Tennessee Press, 1986.

———. "Robert R. Church, Jr. of Memphis." *Tennessee Historical Quarterly* 42 (Winter 1983).

Binzen, Peter. "Business Community Sees Reason for Hope." *Philadelphia Inquirer,* Jan. 8, 1984.

Black, Earl, and Merle Black. *Politics and Society in the South.* Cambridge, Mass.: Harvard Univ. Press, 1987.

Brink, William, and Louis Harris. *Black and White.* New York: Simon and Schuster, 1966.

Brownell, Blaine, and David Goldfield. *The City in Southern History.* Port Washington, N.Y.: Kennikat Press, 1977.

Browning, Rufus, Dale Rogers Marshall, and David Tabb. "Minority Mobilization in Ten Cities: Failures and Success." In *Black Electoral Politics,* edited by Lucius Barker. New Brunswick, N.J.: Transaction Books, 1990.

———. *Protest Is Not Enough.* Berkeley: Univ. of California, 1984.

Bullard, Robert D. *In Search of the New South: The Black Urban Experience in the 1970s and 1980s.* Alabama: Univ. of Alabama Press, 1989.

Bullock, Charles S. "Turnout in Municipal Elections." *Political Studies Review* (Spring 1990).

Bullock, Charles, and Loch Johnson. *Runoff Elections in the United States.* Chapel Hill: Univ. of North Carolina Press, 1992.

Bunche, Ralph. *The Political Status of the Negro in the Age of FDR.* Chicago: Univ. of Chicago Press, 1973.

Capers, Gerald. *The Biography of a River Town.* New York: Vanguard Press, 1966.

———. "Memphis: Satrapy of a Benevolent Despot." In *Our Fair City,* edited by Robert Allen. New York: Vanguard Press, 1947.

Cartwright, Joseph. *The Triumph of Jim Crow.* Knoxville: Univ. of Tennessee Press, 1976.

Church, Annette, and Roberta Church. *The Robert R. Churches.* Ann Arbor: Univ. of Michigan Press, 1974.

City of Memphis. *Charter and Related Laws, City of Memphis.* Tallahassee, Fla.: Municipal Code Corporation, 1967.

———. *CHAS: Five Year Comprehensive Housing Affordability Strategy.* City of Memphis, Division of Housing and Community Development. Oct. 1991.

Clark, Susan. "More Autonomous Policy Orientations." In *The Politics of Urban Development,* edited by Clarence Stone and Heywood Sanders. Lawrence: Univ. Press of Kansas, 1987.

Cleghorn, Reese, and Pat Watters. *Climbing Jacob's Ladder.* New York: Harper, Brace and World, 1967.

Cohen, William. "Negro Involuntary Servitude in the South, 1865–1940." *Journal of Southern History* 42 (Feb. 1976).

Cole, Leonard. "Electing Blacks to Municipal Office: Structural and Social Determinants." *Urban Affairs Quarterly* 10 (Sept. 1974).

Conley, Larry. "Profile: Willie Herenton." *Memphis Magazine,* Dec. 1980.

———. "Willie Herenton Speaks Out." *Memphis Magazine,* Nov. 1989.

Conway, M. Margaret. *Political Participation in the United States.* Washington D.C.: CQ Press, 1991.

Cowan, Thomas. *Values and Policy in Shelby County, Tennessee.* Memphis: Christian Brothers College Study, 1979.

Crawford, Charles. *Yesterday's Memphis.* Miami: Seemann, 1976.

Dahl, Robert. *Democracy in America.* Chicago: Rand McNally, 1976.

Daniel, John. "Memphis 1975: The Campaign Strategy of a Black Political Candidate." Honors thesis, Southwestern at Memphis College, 1976.

Daniels, Jonathan. "He Suits Memphis." *Saturday Evening Post,* June 10, 1939.

Davidson, Chandler. *Biracial Politics.* Baton Rouge: Louisiana State Univ. Press, 1972.

Davis, Denoral. "Against the Odds." Ph.D. dissertation, State Univ. of New York at Binghamton, 1987.

de Tocqueville, Alexis. *Democracy in America.* Edited by Phillips Bradley. New York: Knopf, 1951.

Dollard, John. *Caste and Class in a Southern Town.* New Haven: Yale Univ. Press, 1938.

Doyle, Bertram. *The Etiquette of Race Relations.* Chicago: Univ. of Chicago Press, 1937.

Drake, St. Clair, and Horace Cayton. *Black Metropolis.* New York: Harper and Row, 1945.

DuBois, W. E. B. *The Souls of Black Folks.* Chicago: McClung, 1903.

Duggar, Robert. "The Relation of Local Government Structure to Urban Renewal." *Law and Contemporary Problems* 26 (Jan. 1961).

Dye, Thomas. *Politics in States and Communities.* Englewood Cliffs, N.J.: Prentice-Hall, 1985.

Dye, Thomas, and Theodore Robinson. "Reformism and Black Representation on City Councils." Unpublished paper cited in Dye, *Politics in States and Communities,* 305.

Edwards, Franklin, and Cindy Ma. *Futures and Options.* New York: McGraw-Hill, 1992.

Eisinger, Peter. *The Politics of Displacement.* Madison, Wisc.: Institute for Research on Poverty, 1980.

Elazar, Daniel. *American Federalism.* New York: Crowell, 1972.

Ellis, John. "Disease and the Destiny of a City: The 1878 Yellow Fever Epidemic in Memphis." *The West Tennessee Historical Papers* 28 (1974).

Engstrom, Richard, and Michael McDonald. "The Election of Blacks to City Councils." *American Political Science Review* 75 (June 1981).

Enterprise Foundation. *Memphis Tenn: An Assessment Report on Housing Needs, Programs and Public/Private Partnership Opportunities.* Columbia, Md.: Enterprise Foundation, 1992.

Franklin, Jimmie Lewis. *Back to Birmingham.* Tuscaloosa: Univ. of Alabama Press, 1989.

Franklin, John Hope. *From Slavery to Freedom.* New York: Knopf, 1980.

Frazier, Franklin. *The Negro Church in America.* New York: Schocken Books, 1964.

Friedman, Milton. *Capitalism and Freedom.* Chicago: Univ. of Chicago Press, 1962.

Friesema, Paul. "Black Control of Central Cities: The Hollow Prize." *Journal of the American Institute of Planners* 35 (Mar. 1969).

Fuller, T. O. *The Inter-Racial Blue Book.* Memphis: Inter-Racial League, 1925.

Geschwender, James. "Social Structure and the Negro Revolt." *Social Forces* 43 (1964–65).

Gilder, George. *Wealth and Poverty.* New York: Basic Books, 1981.

Gilliam, Franklin D. "Race, Sociopolitical Participation, and Black Empowerment." *American Political Science Review* 83 (June 1990).

Goings, Kenneth. "Lynching, African-Americans and Memphis." Unpublished paper.

Goldfield, David. *Cotton Fields and Skyscrapers.* Baltimore: Johns Hopkins Univ. Press, 1982.

Grimshaw, William. "Is Chicago Ready for Reform?" In *The Making of the Mayor, Chicago 1983*, edited by Melvin Holli and Paul Green. Grand Rapids, Mich.: Eerdmans, 1984.

Grofman, Bernard, and Chandler Davidson, eds. *Controversies in Minority Voting.* Washington, D.C.: Brookings Institution, 1992.

Grofman, Bernard, Michael Migalski, and Nicholas Noviello. "The Totality of Circumstances Test in Section 2 of the 1982 Extension of the Voting Rights Act: A Social Science Perspective." *Law & Policy* 7 (Apr. 1985).

Hadden, Jeffery, Louis Masotti, and Victor Thiessen. "The Making of the Negro Mayors, 1967." *Trans-action* 5 (Jan./Feb. 1968).

Hamilton, Charles V. *The Black Preacher in American Politics.* New York: Morrow, 1972.

———. "De-Racialization: Examination of a Political Strategy." *First World* 11 (Mar./Apr. 1977).

———. "The Patron-Recipient Relationship and Minority Politics." *Political Science Quarterly* 94 (Summer 1979).

Handy, W. C. *A Treasure of Blues*. New York: C. Boni, 1949.

Harkins, John. *Metropolis of the American Nile*. Oxford, Miss.: The Guild Bindery Press, 1982.

Hartz, Louis. *The Liberal Tradition in American Politics*. New York: Harcourt, Brace, 1955.

Hathaway, James. "A Social History of the Negro in Memphis." Ph.D. diss., Yale Univ., 1934.

Henig, Jeffrey. "Race and Voting." *Urban Affairs Quarterly* 28 (June 1993).

Henson, M. Dale, and James King. "The Atlanta Public-Private Romance." In *Public-Private Partnership in America*, edited by R. Scott Foster and Renee Berger. Lexington, Mass.: Lexington Books, 1982.

Hill, Edward W., and Heidi Marie Rock. "Race and Inner-City Education." In *The Metropolis in Black & White*, edited by George Galster and Edward Hill. New Brunswick, N.J.: Center for Urban Policy Research, 1992.

Holloway, Harry. *The Politics of the Southern Negro*. New York: Random House, 1969.

Holmes, Jack. "The Underlying Causes of the Memphis Riot of 1866." *Tennessee Historical Quarterly* 17 (1958).

Honey, Michael. *Southern Labor and Black Civil Rights*. Champaign: Univ. of Illinois Press, 1993.

Huckfeldt, Robert, and C. W. Kohfeld. *Race and the Decline of Class in American Politics*. Champaign: Univ. of Illinois Press, 1989.

Jackson, Bryan. "Black Political Power in the City of the Angels." In *Black Electoral Politics*, edited by Lucius Barker. New Brunswick, N.J.: Transaction Books, 1990.

Jacob, John. "Black America, 1993: An Overview." In *The State of Black America 1994*, edited by Billy Tidwell. New York: National Urban League, 1994.

Jalenak, James. "Beale Street Politics." Honors thesis, Yale Univ., 1961.

Jones, Mack. "Black Political Empowerment in Atlanta." *Annals of the American Academy of Political and Social Sciences* 439 (Sept. 1978).

Karnig, Albert. "Black Representation on City Councils." *Urban Affairs Quarterly* 12 (Dec. 1976).

Kasarda, John. "Caught in the Web of Change." *Society* 21 (Nov./Dec. 1983).

Katznelson, Ira, and Mark Kesselman. *The Politics of Power*. New York: Harcourt, Brace and Jovanovich, 1987.

Kelley, Robin. "We Are Not What We Seem." *Journal of American History* 80 (June 1993).

Kessel, John. "Governmental Structures and Political Environment." *American Political Science Review* 57 (Sept. 1963).

Key, V. O. *Southern Politics in State and Nation.* New York: Knopf, 1949.

Kirby, Michael. *Memphis Poll 1993.* City of Memphis, Finance Division, 1993.

———. *Memphis Poll 1994.* City of Memphis, Finance Division, 1994.

Kleinmann, Leanne. "Pluck, Luck or Politics?" *Memphis Magazine,* Feb. 1992.

Kristol, Irving. *Two Cheers for Capitalism.* New York: Basic, 1978.

Laffer, Arthur, and James Seymour. *The Economics of the Tax Revolt.* New York: Harcourt, Brace, and Jovanovich, 1979.

Lamon, Lester. *Black Tennesseans, 1900–1930.* Knoxville: Univ. of Tennessee Press, 1977.

Lane, Robert. *Political Life.* Glencoe, Ill.: Free Press, 1959.

Larsen, Lawrence. *The Rise of the Urban South.* Lexington: Univ. Press of Kentucky, 1985.

Lee, George. *Beale Street.* New York: R. O. Ballou, 1934.

Lemann, Nicholas. *The Promised Land: The Great Black Migration and How It Changed America.* New York: Knopf, 1991.

Lewinsohn, Paul. *Race, Class and Party: A History of Negro Suffrage and White Politics in the South.* New York: Russell and Russell, 1963.

Lewis, Selma. "Social Religion and the Memphis Sanitation Strike." Ph.D. diss., Memphis State Univ., 1976.

Logan, Rayford. *The Betrayal of the Negro.* London: Collier and Macmillan, 1965.

Lohse, Deborah. "100 Metro Area Tax Bills." *Money,* Jan. 1993.

Marshall, F. Ray, and Arvil Van Adams. "Negro Employment in Memphis." *Industrial Relations* 9 (May 1970).

Martin, Roscoe. Foreword to V. O. Key, *Southern Politics in State and Nation.* New York: Knopf, 1949.

Matthews, David, and James Prothro. *Negroes and the New Southern Politics.* New York: Harcourt, Brace and World, 1966.

Mays, Benjamin. *Born to Rebel.* New York: Scribner's, 1971.

McFate, Katherine. *The Metropolitan Area Fact Book.* Washington, D.C.: Joint Center for Political Studies, 1989.

McIlwaine, Shields. *Memphis Down in Dixie.* New York: Dutton, 1948.

Melton, Gloria Brown. "Blacks in Memphis, Tennessee, 1920–1955." Ph.D. diss., Washington State Univ., 1982.

Memphis and Shelby County Office of Planning and Development. *Southeast Memphis Annexation Area.* Nov. 1987.

Memphis and Shelby County Planning Commission. *Annexation: A Must for a Growing Memphis.* Sept. 1967.

Miller, William. *Mr. Crump of Memphis.* Baton Rouge: Louisiana State Univ. Press, 1964.

———. *Memphis During the Progressive Era.* Memphis: Memphis State Univ. Press, 1957.

Moeser, John V., and Dennis M. Rutledge. *The Politics of Annexation: Oligarchic Power in a Southern City.* Cambridge, Mass.: Schenkman, 1990.

Moore, Gary. ". . . and the Mall Came Tumbling Down." *Memphis Flyer,* June 24, 1992.

Morris, Aldon. "The Future of Black Politics." *National Political Science Review* 3 (1991).

Murray, Richard, and Arnold Vedlitz. "Race, SES and Voting Participation in Large Southern Cities." *Journal of Politics* 39 (Nov. 1977).

————. "Racial Voting Patterns in the South." *Annals of the American Academy of Political and Social Science* 439 (Sept. 1978).

Myrdal, Gunnar. *The American Dilemma.* New York: Harper and Brothers, 1949.

Neill, Kenneth. "Mr. Crump: The Making of a Boss." *Memphis Magazine* (Oct. 1972).

Nelson, William. "Black Mayors as Urban Managers." *Annals of the American Academy of Political and Social Sciences* 439 (Sept. 1978).

————. "Cleveland: The Rise and Fall of the New Black Politics." In *The New Black Politics,* edited by Michael Preston, Lenneal Henderson Jr., and Paul Puryear. New York: Longman, 1982.

Nelson, William, and Phillip Meranto. *Electing Black Mayors.* Columbus: Ohio State Univ. Press, 1977.

Noblit, George, and Thomas Collins. "School Flight and School Policy: Desegregation and Resegregation in the Memphis City Schools." *Urban Review* 10 (Fall 1978).

Olsen, Marvin E. *Social and Political Participation of Blacks.* Bloomington: Indiana Univ. Press, 1970.

Orfield, Gary, and Carole Ashkinaze. *The Closing Door.* Chicago: Univ. of Chicago Press, 1991.

Parker, Frank R. *Black Votes Count.* Chapel Hill: Univ. of North Carolina Press, 1990.

Parsons, Georgia. "Racial Politics and Black Power in the Cities." In *The Metropolis in Black and White,* edited by George Galster and Edward Hill. New Brunswick, N.J.: Center for Urban Policy Research, 1992.

Pierce, Neal. "Sparking an Economic Comeback in Memphis." *National Journal,* Apr. 11, 1987.

Perry, David, and Alfred Watkins, eds. *The Rise of the Sunbelt Cities.* Beverly Hills: Sage, 1977.

Perry, Huey. "The Evolution and Impact of Biracial Coalitions and Black Mayors in Birmingham and New Orleans." In *Black Electoral Politics,* edited by Lucius Barker. New Brunswick, N.J.: Transaction Books, 1990.

Pettigrew, Thomas. "When a Black Candidate Runs for Mayor: Race and Voting Behavior." In *People and Politics in Urban Society,* edited by Harlan Hahn. Beverly Hills: Sage, 1971.

Plank, David N., and Marcia Turner, "Contrasting Patterns in Black School Politics: Atlanta and Memphis, 1865–1985." *Journal of Negro Education* 60 (1991).

Pohlmann, Marcus. *Black Politics in Conservative America.* New York: Longman, 1990.

————. "The Electoral Impact of Partisanship and Incumbency Reconsidered: An Extension to Low Salience Elections." *Urban Affairs Quarterly* 13 (June 1978).

————. *Governing the Postindustrial City.* New York: Longman, 1993.

Polk's Memphis City Directory. Memphis: R. L. Polk Company, 1990.

Price, Margaret. *The Negro Voter in the South.* Atlanta: Southern Regional Council, 1957.

Rabinowitz, Howard. *Race Relations in the South, 1865–1890.* New York: Oxford Univ. Press, 1978.

Range, Peter Ross. "Capital of Black is Bountiful." *New York Times Magazine,* Apr. 7, 1974.

Ransom, Bruce. "Black Independent Electoral Politics in Philadelphia: The Election of Mayor W. Wilson Goode." In *The New Black Politics: The Search for Political Power,* edited by Michael Preston, Lenneal Henderson, and Paul Puryear. New York: Longman, 1987.

Reed, Adolph. "A Critique of Neo-Progressivism in Theorizing about Local Policy Development." In *The Politics of Urban Development,* edited by Clarence Stone and Heywood Sanders. Lawrence: Univ. Press of Kansas, 1987.

Ripey, Thomas. "Changes in the Formal Structure of Municipal Government and their Effect on Selected Aspects of the Legislative Process." Ph.D. diss., Univ. of Kentucky, 1973.

Roberts, Steven V. "He's One of Us." *New York Times Magazine,* Feb. 24, 1974.

Robinson, Clayton. "Impact of the City on Rural Immigration to Memphis: 1880–1940." Ph.D. diss., Univ. of Minnesota, 1967.

Rosenthal, Donald, and Robert Crain. "Structure and Values in Local Political Systems." *Journal of Politics* 28 (Feb. 1966).

Ryan, James Gilbert. "The Memphis Riots of 1866." *Journal of Negro History* 62 (1977).

Salisbury, Robert. "St. Louis Politics." *Western Political Quarterly* 13 (June 1960).

Scher, Richard K. *Politics in the New South.* New York: Paragon House, 1992.

Schexnider, Alvin J. *Political Mobilization in the South: The Election of a Black Mayor in New Orleans.* New York: Longman, 1982.

Schively, W. Phillips. "Ecological Inference: The Use of Aggregate Data to Study Individuals." *American Political Science Review* 63 (1969).

Sigafoos, Robert. *Cotton Row to Beale Street.* Memphis: Memphis State Univ. Press, 1979.

Smith, Robert. "Recent Elections and Black Politics: The Maturation or Death of Black Politics?" *PS: Political Science & Politics* 23 (June 1990).

Sonenshein, Raphael. "Biracial Coalition Politics in Los Angeles." *PS: Political Science and Politics* 19 (Summer 1986).

———. *Politics in Black and White.* Princeton: Princeton Univ. Press, 1993.

St. Angelo, Douglas, and Paul Puryear. "Fear, Apathy and Other Dimensions of Black Voting." In *The New Black Politics,* edited by Michael Preston, Lenneal Henderson Jr., and Paul Puryear. New York: Longman, 1982.

Stanley, Harold W. *Voter Mobilization and the Politics of Race.* New York: Praeger, 1987.

Starks, Robert, and Michael Preston. "Harold Washington and the Politics of Reform in Chicago: 1983–1987." In *Racial Politics in American Cities,* edited by Rufus Browning, Dale Rogers Marshall, and David Tabb. New York: Longman, 1990.

Starks, Robert, and Michael Preston. "Harold Washington and the Politics of Reform in Chicago: 1983–1987." In *Black Electoral Politics,* edited by Lucius Barker. New Brunswick, N.J.: Transaction Books, 1990.

Stein, Laura, and Carol Kohfeld. "St. Louis' Black-White Elections." *Urban Affairs Quarterly* 26 (Dec. 1991).

Stein, Laura, and Arnold Fleischman. "Newspaper and Business Endorsements in Municipal Elections." *Journal of Urban Affairs* 9 (Fall 1987).

Stone, Clarence. "Race and Regime in Atlanta." In *Black Electoral Politics,* edited by Lucius Barker. New Brunswick, N.J.: Transaction Books, 1990.

———. *Regime Politics: Governing Atlanta, 1946–1988.* Lawrence: Univ. Press of Kansas, 1989.

Stone, Clarence, and Heywood Sanders, eds. *The Politics of Urban Development.* Lawrence: Univ. Press of Kansas, 1987.

Summers, Mary E., and Philip A. Klinkner. "The Daniels Election in New Haven and the Failure of the Deracialization Hypothesis." *Urban Affairs Quarterly* 26 (Dec. 1991).

Symposium. *Urban Affairs Quarterly* 26 (Dec. 1991).

Symposium. *PS: Political Science and Politics* 23 (June 1990).

Taylor, A. A. *The Negro in Tennessee, 1865–1880.* New York: Associated Publishers, 1941.

Terreo, John. "Reporting by Memphis Newspapers Prior to the 1866 Race Riot and During the 1968 Sanitation Strike: A Historical Study." Master's thesis, Memphis State Univ., 1987.

Thompson, Daniel. *Negro Leadership Class.* Englewood Cliffs, N.J.: Prentice-Hall, 1963.

Thompson, J. Phillip. "David Dinkins' Victory in New York City: The Decline of the Democratic Party Organization and the Strengthening of Black Politics." *PS: Political Science and Politics* 23 (June 1990).

Tidwell, Billy. *The State of Black America 1994.* New York: National Urban League, 1994.

Tucker, David. *Black Pastors and Leaders 1819–1972.* Memphis: Memphis State Univ. Press, 1975.

———. *Lieutenant Lee of Beale Street.* Nashville, Tenn.: Vanderbilt Univ. Press, 1971.

———. *Memphis Since Crump.* Knoxville: Univ. of Tennessee Press, 1980.

U.S. Department of Commerce, Bureau of the Census. *Census of the Population, 1990.* Washington, D.C.: Government Printing Office, 1991.

Vaughn, Sandra. "Memphis: Heart of the Mid-South." In *In Search of the New South: The Black Urban Experience in the 1970s and 1980s,* edited by Robert Bullard. Tuscaloosa: Univ. of Alabama Press, 1989.

Wald, Kenneth. "The Electoral Base of Political Machines." *Urban Affairs Quarterly* 16 (Sept. 1980).

Walker, Altina. "Class and Race in the Memphis Riot of 1866." *Journal of Social History* 18 (Winter 1984).

Walker and Associates. *Headliners* 6 (Dec. 1985).

Walker, Randolph Meade. "The Role of the Black Clergy in Memphis During the Crump Era." *West Tennessee Historical Papers* 33 (Oct. 1979).

Wanninski, Jude. *The Way the World Works.* New York: Basic Books, 1978.

Washington, Booker T. *Up from Slavery.* Garden City, N.Y.: Doubleday, 1963.

Weathers, Ed. "A Tale of Two Mayors." *Memphis Magazine,* May, 1984.

———. "Wyeth Chandler: The Man in City Hall." *Memphis Magazine,* July 1981.

Webb, Eugene. *Unobtrusive Measures.* Chicago: Rand McNally, 1966,

Wei, Yung, and H. R. Mahood. "Racial Attitudes and the Wallace Vote." *Polity* 3 (Summer 1971).

Whelan, Robert K., Alma Young, and Mickey Lauria. "Urban Regimes and Racial Politics in New Orleans." *Journal of Urban Affairs* 16 (1994).

Williams, Charles, Jr. "Two Black Communities in Memphis, Tennessee: A Study in Urban Socio-Political Structure." Ph.D. diss., Univ. of Illinois, 1982.

Williams, Linda. "White-Black Perceptions of the Electability of Black Candidates." *National Political Science Review* 2 (1990).

Williams, Roger M. "America's Black Mayors: Are They Saving the Cities?" *Saturday Review/World,* May 4, 1974.

Williamson, Joel. *The Crucible of Race.* New York: Oxford Univ. Press, 1984.

Wilson, William Julius. *The Truly Disadvantaged.* Chicago: Univ. of Chicago Press, 1987.

Winn, Mylon. "The Election of Norm Rice as Mayor of Seattle." *PS: Political Science & Politics* 23 (June 1990).

Worthly, Ford. "Booming American Cities." *Fortune,* Aug. 17, 1987.

Wrenn, Lynette. "Commission Government in the Gilded Age. *Tennessee Historical Quarterly* 47 (Winter 1988).

Wright, William. *Memphis Politics: An Example of Racial Bloc Voting.* New York: McGraw-Hill, 1962.

Zimmerman, Waldo. "Mr. Crump's Legacy." *Memphis Magazine* (Oct. 1984).

Racial Politics at the Crossroads was designed and typeset on a MacIntosh computer system using PageMaker software. The text is set in Bodoni, chapter titles are in Gill Sans Bold, and chapter numbers in Bauer Bodoni. This book was designed by Todd Duren, and composed by Dana West. The recycled paper used in this book is designed for an effective life of at least three hundred years.

Index

Adkins, Bill, 137, 143, 152, 158, 160
African-American People's Convention
  Organization, 143, 144–46, 155–56
African Americans. *See* black mayors;
  blacks; racial politics
Alexander, Bill, 137
Alissandratos, Andy, 39, 171, 191
Anderson, Marian, 63
Arrington, Richard, xviii
Ash, Vernon E., 140, 142

Bahrmand, Mahnaz, 86–88, 149, 157
Bailey, D'Army, 25, 26, 71, 177, 201
Baker, Jackson, 133
Bakke, John, 120–21
Banks, Frank, 151, 152, 159, 182
Banks, Lorenzo, 142, 143
Barksdale, Gene, 172
Barrett, Paul, 66
Barry, Marion, xviii
Barthelemy, Sidney, 203
Bass, Jack, xvi
Beale Street, 44, 54
Beifuss, Joan, 19
Bell, Benjamin, 59
Belz family, 129
Bentley, W. H., 58
Berry, Jimmie, 172
Bethel Grove Elementary School, 77
Biles, Roger, 8
Birch, Joe, 122
Black, Earl, 203
Black, Merle, 203
black mayors: factors contributing to election
  of, xviii–xxi; in the United States, xvii–xxi,
  198–200. *See also* Herenton, W. W.

Blackburn, James, 79, 174, 191
blacks: bloc voting of, 96–98, 177–78, 183; as
  candidates for election, 176–78; and city
  council elections, 168–73; and city court
  elections, 174–75; in early Memphis, 5; in
  electoral politics, 59–73, 178–79; as entre-
  preneurs, 54–55; factionalism among, 70–
  72; income levels, 56; and local economy,
  54–57; in Memphis public schools, 82, 84;
  opposition to annexation, 109; as political force, 53, 57–59, 72–73; political leaders, 26, 52; population in Memphis, 5, 11,
  52, 100; and Program of Progress, 67–69,
  112; and school board elections, 173–74;
  suffrage for, 198; as supporters of
  Hackett, 25, 72, 98, 126–27, 135–37; as
  supporters of Herenton, 142–48, 200;
  voter registration of, 100–104, 153–54;
  voter turnout among, 104–7, 149, 162–63,
  179–82, 185; and voting fall-off, 180–81;
  voting patterns, xvi–xvii, xxii, 92–107
Blanchard, Jerred, 19, 23
bloc voting, 96–98, 177–78, 183
Boyd, William "Bill," 124, 126–27
Boyle family, 129
Bradley, Tom, xviii
Brewster, W. H., 64
Brink, William, 62
Brooks, Henri, 143, 152
Brooks, Thomas, 57
Brooks Art Museum, 43
Broughton, James, 38
Brown, George Jr., 79
Brown, Joe, 177
Brown v. Board of Education, 64
Brownell, Blaine, xv, 5

Browning Farris, 130
Bruce, Bill, 23
Bumpers, Dale, 137
Bunton, Henry, 64
Burch, Lucius, 26, 112
Busby, Gene, 135
Bush, George, 33, 114

Calvary Episcopal Church, 28
Campbell, A. E., 64
Capers, Gerald, 13, 15
Carey, Margaret, 113
Carlook, Levon, 12
Carpenter, Charles, 151, 157, 158, 159
Cartwright, Joseph, 60
Chandler, Wyeth, 32–33, 34, 84, 126; as can-
    didate for mayor, 93, 98; as mayor of
    Memphis, 20–22, 27, 71
Chapman, Buddy, 22
Chism, Sidney, 143
Christian, Cornell, 79
Church, Robert Jr., 16, 58, 60–61, 62, 63
Church, Robert Sr., 54–55, 63
churches, 28; and Herenton campagin, 161–
    62; role of in politics, 64
Citizens for Equal Representation, 113–14
Citizens for Progress, 65
Clark, Dick, 45
Clark, William, 129
Clayburn Ball Temple AME Church, 89, 141
Cleaver, Emanuel, xviii
Cleo, 54
Clouston, James, 54
Clouston, Joseph, 60
Coats, William, 78
Cody, Michael, 25, 35, 93–94, 97, 98, 112, 192
Coe, Clarence, 58
Cole, Kenneth, 141
Coleman, Veronica, 26
Committee on Community Relations, 57–58
Community Development Bloc Grants, 47
Community Welfare League (CWL), 59
Conley, Larry, 84–85
Conway, Margaret, 104
Cook, Ned, 21, 43–44
Cooley, David, 28–29
Cooper, Barbara, 143
Cooper, Sam, 129
Cordova, 109–11, 178
Covington, Jimmie, 82
Cowan, Thomas, 19
Crawford, Robert, 124
Creative Marketing Concepts, 152
Crenshaw, Cornelia, 145
Crenshaw, Jeff, 125
crossover voting, 179, 184; in city council

elections, 168–73; in city court elections,
    174–75; of white liberals, 185–90
Crump, Bessie, 16
Crump, E. H. "Boss," xxiv, 26–27; and black
    voters, 62, 63, 101–2, 198; as mayor of
    Memphis, 14–17; as segregationist, 15–16

Daley, Richard M., xix
Daniel, John, 24
Davis, Bill, 39
Davis, Fred, 69
Day, Clarence, 129
Deaderick, John, 4
Dedicated Citizens' Committee, 14
DeVries, Walter, xvi
Dice, John, 23
Dinkins, David, xviii
Donald, Bernice, 26
Doyle, Bertram, 197–98
Du Bois, W. E. B., 54
Duckett, Greg, 26, 125, 126, 135
Dunavant, William, 44, 128

Edmonds, Oscar, 24, 33, 39, 170, 191
education, 50–51
Elazar, Daniel, 10–11
Ellington, Buford, 112
Estival Place, 47, 122
Evans, Henry, 22
Evers, O. Z., 60, 61, 70

Farnsworth, Thomas Jr., 127, 129
Farris, Jimmy, 123
Farris, William, 33
Federal Express, 54
Felix Walker and Associates, 152
Fields, Richard, 158
Fogelman family, 129
Foote, Will, 63
Ford, Bishop, 136
Ford, Harold, 59, 89, 103, 144, 171; as con-
    gressman, 69–70; and Herenton cam-
    paign, 142, 143, 145–48, 154, 159–60, 162
Ford, James, 39, 103
Ford, John, 25, 59, 71, 72, 95, 98, 103, 144, 162
Ford, N. J., 54
Freedmen's Bureau, 11
Freeman, John, 78
French, Reginald, 145, 151
Fresh Ideas, 152
Fuller, T. O., 63
Fuller, Thomas, 64

Gaia, Pam, 23
Gantt, Harvey, xviii
Gatson, Cheryl, 173

Gattas, Fred, 129
Gibbons, Bill, 72, 95, 98, 129, 171
Gibson, Harry, 16
Gibson, Kenneth, xviii
Gill, Del, 143, 144
Gill, Tom, 87
Gilliam, H. H., 102
Gilliss, Clarence, 54
Gladney, Alexander, 68
Goals for Memphis, 29
Goldfield, David, xv, 3, 5, 9, 11
Goode, Wilson, xviii
Gore, Al, 126
Greiner, Mori, 19
Griggs, Sutton, 64
Gurley, Paul, 33, 126

Hackett, Bill, 31, 32
Hackett, Jason, 32
Hackett, Kathy, 32
Hackett, Mark, 31
Hackett, Mary Shea, 32
Hackett, Richard C. "Dick," xxiii; as administrator, 37–39; black support for, 25, 72, 98, 126–27, 135–37, 160; campaign advertising, 137–38; campaign contributors, 127–30; campaign expenditures, 130–32; campaign issues, 134–37; campaign organization, 124–27; campaign strategy, 121–24, 192; debate with Herenton, 40, 44, 122, 123, 158–59; economic development projects, 42–46, 134; education policy, 50–51; election results (1991), 167, 1779; endorsements of, 138; Ford's attack on, 159; Herenton chosen as opponent of, 141; Herenton's defeat of, 191–92; and Hodges's candidacy, 167–68; housing policy, 46–49; mayoral campaign of (1982), 34–35, 93–94, 97, 112; mayoral campaign of (1987), 95; mayoral campaign of (1991), 90, 119–39; as mayor of Memphis, 24–25, 27, 39–51, 71, 74; motivations for 1991 campaign, 120–21; personal background, 31–32; political life, 32–51; public policies, 39–51; relationship with unions, 36, 138; "Rose Garden Strategy" of, 121–22; as Shelby County clerk, 33–34; tax policy, 40–41; voter registration efforts, 133–34; and voting rights lawsuits, 114; white support for, 119. See also mayoral election (1991)
Hackett, Rosemary, 31
Hackett, William (father of Richard Hackett), 31
Hackett, William (son of Richard Hackett), 32
Hagler, Monice, 135

Hammond, Alan, 141, 151
Harkins, John, 8, 18, 19
Harleson, Larry, 135
Harper, Charlotte, 170
Harris, Joe, 74
Harris, Louis, 62
Harris, Tom, 76
Hatcher, Richard, xviii
Hawkins, William, 141
Hayes, Elton, 12
Hayes, Thomas H., 54
Heiskell, Donelson, Bearman, Adams, Williams and Kirsch, 130
Henley, Hezekiah, 60
Herenton, Andrea, 75
Herenton, Dorothy Elizabeth, 74
Herenton, Errol, 75
Herenton, Ida Jones, 75
Herenton, Rodney, 75
Herenton, Ruby Lee, 74
Herenton, W. W.: and absentee ballots, 182; awards and honors, 83; as boxer, 76–77; campaign contributors, 152–53; campaign expenditures, 130–32; campaign strategy, 154–58; church support for, 161–62; corporate support for, 150; debate with Hackett, 40, 44, 122, 123, 158–59; economic development strategy, 157; educational innovations of, 80–82; election as mayor, xv, xxii, xxiii, 30, 165–93, 197; endorsements of, 160–61; and Hodges's candidacy, 167–68; mayoral campaign of, xxiii–xxiv, 88–91, 122, 134, 135, 139, 148–64; personal background, 74–78; political future of, 202–4; racial reflexivity as factor in election, 201–2; relationship with Mahnaz Bahrmand, 86–88, 149, 157; religious beliefs of, 89, 90; as school principal, 77–78; as school superintendent, 51, 78–88, 158; union support for, 153, 160; and unity movement, 141–48, 180, 184–85, 200; and voter registration, 153–54, 180; voter turnout for, 149, 162; white support for, 187–90. See also mayoral election (1991)
Hickory Area Residents for Tomorrow (HART), 110
Hickory Hills, 109–11, 115, 178, 193
Higgs, W. Otis, 26, 47, 113–14, 126, 144; as mayoral candidate, 22–24, 25, 71, 72, 93, 94, 95, 98, 145, 147, 148
Hinds, M. A., 66
Hnedak Bobo, 130
Hodges, Robert "Prince Mongo," 167–68, 179
Holiday Inn, 156
Hollis, Samuel, 129

Holloway, George, 58
Holloway, Harry, xvi, 13, 52, 57, 61, 66, 164, 198
Holt, John, 36
Hooks, Benjamin, 65, 143
Hooks, Julia, 57
Hooks, Michael, 26, 143–44, 177
Horton, Odell, 26
Howard, Osbie, 151, 182
Howell, Rai, 172, 173
Howery, Donald, 143
Huddleston, Clay, 22
Hughes, Eleanor, 122
Humphrey, Hubert, 8–9
Hunt, Earnestine, 94, 174–75, 177, 184, 191
Hunt, Turner, 60

incumbency: in 1991 elections, 190–91
Independent Political Action Committee (IPAC), 136
Ingram, William, 17, 69, 70, 94
International Paper, 35
Ivy, James, 135

Jackson, Andrew, 4
Jackson, Hattie, 147
Jackson, Jesse, 160–61, 180
Jackson, Mahalia, 65, 164
Jackson, Maynard, xviii, 202
Jalenak, James, 102, 105
James, Bob, 21, 39
Jefferson, Carol, 135
Jefferson, William, 203
Jim Crow laws, xvi, 11–12, 55, 62
Johnican, Minerva, 25, 71–72, 94, 98, 105, 135–36, 160, 177
Johnson, Carl, 85
Johnson, Jerry, 76
Jones, Dolores Elder, 174
Jones, Ed, 137
Jones, George, 125–26, 135–36, 160
Jones, Ida, 75
Jones, Paul Tutor, 128
Jones, Rufus, 75

Karney, Kenneth, 173
Kefauver, Estes, 63, 68
Kelley, Michael, 79
Kennedy Democratic Club, 148
Kerrick, John, 165
Key, V. O., xvi, xvii
King, Alvin, 136, 160
King, James, 132
King, Martin Luther Jr., 89, 141, 164; assassination of, 17–18, 58, 102
King, Martin Luther III, 161
Kirk, Ron, xviii

Knight, Ed, 135
Knox, John, 57
Ku Klux Klan, 8, 13, 16
Kuykendall, Dan, 69
Kyle, Sara, 174, 175, 179, 184
Kyles, Samuel, 160

Lamon, Lester, 14
Langdon, Phillip, 129
Larsen, Lawrence, 26
Lawson, James, 58
Lee, George, 5, 52, 53, 56, 60–61, 62, 63, 102
Lee, Tom, 63
Leffler, Florence, 39, 170, 172, 184
Lemond, Danny, 125
LeMoyne College, 75, 77
LeMoyne High School, 12
Lewinsohn, Paul, 62
Lewis, Clifford, 173, 184
Lewis, Sara, 174, 184
Lewis, Vera, 162–63
Liberty Bowl, 43
Liberty Bowl Festival Association, 130
Lincoln Republican League of West Tennessee, 60–61
Lipman, Ira, 129
Lipscomb, Robert, 26
Lockard, H. T., 66, 68
Loeb, Henry, 112, 141; and black community, 19–20, 58; as mayor of Memphis, 17–20, 27
Long, G. A., 15, 16
Love, Roy, 64
Lowery, Myron, 26, 169–71, 181, 184, 190

Main Street mall, 46
Mallory family, 129
Marshall, Tom, 173, 191
Martin, J. B., 16, 62
Martin, Roscoe, xvi
Mauney, Mal, 80, 191
mayoral election (1991): analysis of, 175–93, 197–202; ballot counting in, 181–82; incumbency factor, 190–91; racial polarization in, 183–85; results of, 167–68, 178–79; voting fall-off in, 180–81; white liberals as factor in, 185–90. See also bloc voting; crossover voting; Hackett, Richard; Herenton, W. W.
McCormick, Mary Rose, 39
McCullar, Meredith, 129
McDaniel, James, 59
McElrath, Roland, 135
McGehee, James, 127, 129
McVean, Charles, 130
McWherter, Ned, 83, 127
Meeman, Edward, 29

Melton, Gloria Brown, 65
Memphis, Tenn.: annexation and, 12, 107–11, 114, 198; black political leaders in, 26, 52; black population in, 5, 11, 52; bloc voting in, 96–98, 99, 183; bond rating of, 41–42; Chandler as mayor of, 20–22; churches in, 28; code enforcement in, 48–49; commerce in, 4, 9–11, 28–29, 53–54; cotton trade, 9, 10, 53–54; Crump as mayor of, 14–17; downtown development, 44; election law in, xxii, 111–13; economic development, 42–46, 54–55; education in, 50–51, 80–85; ethnic mix in, 4, 5–7, 27; Hackett as mayor of, 24–25, 27, 39–51; Herenton as candidate for mayor of, xv, xxii, xxiii–xxiv, 30, 88–91, 122, 134, 135, 139, 148–64; history of, 4–5; housing in, 46–49; Loeb as mayor of, 17–20; Midtown area, 185–90; modernization of, 10; nonpartisan election system, xxii, 96; political change in, 29–30; population growth in, 5–7, 8–9, 99–100; race relations in, 28–29; racial polarization in, 95–96, 183–85; racial politics in, 11–14, 22–24, 34–36, 57–73, 94–95, 115, 198; sanitation in, 7, 53; sanitation strike in, 58; segregation in, 11–14; tax policy in, 40–41; trolley, 46; voter registration in, 100–104; voter turnout in, 104–7; voting patterns in, xxii, 92–107; voting rights lawsuits, 113–15; white political leaders in, 27–28; yellow fever epidemic, 7–8, 53, 199. See also Hackett, Richard; Herenton, W. W.
Memphis Bar Association, 153
Memphis Board of Education, 50; elections (1991), 173–74; Herenton's appointment as superintendent, 78–80
Memphis Chamber of Commerce, 28–29, 42–43
Memphis City Council, 14, 126; and annexation, 109–10; black members of, 60; Hackett's relationship with, 39; impact of at-large elections on, 112–13; incumbency factor, 190–91; race as factor in 1991 elections, 168–73
Memphis City Court elections (1991), 174–75
Memphis Committee on Community Relations, 26, 112
Memphis Convention and Visitors Bureau, 44
Memphis Housing Authority, 46–48
Memphis Inter-Faith Association (MIFA), 28, 47, 122
Memphis Peace and Justice, 29
Memphis Race Relations and Diversity Institute, 29
Memphis Restaurant Association, 122

Memphis school system: budget under Herenton, 83–84; and OCI report, 85–86. See also Memphis Board of Education
Memphis Teachers' Association, 153
Memphis 2000 Plan, 109
Memphis World, 75
Memphis Zoo, 43
Memphis Zoological Society, 43
Miller, William, 13
Mississippi Boulevard Christian Church, 153
Mitchell, Arelya, 148
Mitchell, Curtis, 141
Mitchell, Logan, 141
Moon, Jacob, 60
Moore, Harry, 158
Moore, Jimmy, 86, 87
Morgan Keegan, 129
Morial, Ernest, xviii
Morris, Charlie, 148
Morris, Jack, 67
Morris, William "Bill," 21, 27, 127
Morrison, Mary, 57
Moss, Morrie, 129
Mt. Vernon Baptist Church, 87, 89
Mud Island museum and river walk, 44, 134
Muhammad, Talib-Karim, 113, 144, 145, 148
Murray, Richard, 201

National Association for the Advancement of Colored People (NAACP), 58–59
National Council of Christians and Jews, 29
National Football League team: as campaign issue, 156
National Urban League (NUL), 59
Nelson, William E. Jr., 146
Netters, James, 69, 87, 89, 151
Newsum, Floyd, 151
Nicholson, Phillip, 54
Nixon, Richard, 9
Nonaconah Parkway, 50
North Parkway, 49–50
Northcross, Amber, 124
Northcross, Phillip, 124
Norwood, Dan, 24, 110

Oliver, Jerry, 33, 135
optional schools, 80–81
Organization Consultants, Inc. (OCI), 85–86
Orgill, Edmund, 29, 64
Osman, John, 29
Overton, John, 4
Overton Park expressway, 50

Pace, Harry, 62
Page, G. E., 60
Parker, Frank, 104–5

Parks, Charley, 57
Pat Carter Pontiac, 55
Patterson, J. O., 24–25, 35, 69, 71, 109, 112
Peabody Hotel, 44
Pearson, Peggy, 123
People's Convention. *See* African-American People's Convention Organization
Perry, Howard, 16
Persons, Ell, 58
Pete, Floyd, 182
Pink Palace Museum, 43
Pleasant, O. C., 72, 103, 181–82
Plunkitt, George Washington, xx
politics: churches' role in, 64, 161–62; race as factor in, xv–xvii, 11–14, 22–24, 34–36, 59–73. *See also* Hackett, Richard; Herenton, W. W.
Pontius, John, 125
Prescott, Barbara, 191
Preston, Michael, xix
Price, Margaret, 59
Prim, H. S., 60
Program of Progress (POP), 67–69, 111–13
Pryor, Downing, 21, 126
Pyramid Arena, 45–46, 119

race: as factor in city council elections, 168–73; as factor in Memphis politics, 11–14, 22–24, 34–36, 59–73; as factor in southern politics, xv–xvii; and Memphis school board, 78–80. *See also* blacks; Hackett, Richard; Herenton, W. W.; mayoral election (1991)
racial politics: in Memphis, 11–14, 22–24, 34–36, 57–73, 94–95, 115; in southern cities, 197–98. *See also* blacks; Hackett, Richard; Herenton, W. W.; mayoral election (1991)
racial reflexivity, xxi, 94–95; in Hackett campaign, 136, 140; in 1991 mayoral race, 200–202
Ramses exhibit, 43
Randolph, A. Phillip, 15, 63
Rankin, Myrtis, 151
Reagan, Ronald, 82
Redwin, Ron, 151
Rhodes, Gail, 174
Rice, John, 4
Rice, Norman, xviii
Richmond, Isaac, 145
Robinson, Clayton, 6
Robinson, Halloe, 141
Robinson, Jim, 174
Robinson, Joseph, 35–36
Roddy, Bert, 54, 58
Roosevelt, Franklin, 63
Ryans, Jerome, 26

Sabato, Larry, 122
St. Jude Children's Research Hospital, 33, 35, 42, 129
St. Louis, Mo.: racial politics in, 199
Sam Cooper Boulevard, 49
Sammons, Jack, 27, 130
Sanford, Jeff, 125–26
Schmoke, Kurt, xviii
Seesel family, 129
segregation: federal laws affecting, 64; in Memphis, 11–14; in the South, xvi
Shadyac, Richard, 129
Shannon Elementary School, 77
Shannon Street Seven, 12, 35, 36
Shappley, Ken, 130
Shaw, Ed, 60, 69
Shea, John, 129
Shelby County Board of Commissioners, 60
Shelby County Democratic Club, 25
Shelby County Interfaith, 28, 123
Shelby Farms, 50
Shlenker, Sidney, 45–46, 119, 130
Simone, Joseph, 129
Sisson, Pete, 86, 87
Smith, Connie, 124
Smith, Fred, 27, 44
Smith, James, 72, 135–36, 138, 160
Smith, Maxine, 59, 79, 89, 90
Smith, Robert, xx
Smith, Vasco, 68, 113
Smith, Vincent, 124
Smith v. Allwright, 64
Smoky City, 47
Snoden, Jack, 130
Snowden, Robert, 129
Solvent Savings Bank, 55
Sonenshein, Raphael, 204
Sonnenberg, Barbara, 27, 39, 50, 80, 170, 171, 184, 191
Starks, Robert, xix
Stiles, Maynard, 22
Stokes, Carl, xviii
Strictland, Hazel, 182
Strong, Hugh, 141
Sugarmon, Russell, 20, 65–66, 68, 112
Supreme Court. *See* U.S. Supreme Court
Supreme Liberty Life Insurance Co., 54
Swearengen, James, 182

Tanner, John, 127
Taylor, Danny, 171, 190
Teamsters' union, 153
Terreo, John, 13
Terry, Ron, 88
T. H. Hayes and Sons Funeral Home, 54
Thomas, Chris, 191
Thomas, J., 60

Thornton, Matthew, 62
Tigrett, John, 130
Tigrett, Pat, 130
Todd, Bill, 174
Tom Lee Park, 43, 63
Tri-State Bank, 55
Tri-State Defender, 136, 137
trolley, 46
Tucker, David, 64, 108
Turley, Henry, 27
Turner, Jerome, 115
Turner, Jesse, 26, 59, 66, 67, 68, 152
Turner, Johnnie, 152
Turner, Kenneth, 21–22, 23, 24, 94, 98

unions: and black workers, 58; and Hackett
    as mayor, 36; sanitation strike, 58; as
    supporters of Herenton, 153, 160
Unity League, 61
Unity Summit, 146–48
Universal Life Insurance Co., 55
Urban Policy Institute, 29
U.S. Supreme Court: decisions affecting
    segregation, 64

Vander Schaaf, Pat, 144, 170, 172–73, 179,
    184, 191
VECA, 28
Vedlitz, Arnold, 201
Vergos, Charlie, 129
voter registration, 100–104; and Hackett
    campaign, 133–34; and Herenton cam-
    paign, 153–54, 162–63
voter turnout, 104–7; for Herenton, 149, 162–
    63, 185
voting fall-off, 180–81
Voting Rights Act of 1965, 114

Wade, Lawrence, 47
Walker, Delos, 129, 137
Walker, Felix, 152
Walker, Joseph E., 63–64, 65
Walker and Associates, 137
Wallace, George, 9, 13

Wallace, Lucius, 66
Walsh, Eddie, 89, 90, 141, 151, 156, 163, 166
Ware, Charles, 66
Washington, Booker T., 13, 57
Washington, Harold, xvii, xviii, xix, 143
Waters, J. D., 60
Watkins, Thomas, 58
WDIA, 136
Webb, Wellington, xviii
Welford, Buckner "Buck," 173, 192
Welford, Harry, 173
Wells, Ida B., 58
West Tennessee Annual Conference of the
    CME Church, 153
Whalum, Kenneth, 39, 144, 154, 169, 170,
    184, 185, 190
Wharton, A. C., 26, 144
White, Michael, 203
White, Ralph, 147
White Citizens Council, 13
Wilbun, Shep, 26, 39, 65, 143, 144, 145, 154
Wilkens, Jim, 162
William, Charles Jr., 70, 71
Williams, Eldredge, 141
Williams, J. C., 191
Williams, Joseph, 14
Willis, A. W., 20, 26, 65, 66, 68, 69, 126
Willis, Archie, 152
Wilson, Lionel, xviii
Winchester, James, 4
Withers, Teddy, 25, 71–72, 98, 142, 143, 144,
    147
Witherspoon, Willie, 74–75
WLOK, 136, 137, 160
Wolbrecht, William, 129
Wonders Series, 43–44
Woodruff, David, 54
Woods, Cary, 46, 47
Woodson, Roland, 141

Yacoubian, Berje, 23
yellow fever epidemic, 7–8, 53, 199
Young, Andrew, 202
Young, Coleman, xviii